Pews, Prayers, and Participation

Pews, Prayers, and Participation

Religion and Civic Responsibility in America

Corwin E. Smidt

Kevin R. den Dulk

James M. Penning

Stephen V. Monsma

Douglas L. Koopman

Georgetown University Press ✸ Washington, DC

Georgetown University Press, Washington, D.C. www.press.georgetown.edu

Library of Congress Cataloging-in-Publication Data

Smidt, Corwin E., 1946-
  Pews, prayers, and participation : religion and civic responsibility in America / Corwin E. Smidt . . . [et al.].
     p. cm. — (Religion and politics)
  Includes bibliographical references and index.
  ISBN-13: 978-1-58901-218-9 (hardcover : alk. paper)
  ISBN-13: 978-1-58901-217-2 (pbk. : alk. paper)
  1. Christianity—United States.   2. Christianity and politics—United States.   I. Title.
  BR515.S55 2008
  241'.621—dc22   2008004643

15 14 13 12 11 10 09 08   9 8 7 6 5 4 3 2
First printing

Printed in the United States of America

To our students—past and future civic leaders

Contents

Illustrations

Acknowledgments

We want to acknowledge and express our appreciation for the generous support of The Lynde and Harry Bradley Foundation, which initiated this project and enabled us to engage in the research and writing that stands behind this book. In addition, we wish to thank the Paul B. Henry Institute for the Study of Christianity and Politics at Calvin College for its support and services that helped to bring the effort to its completion.

Introduction
Religion and Civic Responsibility

During election campaigns, it is commonplace for religious leaders to exhort their followers to a more robust and thoughtful participation in public life. In the 2004 presidential election, for example, the U.S. Conference of Catholic Bishops distributed its quadrennial statement on "faithful citizenship," and the National Association of Evangelicals issued a call for greater "civic responsibility."[1] What these statements share is the language of duty and obligation, a profoundly others-centered orientation that is reflected in their repeated invocations of the "public interest" or "common good." By implying that one is obligated or duty bound to act on behalf of members of one's community, these statements strongly suggest that one's moral obligations entail civic engagement.

Yet do the intended audiences heed these messages? Have the interpretations of civic responsibility reflected in these and many other documents seeped into the moral consciousness of religious believers and served to motivate their activism? The authors of this book consider these questions by exploring a variety of ways in which religious people in the United States give expression to their civic responsibilities. We treat religion as a key part of that cluster of associations and institutions that is sometimes termed civil society. We suggest that the role of religion in fostering "civic responsibility" is real and consequential but also remarkably complex and subject to "privatizing" pressures that lessen religion's public witness.

Our examination of religion and civic responsibility draws from, but also extends, recent scholarly discussions about civil society and its contribution to the democratic experience in the United States. Interest in civil society

1

has "exploded" over the past two decades (Cohen 1999, 263). In their analyses, scholars have given attention to a wide range of concerns related to American social and political life, examining such matters as the nature and extent of social interaction among American citizens, the kinds of social relationships that serve to build and sustain moral commitment and character, and the shared values that serve to define us, either implicitly or explicitly, as a people (Wuthnow 1996, 2).

While scholarly inquiry into civil society has cast a wide net, it has nevertheless focused on two major and related matters. First, in their efforts to assess the general health of American civil society, scholars have addressed the quality of the experience shared by the American people. They have raised questions that have both a descriptive and normative cast: Are Americans exhibiting declining levels of civic engagement and social compassion across a spectrum of social life? Is the vitality of participation in voluntary associations diminishing? Are the American people less willing to cooperate, help, and serve their neighbors today than in the past? Are today's Americans less social, more individualistic, and less trusting than previous generations?

A second focus has been the specific relationship of civil society to democratic citizenship in the United States. In the eyes of some analysts, democracy in America is at risk. This risk, however, does not stem from potential acts of terrorism or any external threat; rather, it results from disturbing changes among the American people, namely, "an erosion of activities and capacities of citizenship" (Macedo et al. 2005, 1). Central to this concern are some fundamental questions about democracy itself: Is democracy defined by nothing more than the presence of certain procedural guarantees and the aggregation of individual self-interests? Or is a truly robust democracy secured through, and largely dependent on, the virtue and public spirit of its citizens? For those who answer "yes" to the former question, civil society is simply a place where citizens may freely pursue their own interests with few impediments from the state and with the aid of likeminded individuals. For those who respond affirmatively to the latter question, civil society is—or at least can and should be—a place to foster a stronger sense of civic responsibility through moral development.

Given these issues, one might anticipate that religion would be at the heart of the recent debate on civil society. After all, social observers from the nation's founding to the present have marveled at the comparatively high levels of religious engagement in the United States, and analysts have long recognized that members of religious congregations are more likely than nonmembers to join voluntary associations (e.g., Moberg 1962, 393–94). Moreover, those who see civil society as a place to develop freely without the state's coercive control frequently cite the role civil society can play as a check on and buffer against the state, particularly in terms of serving as "sites of resistance against tyranny and oppression" (Galston 2000, 69). For example, various analysts and commentators have noted the central role that churches, synagogues, and other places of worship played in the demise of the Soviet bloc and in fostering democratic life and self-government in Eastern Europe (e.g., Weigel 1992; Steele 1994). Others who emphasize civil society as a seedbed for moral development frequently suggest that religion is an important means to inculcate the habits of self-control, moral decency, and regard for others that are crucial for the effective functioning of democratic life (e.g., Eberly 1998; Himmelfarb 1999).

There is, in fact, a rich research tradition on civil society that links religion to active civic engagement. So if that is the case, why should we pursue still another study on the topic? Several factors provide a justification. First, while data patterns revealing the relationship between religion and civic engagement have long been demonstrated, the nature of that relationship is complex and not fully understood (Miller 2003, 51).

Beyond providing a more complete understanding, this study offers several unique elements that merit further consideration. First, our discussion and analysis of the "dependent variable" is framed in a distinctive way, as we focus on civic *responsibility* rather than on the narrower category of civic *engagement*. Certainly, the study of civic engagement is important, but the notion of civic responsibility adds a moral, or value-oriented, dimension to the analysis. As we discuss in the next chapter, civic responsibility entails certain kinds of behavior, capacities, and virtues. For example, to exhibit civic responsibility, individuals must act in ways that reveal that they see themselves as part of a broader community with its own "public" or "common" good, that they seek to develop their capacities to participate in public life, and that they recognize their obligation to act in good faith and in ways that engender trust. Because we seek to assess the role of religion in fostering broad civic responsibility, our study moves beyond what researchers typically assess when examining the relationship between religion and civic engagement.

Second, our analysis takes a new approach in its conceptualization and measurement of religion. Because religion is multifaceted, there has been little consistency in the religious measures employed across previous studies on religion and civic engagement. Some have focused in part on the effects of church membership (e.g., Nemeth and Luidens 2003), others on church attendance (e.g., Lazerwitz 1962; Smidt 1999; Campbell and Yonish 2003), others on the tradition of one's religious affiliation (e.g., Wuthnow 1999a; Smidt, Green et al. 2003), and still others on various combinations of particular variables (e.g., Park and Smith 2000; Lam 2002). But what is it specifically about religion that contributes to civic engagement and civic responsibility? Is it religious belief, religious commitment, religious networks, or some combination of such factors? We have chosen to analyze religion in a new way, taking into account both the public and private dimensions of religious life—an approach we believe has direct theoretical relevance for an analysis of public engagement more generally.

Third, our study is based on the analysis of many surveys gathered over the past seven decades. Most studies analyzing the role of religion in fostering civic engagement have drawn on the results obtained through a single survey. While such studies can reveal important findings and insights, their conclusions are necessarily limited, and confirmation of patterns across studies largely occurs in a serial fashion, with the findings of one study being compared to findings from earlier research. To date there has been little effort to validate findings across surveys, something this book seeks to do.

Finally, our study seeks to assess whether engagement in religious life makes any contribution beyond that linked to participation in other voluntary associations. Many previous studies have employed multivariate analysis to assess whether a particular religious variable necessarily remains as a significant predictor of civic engagement once the effects of other variables are taken into account. But there is a deeper issue. Is there anything inherent in religion that contributes to such engagement, or do religious variables, even when they account for unique variation in the dependent variable, simply reflect other social forces at play? For example, Putnam (2000, 67) has contended (without demonstrating) that it is the social connectedness of religious people, and not necessarily religion itself, that contributes to relatively high levels of social trust and reciprocity among believers. Moreover, little, if any, research has been done to assess whether participation in religious life has social effects distinct from participation in other voluntary associations. This study seeks to move the analysis of religion in fostering civic responsibility beyond simply explaining the relationship among variables to answering questions about whether there is anything inherent in religion itself that fosters civic responsibility.

Religion and Public Life

Public life is essential to human flourishing. To participate in, share responsibility for, and develop affective ties to some social entity outside oneself, whether a voluntary association, a church, a neighborhood, or a workplace, adds a dimension to human experience beyond that present in the private realm. Moreover, such participation in public life not only serves to balance the limitations of private life but it also moderates its negative tendencies.[2]

It is important to recognize that the political engagement of citizens does not encompass the whole of their public or "civic" life.[3] Social scientists and commentators are often inclined "to identify public life with politics" (Cochran 1990, 51), but political life is more narrowly focused than public life. Political life is aimed at "influencing the selection of governmental personnel and/or the actions they take," while civic life reflects "publicly spirited collective action," generally nonremunerative in nature, that is *not* guided, at least directly, "by some desire to shape public policy" (Campbell 2004b, 7). Thus the public role of religion is much broader and deeper than the political role of religion.

Participation in civic life can be exhibited in various ways—for example, through joining associations and organizations, volunteering, or making charitable contributions. It can also encompass a range of activities, such as working as a volunteer in a soup kitchen, participating in a book club, leading a boys or girls club, or organizing some charitable event. These efforts and associations may make many of the same contributions to personal and political development as those that are directly political in nature. But while the byproducts of these activities may have political implications, these endeavors are not directly political in nature.

Generally speaking, a citizenry that actively participates in civic life is lauded by analysts and practitioners alike. But when one shifts to a discussion of the role of religion in the public square, the topic becomes much more controversial. Subsequent differences in perspective partially stem from the fact that religion in public life can have both beneficial and detrimental effects. Certainly, the framers of the American Constitution were well aware of these divergent effects and understood their complexity and nuance. The framers recognized that, institutionally, the church can be separated from the state, but that ultimately religion cannot be separated from politics because the two are intertwined in ways that cannot be overcome simply by preventing the establishment of religion.[4] Nevertheless, while it may be impossible to separate religion completely from public life, the framers remembered very well the religious wars in England—the bloody conflict that centered on whether the established church should be the Church of England or the Roman Catholic Church. Not only did privileging one church over another lead to various kinds of political problems and violence, but the state itself was (and is) not in a position to determine religious truth.

Yet the framers were engaged in a noble experiment that sought to create a republic in which the people governed and enjoyed personal liberty. In the eyes of most, if not all, of these framers, a democratic republic required that its people exhibit moral constraint and behavior. Only a moral people, who willingly obeyed the law (and were not compelled to do so through the coercive power of the state) and who exhibited honesty and honored their commitments in their personal relationships and business dealings, could ensure that a democratic republic would stand.

But what were the sources of that morality? Largely, the founders saw it arising from the religious—and especially Christian—faith of the people; the particular denominational expression was not so crucial as the need for religion to be thoroughly rooted in the lives of the people of a democratic republic. Hence the free-exercise-of-religion clause of the First Amendment was written, in part, to enable religion both to flourish and to take firm root in the lives of the citizens of the land (because the effects of religion in the lives of the people would be stronger when citizens were free to embrace the religion of their choice). In other words, by diminishing the official standing of religion through nonestablishment, the social strength of religion was enhanced (Elshtain 2002, 18).

The Detrimental Effects of Religion in Public Life

Historically, liberal political thought has been committed to the central value of individual freedom and the need to protect and advance such freedom through state action.[5] For liberal theorists, one's freedom is potentially threatened by any established power and privilege, whether the locus of that power is within or outside the state. As a result, liberalism fights to protect individual freedom from established and dominant institutional structures of social and political power.

Given this normative orientation, liberals within the American context have worked to protect religious liberty, relying on religious disestablishment as one way to protect the liberties of American citizens. An established church could well constitute a concentrated—and perhaps dominant—institutional power capable of threatening the polity's religious freedom. Through mechanisms such as the "no establishment" clause of the First Amendment, liberals have sought to harmonize religion and politics through institutional separation. Indeed, some theorists have even objected to any presence of religion in public life on the grounds that religion tends to be divisive and disruptive, reinforcing and strengthening political divisions rather than bridging or healing them. In fact, religion's effects in this regard may actually be more detrimental than those of other social divisions, for as Pascal stated more than three centuries ago: "Men never do evil so completely and so cheerfully as when they do it from religious conviction" (Pascal 2004, 243).

More recent versions of liberalism have emphasized the importance of reason in discussions related to public policies. For example, Rawls (1971) contended that one of liberalism's major contributions was its commitment to tolerance that served to establish a society of civility and provided the personal freedom that enabled individuals to pursue their own life plans (the "unencumbered" self). But to achieve this tolerance, Rawls contended that public policies had to be premised on public reason, that is, on arguments and evidence that are accessible to all. The use of religious arguments is therefore inappropriate, as the public airing of such religious views supposedly "promotes a sense of separation between the speaker and those who do not share his religious convictions and is likely to produce both religious and political divisiveness" (Greenawalt 1988, 219).

Other political philosophers have also argued that public reason in a pluralistic society cannot include any religious doctrines that presuppose comprehensive conceptions of the good life, holding that religion should exist primarily in the private rather than in the public realm (e.g., Ackerman 1980; Dworkin 1985; Macedo 1990, 1995; Nagel 1991; Audi 2000). Accordingly, religious considerations should be clearly distinguished from political ones: Believers who accept the requirements of public reason, who are able and willing to speak a common civic language, are welcome in the public sphere. But those who do not must remain in the private one: "They must pay a price for living in a free pluralistic society" (Macedo 1995, 496).

Other theorists have criticized the Rawlsian conception of the "unencumbered" self and the requirement of public reason in political discourse, insisting that any complete conception of personhood requires an understanding of the roles that family, friendship, and faith play in common democratic experience (Sandel 1982; Walzer 1983; Glendon 1991). Applying this communitarian assumption to contemporary legal debates, they argued that faith is hardly a simple matter of personal choice but is, for most believers, more a duty than a choice, less a matter of personal right than public responsibility. By seeking to remove religion from the public realm, Rawlsian liberalism only serves to undercut liberal society by "impoverishing political discourse and eroding the moral and civic resources necessary to self-government" (Sandel 1996, 23).

Whatever the proper role of religion in public discourse, liberal political thought has generally emphasized that the state should act as a pragmatic broker between countervailing interests rather than serve as the generator or promulgator of values. For most classical liberals, it is not the state's role to provide moral vision; rather, it is primarily the institutions of civil society that are responsible for the generation and promulgation of moral visions (Neuhaus 1984, 133). Such a procedural notion of democratic government, however, tends to be highly unsatisfactory to those who want politics to deal not only with process but also with matters related to justice, the common good, and the nation's role in history.

Consequently, one of the most fundamental debates about the meaning of the American Constitution, as well as the nature of American civic and political experience, is the extent to which religion and public life should have anything to do with each other. This question presented itself even before the ratification of the First Amendment, and our answers have changed over time. Some have even suggested that we are currently witnessing an important renegotiation of the relationship between religion and public life (Dionne 2001, 24). Clearly, however, no consensus exists on how or to what extent church and state, or religion and politics, are to operate together within the public square.

Still, we easily forget that on some matters related to this issue there is very little controversy. For example, there is near universal agreement that there should be no state church and that no particular faith or religious tradition should be privileged under the law. Likewise, there is consensus that the state should not be involved in the operation of church matters, whether in terms of writing church doctrine, selecting church leaders, or determining the bases of church membership. Nor are there any serious advocates for the position that the state should compel religious belief.

Thus the difficulties related to the relationship between religion and politics in the American context arise from other facets of this issue. In particular, these difficulties relate to the extent to which a democratic and representative system of government should accommodate itself to the religious character of its people. To what extent should the state be secular in its goals, orientations, and policymaking? Should the Jeffersonian "wall of separation" between church and state be relatively high or low? Should any such wall serve primarily to protect the church from the state or the state from the church?

The Beneficial Effects of Religion in Public Life

Answers to these questions are difficult because although religion can have detrimental effects on public life, it can also be beneficial. First, religion can contribute to the foundation of democratic society by shaping individual character and virtue. Every individual possesses and exhibits particular moral values; even the position that all values are socially constructed and are therefore equal in social standing, with none "truer" or better than another, reflects a moral value. Yet even if one grants such a position, not all moral values are equivalent in their social effects, as some offer greater benefits socially and politically than others. Many analysts therefore view religion generally as a positive good, not simply because it may provide comfort and reassurance to those who are religious, but because it "upholds moral and ethical standards, such as loving your neighbor and being kind to the needy" (Wuthnow 2005, 101).

For many individuals, religion serves as the primary, though not necessarily exclusive, basis of their moral values. This relationship was recognized by many Founding Fathers, who viewed religion as an indispensable prop to republican virtue, in that "moral virtue underpins civic virtue, and religion fosters moral virtue" (Cochran 1990, 56). Moreover, regardless of whether or not one's values are derived from a particular religious faith, they affect the way one views the purposes of government, the policy goals government should pursue, and the means, or procedures, to be employed. In this sense religious values, like all other values, help to shape democratic political life (Smidt 2001, 98), and not even the presence of a very high wall of separation between church and state can prevent values, including religious values, from doing so.

In addition to fostering individual character, religion can shape public life through its moral voice. Religion's emphasis on transcendence relativizes and limits the political sphere of activity (Cochran 1990, 150–52). Religion points to a sovereignty beyond that of the state. It also points to a life beyond politics, because ultimate spiritual meaning cannot be obtained through political means. Thus religion can legitimately operate within democratic political systems as a "voice," because many religious traditions call their adherents to engage in prophetic politics—to speak out against evil in all its forms, including its political forms—and call their adherents to live lives that reflect more fully the "kingdom of God."

Religion further contributes to public life through associational and participatory activities of religious life. Corporate worship is a public occasion, and interaction with other believers occurs in a public space. Participation in these public events and spaces provides a wide variety of opportunities in which to develop an interest in and concern for public life, as well as provides numerous opportunities to learn important civic values and skills. For example, those who gather to worship may be reminded in sermons, prayers, and other proclamations of the ethical imperative to minister to those in need. Similarly they may learn of opportunities to volunteer and serve others in their community through announcements, classes, or informal conversation with fellow worshippers. And regardless of whether such members participate in church governance, lead worship, teach classes, organize liturgies and celebrations, or engage in church-sponsored community service or civic projects, all such endeavors provide opportunities for individuals to learn how to take responsibility, make collective decisions, express their views, acknowledge the contrasting views of others, and compromise. Thus religion can undergird civic life through the moral and civic virtues it inculcates in individuals, the civic skills it imparts, and the public engagement it encourages.

Contemporary American Civic and Religious Life

From the earliest days of the republic, one of the key characteristics of American society has been Americans' relatively high level of civic engagement, a willingness to join groups and associations in an effort to pursue common interests and the broader public good. This tradition of volunteerism and civic engagement is deeply rooted in American society, tracing its origins to the nation's Puritan heritage (Ahlstrom 1963). The French social observer Alexis de Tocqueville noted already in 1835 that "as soon as several Americans have conceived a sentiment or an idea that they want to produce before the world, they seek each other out, and when found, they unite" (Tocqueville 1969, 516).

The Changing Nature of Civic Engagement

Over the past decade, a number of important scholarly studies of Americans have revealed the vital role that religion plays in the public square (e.g., Verba, Schlozman, and Brady 1995; Wuthnow 1996; Putnam 2000).

Religious people are deeply social beings, as almost "half of all associational memberships in America are church related" (Putnam 2000, 66), and religious people exhibit pro-social behaviors such as altruism and compassion, as "half of all personal philanthropy is religious in character, and half of all volunteering occurs in a religious context" (Putnam 2000, 66). As we will discuss later in the book, people are more likely to give money and time, even to secular efforts, if they are church members (Wuthnow 1996, 87; Campbell and Yonish 2003; Brooks 2006).

Nonetheless, there is growing concern today about an apparent decline in civic engagement among the American people, revealed in part by diminished rates of civic volunteerism and low levels of political participation (e.g., Becker and Dhingra 2001; Skocpol 2003). Evidence documenting the decline of civic engagement comes from a number of sources. The membership records of many long-standing, diverse organizations (e.g., the PTA, the Elks, and the League of Women Voters) reveal a decline in participation over the past three decades, and the amount of time Americans spend socializing informally and visiting with others has declined as well (Putnam 2000).

Similarly there has been a decline in most levels of political participation over the past several decades. Such activities as attending political rallies and speeches, attending meetings that address civic concerns, and working for political parties or candidates during elections have seen a marked decline—roughly between one-third to one-half, depending on the particular indicator examined (Putnam 2000, chapter 3). Generally speaking, there has also been a slow erosion of voter-turnout rates in American presidential elections, as turnout has dropped from approximately 60 percent to 50 percent over the course of four decades.[6]

In addition, we appear to be witnessing privatization of moral convictions within American public life, as well as a growing sense that moral convictions are deemed either irrelevant or inappropriate within public discussion and debate (Wuthnow 1999b, 22). For some, religious beliefs are treated as personal opinions that are best kept to oneself, thereby rendering them irrelevant to civic deliberation (Carter 1993; Casanova 1994). For others, deliberative democracy requires that citizens make their arguments based on publicly accessible (i.e., non–faith-based) reason, with the role of religious perspectives in democratic deliberations restricted to a "nonpublic" arena (e.g., Rawls 1999; Audi 1997). Whatever the reason, many analysts consider the deeper values and traditions that were once part of the public debate to be no longer appropriate within the boundaries of public discussion and increasingly push them into the personal realm, resulting in what might be labeled a "thin consensus" (Walzer 1994). But this separation of one's deepest convictions from public life has negative civic consequences, as it tends to reduce the motivation to come together, to organize around deeply held beliefs, and to bring these beliefs to bear on public issues—perhaps generating lower levels of civic and political engagement.

It should be noted that not all scholars share the perspective that America is witnessing a decline in social and political engagement (e.g., Skocpol and Fiorina 1999; Skocpol 2003; Becker and Dhingra 2001). Some point out that focusing on the historic trends in membership in long-standing organizations may lead researchers to neglect the rise of membership in newly forged organizations, a rise that may well offset declines elsewhere. Others contend that, given existing data, "it is probably impossible to know what have been the trends in group membership since the 1950s" (Smith 1990, 651). Still other analysts point to the explosive growth of interest groups represented in Washington, D.C. (e.g., Berry 1999; Berry and Wilcox 2007); in addition, they note the establishment and membership growth of what might be labeled "mailing list" organizations (e.g., the American Association of Retired People or the Sierra Club) as counterevidence to the contention that civic engagement has declined over the course of the past several decades.

Despite these counterarguments, it would appear that Americans are, at minimum, less socially connected through face-to-face interaction with others outside their family than they were several decades ago. This decline in social interaction among individuals, families, and voluntary associations raises concerns that America's "social capital" is in decline (Putnam 1995a; Putnam 2000), as any diminution in social ties is likely to lead to subsequent decline in civic engagement. Moreover, whatever the relationship between social interaction and civic engagement, little countervailing data has been generated to demonstrate that there has not been a decline in political participation over the past several decades.[7]

Finally, whether or not the level of civic engagement has declined among the American people over the course of the past fifty years, the nature of such engagement appears to have changed in important ways.

Perhaps "the volume of civic engagement" has not so much declined "as it has spread to a wide variety of channels," creating a new mix of civic activities in which citizens are participating (Zukin et al. 2006, 3).

The Changing Nature of Religion in Public Life

Important changes appear to be taking place within American religious life. While certain aspects of American religion appear to have remained relatively stable over the past half century,[8] the nature of religious experience may be changing as religion has become largely detached from its older social moorings. Rising educational levels and increased geographical mobility have weakened traditional relationships between membership in a particular social or ethnic group and its religious affiliation at the same time that increased social and cultural assimilation has diminished many religious differences linked to custom and heritage. In the wake of these changes, old loyalties have weakened, enabling new religious identities to emerge. In this sense, contemporary religion in America is less bound than it was several decades ago by custom or social ties, less rooted in webs of cultural heritage and childhood socialization, and more fully anchored in private and subjective spheres of life.

Religion in America today is more fluid and driven by personal preference and personal values than in the past. While these changes are not likely to lead to the disappearance of religion, they certainly serve to redefine its public expression. Even now we are seeing a shift from "the religious" to "the spiritual," as many Americans willingly define themselves as spiritual while rejecting ties to "organized religion." Just as politics does not encompass all of civic life, neither does the church, as an organizational reflection of religious life, encompass all of religion. Accordingly, there appears to be some growth among those who have what might be described as a privatized faith, that is, Americans who claim a set of religious beliefs and engage in private religious activity but who are disconnected from religious institutions.[9] These "believers but not belongers" often distinguish between the "religious" and the "spiritual," defining themselves in terms of their own religious preferences while largely eschewing any involvement in an "organized" form of religion (Davie 1994).

Are the broad changes in American public life discussed earlier linked to these changes in American religious life? Do those who exhibit a privatized religious faith tend to withdraw from civic and political life? Even as some analysts hold that it is desirable that religious beliefs and values remain private and removed from the public square, might it be true that privatized religion leads to lower levels of public engagement? In other words, might privatized religion work at cross-purposes with the normative value of public engagement? In fact, Elshtain (2002, 24) has suggested that participation in public religious life and participation in political life are related, in so far as "contemporary distrust of organized politics and organized religion goes hand in hand." She notes that both organized religion and organized politics are public expressions, involving groups of people engaging in a shared enterprise, operating under particular rules, and expressing particular convictions. She argues that religious believers who devalue organizational life within the religious arena may express diminished enthusiasm for organizational endeavors within the civic and political spheres of life as well.

Because of our interest in civic and political engagement, and civic responsibility more generally, we analyze religion in terms of one's *form of religious expression*, a variable that reflects both public and private dimensions of religious life. Our study analyzes respondents in terms of a fourfold categorization reflecting whether one exhibits a diminished, a privatized, a public, or an integrated form of religious expression (for a fuller discussion, see chapter 2), and it reveals that the way in which one is religious relates to a wide range of characteristics associated with civic responsibility. Not all who regularly attend public worship services manifest the same behaviors, capacities, and virtues associated with civic responsibility, but neither do all who exhibit low levels of church attendance express like civic responsibility. In short, our study identifies both patterns and variance in the relationship between forms of religious expression and individuals' expression of civic responsibility.

Using this approach, we found that religion nevertheless plays an important role across a wide landscape. Much of the remaining portion of this book demonstrates that fact by examining how religion shapes various behaviors related to civic responsibility, capacities that facilitate civic responsibility, and particular virtues generally seen to undergird civic responsibility.

The analysis is wide ranging, but the results are, for the most part, consistent. In broad strokes, our story is that religion matters, and that it matters significantly, within American civic life. Religion serves to connect people across various social and cultural divides, assists and helps those in need through volunteering or charitable contributions, imparts important civic skills, and fosters important virtues, such as law-abidingness, honesty, and trustworthiness.

Outline of the Book

Chapter 1 focuses primarily on analytical issues and seeks to place the study of civic responsibility within a wider theoretical and analytical context. We first examine the concept of civil society and how it relates to the other two major facets of public life: the state and the market. We then explicate the concept of civic responsibility, noting various components of such responsibility in terms of particular behaviors, capacities, and virtues. Finally, we examine the notion of citizenship and the relationship between citizenship and civic responsibility.

Chapter 2 provides the explication and justification for our use of the "forms of religious expression" measure that we employ in the subsequent chapters. First, we examine the relative vitality of religious life in the United States and the extent to which religious changes may be taking place within American society. On the basis of that discussion, we identify four distinct forms of religious expression (namely, what we term diminished, privatized, public, and integrated forms) and reveal how we assigned individuals to each. Next we validate that the various theoretical expectations tied to these particular forms of religious expression were indeed tapped through the measurement strategy we employ. We conclude the chapter with a sociodemographic profile of each of our four categories.

The next two chapters examine the behavioral facets of civic responsibility. Chapter 3 examines the role of religion in fostering one aspect of civic engagement: involvement in voluntary associations. We analyze the central role that religion plays in American associational life, not simply within organizations related to church life, but also its role in shaping involvement in other voluntary associations. We particularly assess how the different forms of religious expression influence involvement in public life and foster membership in different kinds of voluntary associations.

Chapter 4 shifts the analysis to two other expressions of civic responsibility: volunteering and philanthropic giving. We address how one's form of religious expression serves to shape "giving behaviors" (volunteering and donating), and we examine the extent to which giving behaviors spill over from religious to more secular concerns. Finally, we examine the relative importance of religion in shaping contributions of time and money.

Chapter 5 addresses the role of religion in enhancing the civic capacities of individuals. Using the forms of religious expression, we assess the role of religion in promoting the development and exercise of civic skills as well as the role of religion in fostering cognitive engagement in public life—particularly, greater attention to public affairs and enhanced political knowledge. More specifically, we compare the role of religion in enhancing the civic capacities of Americans to the role played by membership in non-religious voluntary associations. In other words, we attempt to answer the question of how central the role of religion is in American civic life.

Chapter 6 examines the role of religion in fostering civic virtues. Drawing from various sources, we identify multiple manifestations of civic virtue, including the general virtue of law-abidingness, the political virtue of political tolerance, and the economic virtue of a work ethic. The role of religion in shaping propensities to exhibit each virtue is assessed both in terms of its general association and in terms of its relative importance in contributing to such civic virtues.

Chapter 7 concludes our discussion and analysis. In the first part of the chapter, we examine the relationship between civic engagement and political participation, seeking to determine the extent to which religion's role in fostering civic engagement leads to involvement in political life. In the second part of the chapter, we present our concluding thoughts and assessments, and address the implications that our findings have for the larger debate on the role of religion in American public life.

Notes

1. This statement by the National Association of Evangelicals also called for heightened evangelical attention to world affairs and the environment.

2. Of course, this statement reflects more a general quality of associational involvement than some universal causal property, as the statement is partially dependent on the nature of the association (e.g., Hitler youth organizations) with which individuals may be affiliated. For a discussion of various characteristics of private life, along with some of its limitations and negative tendencies, see Cochran (1990, particularly chapters 2 and 3).

3. Civic (or public) life is more than "social life," which is simply the life two or more people share in common (e.g., sharing a common language). Public life "adds to social life a reference to power, especially shared power" and "demands active participation" (Cochran 1990, 46).

4. For example, political choices involve values, and values are linked to moral choices, and morality, for many, is tied to religion; no law can prevent someone from relying on their religious faith as a basis for supporting a piece of legislation or voting for a particular candidate.

5. Fowler (1989, 4), for example, identifies three characteristics of liberal political thought: (1) a commitment to skeptical reason; (2) enthusiasm in principle and, increasingly, in practice for tolerance in political matters and, increasingly, in matters of lifestyle and social norms; and (3) the affirmation of the central importance of the individual and individual freedom. See also MacDonald and Popkin 2001.

6. However, while turnout consistently declined in presidential elections between 1960 and 2000, it did increase dramatically (to approximately 60 percent) in the 2004 presidential election.

7. The notable exception to this pattern was the sharp upturn in voter turnout in the 2004 presidential election.

8. For evidence of this relative stability in reported levels of church attendance, see chapter 2, table 2.2.

9. As Grenville (2000, 213) has noted, the notion of a private Christianity is, strictly speaking, an oxymoron.

1

❈

Civil Society, Civic Responsibility, and Citizenship

Democracy is associated with institutions that foster "rule by the people," yet these kinds of institutions (e.g., legislatures, the franchise) do not operate in a vacuum, isolated from the society of which they are a part. Culture shapes the design and operation of democratic institutions, sometimes by defining the very notion of "the people" itself. The United States' ignominious history of slavery illustrates the point. A set of cultural norms, values, and practices regarding the basic humanity of black Africans led to their systematic exclusion from the vote and from access to other democratic institutions.

One of the first, and in many respects the most prescient, observers of American culture was Alexis de Tocqueville, whose *Democracy in America* assessed democratic practice in early Jacksonian America. Tocqueville acknowledged the significance of the institutions of American democracy as enshrined in the Constitution, but what most impressed him were the causes and effects (for good and ill) of democratic culture, those peculiar habits of mind formed in a society that seemed remarkably egalitarian compared to his native France and the rest of the European continent. Tocqueville was exhilarated by this new democratic "spirit," but he was also deeply concerned about its tendencies toward tyranny and individualism. What intrigued Tocqueville were the many ways American culture moved democratic practice away from these tendencies. In particular, he contended that democracy requires the vitality of civic associations that are not necessarily political in nature but that serve as sources of collective purpose and active social engagement. For Tocqueville, associational life was the lifeblood of democracy, which could not survive unless citizens continued to participate actively, joining with others of similar mind and interest to address matters of common concern or, as he put it, "self-interest *properly* understood" (1969, 526).

It is no wonder that the past few decades have seen renewed interest in Tocqueville's understanding of democratic culture. As we discussed in the introduction, many contemporary scholars and social critics argue that Americans are increasingly uninterested in and ill-prepared for public life and that diminished attachments to voluntary associations are partly to blame. Yet even as many scholars speak in broadly Tocquevillian tones, there has been intense debate about the nature and scope of our civic disengagement, as well as about how we should respond to it. Even the terms of the debate are not always clear. For example, what are the relationships between civil society—quite often described as the realm of "voluntary associations"—and other forms of social organization? Is civil society, for example, distinct from the state and the market? If so, precisely how do one's identity and actions as a citizen or as a consumer differ from one's life in civil society?

In this chapter we develop several ideas that help answer these questions. First, we describe the nature of American civil society by distinguishing it from the state and the market and by locating the place of religion within it. Second, we explicate the components of civic responsibility and suggest the role that religion may play in fostering it. Finally, we examine the nature of the relationship between civic responsibility and the narrower responsibilities of citizenship.

Civil Society, the State, and the Market

The term civil society can assume a variety of meanings (Edwards 2004; DeLue 2002).[1] For some, it is a broad term that encompasses the whole of public life, including the state apparatus and the rights and duties of the citizenry; in this sense, civil society is something akin to political community or the body politic. For others, civil society takes on a moral cast, referring to public institutions that are "good" or "virtuous" or that pursue the "common good." Our understanding of civil society starts with a different, though widely employed, emphasis, namely, that civil society encompasses those particular social relations that reside between the individual on the one hand and the state and market on the other (see also Cohen and Arato 1992, ix; Wuthnow 1996, 30–31; Wolfe 1998, 9; Ehrenberg 1999, 235; Warren 2001, 58). From this perspective, civil society is composed of a variety of associations, including voluntary associations such as religious affiliations, that are distinct from the social organizations that comprise the state or market.

How are the nature and scope of civil society distinct from that of the state or market? The answer is complex because of the nearly constant interactions among the three spheres. An association in civil society—for example, a social club or a religious congregation—is not immune from the forces of the market or the state; as we discuss later in this chapter, associations in civil society are clearly shaped by economic pressures and governmental regulation and protection. Conversely, most scholars of civil society suggest that civil society can exercise profound influence over the norms and values that dominate the market or the state. Nevertheless, the three spheres remain analytically and empirically distinct, even when they appear to be codependent. Civil society differs from the state and market in terms of its motivational bases, its public purposes, and its effects on individual identity.

First, memberships in the associations of civil society are uncoerced. In civil society, the "voluntary social qualities of associative attachments are dominant, as compared to the legally compelled attachments of the state or the money-based attachments to the market" (Warren 2001, 58). On the surface, this characteristic might not seem to distinguish civil society from the state or market because one can voluntarily disengage from activities associated with both the state (e.g., by choosing not to vote) and the market (e.g., by choosing not to seek employment). Yet it is nearly impossible to entirely escape obligations in either sphere: A citizen who refuses to vote is still obligated to obey the state or risk its coercive power, and the average consumer must still find means of sustenance in the market. Generally, voluntary associational relationships within civil society imply not only that membership is consensual but that it is possible to leave such associations without either the loss of social status or public standing in terms of rights and benefits (Post and Rosenblum 2002, 4).

This voluntary nature means that civil society is characterized by varying degrees of fluidity and segmentation. Civil society is fluid in so far as involvement in particular associations, both personal and corporate, waxes and wanes. Individuals may, and frequently do, join more than one group, resulting in loyalties to multiple associations and cross-cutting identities. Individuals may also refuse to join any associations, while retaining their right to participate in the future. But civil society is also more or less fluid to the extent that it segments different sectors of society, that is, the extent to which associational ties serve to cut across social groups or deepen existing cleavages in society. Civil society particularly segments the larger society when associational membership reinforces preexisting social ties with members of the same social, ethnic, or religious groups.

Civil society also differs from the market and the state in its public purposes, which "are organized neither by the self-interest of the market nor by the coercive potential of the state" (Wolfe 1998, 9). Unlike the state, civil society provides a space for uncoerced human association, allowing the individual to join with others of similar mind and interest to address matters of broader concern to members of the group; civil society is "a realm of free choice and voluntary participation" (Walzer 2004, 70). Unlike the market, civil society is *not necessarily* governed by the logic of self-interest, which can be differentiated from the values of camaraderie and public spiritedness (Wuthnow 1996, 32).

Finally, identity is more narrowly cast within civil society than it is within the state, as membership in civil society is linked to *particular* groups and associations. While identity in civil society is therefore always specific, springing from the contingencies of socialization or choice related to particular groups and associations, the state is a domain that seeks common purpose and identity (Post and Rosenblum 2002, 3). Of course, the state may fail to achieve common purposes, but what distinguishes the state is its claim of "the right to speak in the name of a common good and identity," a claim that is captured in the distinction between being a citizen and being a member in civil society (Post and Rosenblum 2002, 9).

Thus, in contrast to the state, civil society constitutes a realm of social life that is characterized by plural and particularistic identities. On the one hand, within civil society, individuals are free to choose with whom to associate, and such associations are free to determine their particular purposes, develop their unique norms, and forge their specific organizational structures and group identities. On the other hand, the state constitutes an "inclusive sphere, which, when viewed from the perspective of civil society, is characterized by overarching public norms made and enforced by official institutions" (Post and Rosenblum 2002, 3). Put another way, associations in civil society are "partial publics" rather than the whole. The state, at least in terms of democratic theory (though not always democratic practice), seeks to represent aggregated interests or the common good.

To this point we have sought to differentiate between the state, the market, and civil society. Yet the boundaries that divide these three domains, while analytically distinct, are fluid and dynamic, not fixed and static. Each sphere can expand or contract. As a result, vigilance is required lest "the distinctive values on which civil society depends become subverted" (Wuthnow 1996, 30–31). In fact, some observers have argued that the freedom found within civil society is increasingly being squeezed from both directions—on the one side "by the bureaucracy of the administrative state" and on the other "by powerful determinism of markets linked in an increasingly global network" (Hollenbach 2003, 151).

Nevertheless, while the various forms of voluntary associations found within civil society "always strive to maintain a measure of autonomy from the public affairs of politics and the private concerns of economics," they are at the same time "partially determined by the state and the market" (Ehrenberg 1999, 235). The state provides the space within which civil society operates and the rules within which it may function. For example, within the American context the First Amendment guarantees of freedom of religion, speech, and association, as well as the qualified protection of private spaces and communications in the Fourth Amendment, are vital for the formation of voluntary associations. The state's legal framework thereby transforms "arrant pluralism into civil society." But the rule of law also "sets limits to the authority of associations over their members" (Post and Rosenblum 2002, 8). Should the boundaries of the state expand too far, civil society can be manipulated, co-opted, and repressed to the point that it will eventually simply whither away. Conversely, while civil society generally thrives in the absence of political encroachments and frequently falters when supplanted by the government (Eberly 1994, xxxi), if civil society expands too far, the state may simply collapse and anarchy result. Of course, where to draw the boundary between the two spheres "is a matter of judgment, which means that it is subject to perennial dispute and contestation" (Post and Rosenblum 2002, 11).

Likewise, civil society is dependent on yet distinct from economic life. When jobs disappear, civic life dissipates. Civil society also draws on "the habits, discipline, and schedules required for productive involvement with the outside world" (Ehrenberg 1999, 247), not to mention the basic resource of financial support. Discussions of the relationship between civil society and the market, however, rarely go beyond the view that the marketplace is either neutral toward or a friend of civil society. Along with this perspective comes the tendency to assume that society will move spontaneously and rationally toward self-organization and harmony if the state is curtailed and individuals are allowed greater freedom (Eberly 1998, 138). Civil society, however, can be overwhelmed by the market and commercial institutions. Hollenbach notes: "It is at least a plausible hypothesis that . . . the more immediate threat to a civil society capable of nurturing freedom is not an authoritarian state but the dominance of the market and its instrumental rationality over increasingly large domains of social and cultural life" (2003, 156). Over time, market economies generate and reinforce social relations that are ordered in light of an instrumental logic that rewards self-interest and even self-aggrandizement. Some social analysts have argued that numerous relationships that traditionally were organized by civil society (e.g., family, community groups) have lately begun to be organized instead by the logic of the market. Even churches, especially in the age of televangelism, often put mammon before God. Thus, the ties of affection and loyalty on which social relations within local communities rest, if not thrive, can easily be replaced by market consumerism (Eberly 1998, 154).

Still, while civil society is partially dependent on the state and the market, both the state and the market are also dependent on civil society as both rest on a moral order defined by noneconomic, noncoercive ties of trust and solidarity (Wolfe 1989, 18). Such ties—what we describe later in this chapter as examples of "civic virtue"—are largely forged within the social and associational life that transpires within civil society. Thus, civil society becomes "the arena in which individual freedoms, even those that are self-interested, are kept in tension with collective values and community participation" (Wuthnow 1996, 7).

Civic Responsibility

As a concept, liberal democracy emphasizes the freedom of individuals to determine their own fates with minimal intrusion by government. Exercising that freedom, however, invites conflict among citizens. Consequently, many liberal theorists have suggested that liberal democracies require virtuous and engaged citizens. The character of the members of a polity affects the operation of its institutions. A collective decline of individual virtue will, at some point, foster social pathologies with which liberal institutions, no matter how well designed, cannot cope. In the end, "the viability of liberal society depends on its ability to engender a virtuous citizenry" (Galston 1995, 39). People are not, however, born virtuous citizens; habits and dispositions need to be forged and, on occasion, renewed or restored. This socialization can occur through different means: the transmission of values from one generation to the next, religious revitalization, public exhortation and advocacy, and the learning that transpires through associational life. Cultural practices can either facilitate or hinder this renewal of the character of citizens.

"Civic responsibility" is another name for virtuous civic engagement. Yet civic responsibility is a contested term, to the point that some scholars assert that it cannot be defined because its meaning is constantly being renegotiated (Astin 2000). Nevertheless, we can identify certain factors typically considered inherent in the concept of civic responsibility. Civic responsibility is best understood as a multidimensional concept that entails certain behavior, capacities, and virtues.

Behavior

As we understand the term, civic responsibility entails civic participation or engagement. It emphasizes being an active, rather than a passive, member of the community. To exhibit civic responsibility is to be a participant, not a spectator—a citizen, not a subject. Actual involvement is the central indicator of civic engagement. Such active participation, however, may take a variety of forms. "Showing up" is a basic level of civic activity, but civic responsibility encompasses more than the mere presence of an individual at a meeting, gathering, or public event. There must also be some psychological engagement to the collective discussion and action.

Volunteerism has long been seen by Americans as a staple of civic responsibility (e.g., Boyte and Kari 2000). Through volunteering, individuals create the possibility of making a mark on their communities by working with their neighbors, by making judgments to facilitate action, and by being involved in decision making (Chopyak 2001). Moreover, many observers have drawn a connection between associational life and the health of American democracy (e.g., Tocqueville 1969; Almond and Verba 1963; Putnam 1995a, 2000). Participation in voluntary associations is believed to strengthen social bonds and enable those involved to develop a sense of community (Galston 2000). In addition, involvement in voluntary associations is thought to foster trust, cooperation, and reciprocity (Brehm and Rahn 1997). In such ways, volunteering serves "to instill civic values, enhance political behavior, and improve democracy and society" (Theiss-Morse and Hibbing 2005, 230).

Naturally, people differ in their perspectives on the role voluntary associations play in democratic society.[2] Some (e.g., political conservatives) are more inclined to see voluntary associations "as a means of devolving power to local communities and as an alternative to government-sponsored programs," while others (e.g., political liberals) are more likely to view such associations "as a means of fostering grassroots politics and increasing the voice of ordinary people" (Theiss-Morse and Hibbing 2005, 229). Similarly, while liberals are likely to view volunteering as a means to buttress or complement action by the state, conservatives are more inclined to contend that such activity substitutes for government programs (Campbell and Yonish 2003, 88). Regardless of these differences in perspective, however, both sides readily acknowledge that involvement in voluntary associations, volunteerism, and philanthropy is something to be valued.

Capacities

A second component of civic responsibility is *capacity* for civic engagement. While capacity entails various qualities, one can argue that it includes at minimum some level of civic interest and knowledge as well as the possession of certain skills relevant to public life.

In terms of fulfilling one's civic responsibility, then, not all civic engagement is necessarily of equal value. For example, some citizens who participate actively may possess relatively little awareness or understanding of the issues under discussion, while other active participants may bring a depth of knowledge and understanding. Citizens need not become policy experts to fulfill their civic responsibilities, but "there is a level of basic knowledge below which the ability to make a full range of reasoned civic judgments is impaired" (Galston 2001, 218). Of course, increased civic capacity does not necessarily translate into increased civic consensus; not all who exhibit deep knowledge and understanding adopt the same position on issues. Nevertheless, the quality of civic discussion and deliberation can only be enhanced by greater capacity.

The interrelationship between civic capacity and civic engagement can also be seen in the manner in which civic knowledge promotes participation in public affairs (Galston 2001, 225; Delli Carpini and Keeter 1996). The likelihood of civic involvement is increased by the possession of knowledge about the means by which to participate in the process (Ecklund 2005), as well as the possession of the civic skills that facilitate such engagement (Verba, Schlozman, and Brady 1995). Without some minimal skill level, individuals are not as likely either to aspire to be involved in public life or to become involved.

The symbiosis between civic engagement and capacity also means that engagement nurtures capacity: active participants become more informed and learn requisite knowledge about matters under discussion, and participation in voluntary associations can play a major role in imparting civic skills by providing opportunities to learn and practice participatory abilities. Thus, Wuthnow notes that "participation in civic organizations is often thought to be beneficial to the functioning of American democracy because it generates civic skills" (1999a, 346).

Virtues

Finally, there is a communal element to civic responsibility: To be responsible implies the presence of others. Being responsible to others relates to the development of character and behavioral habits—a set of other-centered dispositions. Exhibiting civic virtue entails not just the recognition and acceptance of the rights and liberties that one possesses as a citizen, but the willingness to see that others possess these same rights and liberties, and to act accordingly. When cast within this framework, civic responsibility can be defined largely in terms of the obligations one has toward others. Such obligations involve being "respectful, tolerant, and civil" as fundamental duties and being "reciprocal, caring, and benevolent" as desired practices (Mathews 2000, 149). Civic responsibility also entails exhibiting certain moral characteristics or "habits of the heart," such as being honest and trustworthy (Bellah et al. 1985). In fact, civic responsibility and moral responsibility are inseparable, as democratic principles (e.g., tolerance and respect for others, procedural impartiality, concerns for the rights of the individuals and the welfare of the group) are grounded in moral principles (Colby et al. 2000, xxi).

But civic responsibility requires more than qualities related to one's interpersonal relationships; it also entails considerations of the goals or ends of one's actions. To be responsible within a communal context suggests that the problems of and the desires for the larger community become part of the individual's concerns and aspirations (Colby et al. 2000, xxvi). Civic responsibility cannot be exercised purely within the limited scope of one's own interests and desires; to be civically responsible is to be motivated by the good of others, and perhaps even by the common good (Singer et al. 2002).[3]

Thus, civic responsibility entails the recognition that humans are inter-dependent *and* that one has some responsibility for the well-being of others. It also requires one to act on the basis of this recognition by supporting those local efforts and organizations that enable individuals to have a worthwhile, dignified existence. To be sure, modern notions of justice require that there be a system for distributing rewards based on individual merit and initiative. But because that same system leads to inequalities sufficiently severe to prevent some members of society from obtaining the basic conditions linked to a dignified life, justice also requires moral people to object to the excesses of individual pursuits, consumerism, and materialism on the grounds of human dignity and the common good.

Democratic Citizenship and Civic Responsibility

Civil society does not exist in a moral vacuum; it is "shaped and reshaped in a milieu of cultural values and beliefs" (Eberly 1998, 154). In our decidedly pluralistic social context, civil society is colored by a bewildering array of cultural values and beliefs. If we accept Tocqueville's culturalist assumption—and this book is in many ways an extended argument for doing so—then democratic values themselves are part of that contentious milieu. How then does civil society relate to democratic culture and institutions?

Many liberal theorists contend that the key purpose of democratic government is the protection of human freedom or autonomy. Given a fundamental value of individual freedom, liberal theorists fear the unwarranted accumulation of centralized power—particularly totalitarianism, with its threat to freedom "from above." As the state is often tempted to take the route of centralization, the primary way to combat this threat is to craft careful procedures and institutional mechanisms such as periodic elections, separation of power, checks and balances, term limits, referendums, and recall elections. In fact, many classical liberals have held that "a liberal democracy could be made secure, even in the absence of an especially virtuous citizenry, by creating checks and balances" (Kymlicka and Norman 1995, 291). From this perspective, civil society is less a bulwark against centralized power than a space for self-development; it is an arena for enabling and realizing autonomy, a space where individuals can choose a path to develop their own identity. Indeed, as we discuss later in this chapter, while liberal theorists accept the opportunities for voluntary association that civil society provides, they are also often wary of civil society when it appears to take on too much power itself.

To other social theorists, including many in the republican tradition, this liberal position ultimately fosters a "politics of interest" in which politics becomes no more than individuals pursuing "different interests according to agreed-upon neutral rules" (Bellah et al. 1985, 200). While these theorists agree that electoral processes and the Constitution's separation of powers are central to legitimizing U.S. democracy, they argue that democracy is more than a set of procedures and that civic life requires more than institutional safeguards. Democratic life is deeply shaped by the character of the people, as democratic governments are "of the people, by the people, for the people." To ensure that democratic life is healthy and vibrant, citizens must be virtuous and ever vigilant, guarding against complacency and corruption.

Citizenship

These different views of civil society and democratic government become clearer when we look at them in light of recent debates about the role of the individual within the state, that is, in light of debates about the notion of what it means to be a citizen. For our purposes, the concept of citizenship—and particularly of *democratic* citizenship—encompasses a set of behaviors, capacities, and virtues that define the relationship of an individual to the state. In other words, citizenship is not merely a legal status but a particular set of attitudes, dispositions, and forms of engagement. Accordingly, we might recognize certain practices as embodying good citizenship even if the practitioner—a new immigrant, for example—lacked the legal status of citizen.

The nature and scope of citizenship have been central questions in political theory and practice since the ancient Greeks, but recent democratic theorists and empirical political scientists have revived an interest in the concept. This renewed attention is partly a response to a changing environment in which processes of globalization, economic integration, and mass migration (see essays in Beiner 1995), not to mention pockets of nationalist fervor and intrastate ethnic conflict (Kymlicka and Norman 2000), have challenged traditional understandings of the citizen and raised many questions about the role of civil society in shaping "good" citizens.

Contemporary theoretical discussions of the concept of citizenship have sought to address how the individual relates to the modern imperatives of political community. Drawing from John Locke, Immanuel Kant, John Stuart Mill, and others, liberal democratic theorists of the 1960s and 1970s began to ask whether and how the concept of justice governed the role of individuals vis-à-vis both the state and the market (e.g., Rawls 1971; Nozick 1974). Critics of this liberal project countered that liberal understandings of individual rights and freedoms do not fully account for the "thick" social bonds and obligations—what Tocqueville called "habits of the heart"—that are necessary among members of a healthy and stable polity (e.g., Sandel 1982; Bellah et al. 1985).

The formal study of citizenship developed out of this intellectual environment; it was "a natural evolution in political discourse because the concept of citizenship seems to integrate the demands of justice and community membership" (Kymlicka and Norman 1995, 283). While this new emphasis on citizenship is characterized by an array of approaches and arguments, it is framed by common themes of the political obligations and expectations of the individual in complex societies. These contemporary theorists of citizenship also seem to share certain common concerns, most notably the widely held belief that the levels of engagement, capacities, and virtues of citizens in the United States and abroad have slowly diminished during the last few decades (Barber 1984; Popenoe 1995; Sanders and Putnam 2006).

Scholars such as Robert Putnam (2000), Theda Skocpol (2003), and Verba, Schlozman, and Brady (1995), using a variety of methods and focusing on a range of research subjects, have in a more empirical vein arrived at a similar conclusion, namely, that there has been a slow yet determinative erosion not only in civic activity (encompassing, in these studies, both political participation and involvement in civil society) but in the development of citizen competency to engage in that activity as well. From this point of view, the problem is not simply that there is less voting, grassroots organizing, or identification with political organizations but there is also less political knowledge, discussion, and expertise, leading to historically low levels of political efficacy among large swaths of the citizenry. In response, innumerable books, reports, and private and public initiatives have been developed to reinvigorate citizenship in the United States (Eberly 1994; Barber 1998; Putnam 2003; Macedo et al. 2005).

Good Citizens

Several currents run through the scholarship on democratic citizenship that intersect with our themes of civic responsibility and civil society. Many scholars identify a set of dispositions and aptitudes that define good citizenship, including what we have called "civic capacities" and "civic virtues." Others emphasize the behavioral dimensions of citizenship, pointing to voting, acquisition of information, membership in voluntary associations, and other forms of engagement as the marks of the good citizen. Still others have an institutional or organizational focus: They examine institutions and associations such as the rule of law, the right to vote, and civil society itself, all of which provide a framework for exercising citizenship and help to foster it.

Despite such varied approaches to citizenship, several common key assumptions underlie the concept. First, while democratic citizenship enables (and even celebrates) mass participation, this participation requires collective acceptance of important values and faculties. The word "democracy" is a combination of the Greek words for "the people" (*demos*, or, more precisely, citizens of the *polis*) and "rule" or "power" (*kratos*). Hence democracy is often defined as "rule by the people" or "rule by the many" or what we might call popular sovereignty today. Yet citizenship in the classical world was severely limited to those who were thought to have the *capacity* to rule, which excluded (from an ancient point of view) women, slaves, artisans, and many others. Modern democracies, of course, have a more capacious understanding of the terms of membership, but contemporary theorists still tend to conceptualize ideal citizens as "informed participants" who possess key "civic skills" (Verba, Schlozman, and Brady 1995) as well as adequate knowledge about political elites and political processes (Delli Carpini and Keeter 1996). Indeed, this understanding of the "good citizen" as being informed and capable has a deep historical resonance in American civic life (Schudson 1998).

In addition to the basic capacities of citizens, many commentators on democratic citizenship suggest that good citizens exhibit a set of civic virtues—that is, internal dispositions or orientations of action that form an individual's character and lend themselves to concern for public life. James Madison, for example, suggested that the separation of powers and federalism institutionalized in the Constitution would fail to sustain the republic without "sufficient virtue among men for self-government." He continued: "Republican government presupposes the existence of these qualities [virtues] to a higher degree than any other form" (Madison 1987, Federalist 55). Like the ideal of the informed citizen, this belief that democratic governments require virtuous citizens to succeed also resonates with the public, as 90 percent of Americans cite "moral character" as the key defining trait of the good citizen (Wuthnow 1996, 157).

As Madison's words suggest, the concept of a "virtuous" citizenry is most often associated with the republican tradition of political thought, in contrast to the liberal view. Michael Sandel, a contemporary proponent of the republican perspective, sees the prevailing American public philosophy as a kind of liberal proceduralism, in which the contemporary political community is little more than "a framework of rights." He acknowledges that this framework "respects persons as free and independent selves, capable of choosing their own values and ends" but argues for a republican version of self-rule that entails "a sense of belonging, a concern for the whole, a moral bond with the community whose fate is at stake" (Sandel 1996, 4). Thus, it is prudent that citizens who engage in self-rule "possess, or come to acquire, certain qualities of character, or civic virtues." Sandel's view means, however, that "republican politics cannot be neutral toward the values and ends its citizens espouse," but rather "requires a formative politics, a politics that cultivates in citizens the qualities of character self-government requires" (Sandel 1996, 5–6). Other critics have criticized liberal "rights-based" notions of citizenship along similar lines (e.g., Glendon 1991; Galston 1995; Wilson 1995).[4]

Some liberal theorists have suggested that the republican critique caricatures their positions: Liberal democracy, they insist, is not indifferent to the character of its citizens, nor has it ever been. Some of the leading figures in liberal theory and practice—notably John Locke, John Stuart Mill, and even Adam Smith—suggested that their versions of democracy would fail without the moral education of citizens in the civic virtues (Berkowitz 1999). Moreover, from the perspective of liberal virtue theorists, liberal democracies do not merely require virtuous citizens, they also are well suited to develop those virtues (Galston 1991, 1992; Macedo 1990). The virtues supposedly engendered through the formative politics of liberal democracies include reliability, trust, and a strong work ethic, as well as a set of such distinctively *liberal* virtues as autonomy, tolerance, and mutual respect. Given these formative goals, it is not surprising that the project of liberal virtue theorists has recently moved in the direction of civic education (see, e.g., Macedo 2000; Macedo et al. 2005).

We need not settle the argument between liberal and republican theorists on the importance of a virtuous citizenry here (see chapter 6 for an expanded discussion). The key point is that both traditions lay claim to the idea that civic virtue is both important to the health of democracy and currently in decline. In that sense, these theoretical contentions dovetail with the recent scholarly work on social capital and civic engagement. It is not so far-fetched to describe some of the benefits of a robust civic life identified by Putnam (2000) in terms of civic virtue, including his argument that democratic citizenship requires social trust, some measure of toleration of differences, and an acceptance of mutual obligations (i.e., reciprocity).

The Common Good

Related to these matters of citizens' character and civic virtue is another key assumption of most democratic theory: the role of the individual citizen in pursuing collective goals. As noted earlier, civic responsibility is not merely a matter of possessing a certain character that shapes the quality of one's interpersonal relationships; it also entails the articulation and advancement of collective goals or ends. What counts as an appropriate collective goal, however, is generally a matter of great controversy in modern democracies, to the point that many theorists avoid the topic altogether. Unlike the classical understanding of citizenship, which was tied to membership in relatively homogeneous city-states (the Greek *polis* or Roman *res publica*), citizens of modern democracies are beset with societal complexity and diversity that renders collective decision-making more difficult. Compounding the problem is that, if Sandel's argument is correct (i.e., if the prevailing American public philosophy focuses more on individual rights than the responsibilities of citizenship), then talk of the state pursuing a "common good" or "public interest" may be misplaced.

In fact, some commentators argue that the current lack of more sub-stantive discourse about the common good actually serves to diminish citizens' connections with political life. For example, Hollenbach contends that the lack of such discourse serves as "a source of the alienation of many citizens" and reduces their level of political participation (2003, 160), and E. J. Dionne argues that current political discourse largely fails to address the real needs of communities (1991). Thus, the principled conviction on the part of many political philosophers and scholars to avoid, on the basis of ideological or scientific neutrality, any discussion or analysis of the common good leads to a downward spiral in which shared meaning, understanding, and community become even harder to achieve (Hollenbach 2003, 160). As we saw earlier, rejecting the possibility of the common good fosters an "interest-group politics" in which politics becomes simply a contest among private self-interests that exhibit little, if any, concern for the wider society and its problems (see, e.g., Elshtain 1995).

Tocqueville recognized that the interaction of individual self-interest and the public interest could create an intriguing paradox. On the one hand, mass participation to advance public goods requires individual freedom; on the other hand, that same freedom can foster an individualism that gravitates against mass participation to advance public goods. At the same time, Tocqueville noted that religion and other features of civil society contributed to a "public morality" or, in our terms, a sense of civic responsibility that directs the attention of citizens away from the self. Religion, among other aspects of civil society, can form an "unconventional partnership" with democracy in which civil society relies on democracy for its own freedom, while democracy uses civil society to overcome its own excesses (see Fowler 1989).

This brings us to a final point. Most theories of democratic citizenship recognize the unique role of the state in framing public purposes, as well as the importance of the institutions of civil society in pursuing those purposes. The literature is voluminous on the link between the networks of civil society and citizenship. Some speak of civil society as a "seedbed" for civic virtue and the emergence of civic goals (Glendon 1991, 109; see also Glendon and Blankenhoorn 2005); others describe the "mediating" role that civil society plays between the individual and the state or the market (Berger and Neuhaus 1977). All of these perspectives share a commitment to the idea that civil society is a key incubator of healthy citizenship. Eberly neatly summarizes the basic argument of proponents of a strong civil society when he states: "Democracy feeds on the qualities of citizenship that are nourished through the institutions of civil society" (1998, 142).

A cross-national perspective on civil society illustrates its potential for fostering democratic institutions and values. Civil society played a key role in challenging authoritarian regimes in such places as South Africa and Poland in the 1980s and 1990s. In particular, organizations within civil society reached across borders for international support, generating intense pressure that ultimately resulted in democratic transition (Keck and Sikkink 1998). As part of civil society, religion has often played a part in such sociopolitical transitions. Religious institutions have a relatively strong capacity for retaining their autonomy against state encroachment, which makes them uniquely situated to challenge nondemocratic regimes (Gautier 1998). Indeed, religious institutions' ability to protect political space—and to mobilize from within that space—"most strikingly differentiates religiously motivated movements from their secular counterparts" (Wald, Silverman, and Fridy 2005).

Of course, the power of civil society as a space for mobilization can also be put to nondemocratic use. One need only point to the Taliban in Afghanistan, the Shia movement that led to the Iranian revolution, or the many other instances in which religion has justified authoritarian regimes. Some libertarian and conservative critics argue that civil society poses a real threat to individual freedom. From this point of view, civil society can be an uninvited imposition, at best, or a subtle means of insidious social control, at worst. Moreover, even where civil society does challenge authoritarianism, an opposite argument can be made by the left, namely that civil society diminishes the role of the government—and therefore the importance of active citizenship—in addressing widespread inequality through public policy. From this point of view, civil society is a conservative, antipolitical, and privatizing distraction from the most effective means of social change: the state. After all, liberal theorists argue, many of the problems confronting American society—whether poverty or power disparity—cannot be solved by interacting with one's neighbors, volunteering, or programs offered by religious congregations or nonprofit agencies (Skocpol 2003, 259).

Nevertheless, critics from both the right and left acknowledge that there is real power in civil society, and neither side seriously contends that civil society should be discarded altogether (see Walzer 1995). Their arguments are largely cautionary tales about the ways civil society, like any other form of social organization or control, can degrade equality and freedom if misused. These critics cannot—and rarely try to—argue plausibly that institutions other than the state and market have no place in shaping how citizens understand their role in public life.

In summary, citizenship has its own set of distinctive capacities, virtues, and forms of engagement. But citizenship also raises the broader question of the responsibilities of civic life and the role of civil society in shaping those responsibilities. Citizenship brings to the fore the highly contested status of the individual within political community—not only the citizen's rights and freedom but also expectations and obligations toward the common good. The concept of citizenship also highlights the importance of civil society as a set of institutions and associations that, though distinct from the state, have a role in shaping the quality of a citizen's interaction with the state.

Conclusion

Liberal democratic theorists often make a distinction between public and private spheres. These theorists insist that citizens are autonomous in their private lives and that they ought to be left alone to determine their own fates without constraints placed on them by external authority, especially the state. What is "public," in contrast, is defined as being open to governmental inquiry and regulation, and ordinary citizens are expected to have some input into and control over the way democratic government performs its role.

Civil society occupies the space between the public and private. On the one hand, it exists primarily as a domain for private action. Citizens can join the associations of civil society without coercion and for mutual benefit, and they can voluntarily exit those associations. On the other hand, the citizen's experience within civil society often has public effects. In their group experiences, citizens gain knowledge and develop skills that are applicable in public life, and they also develop dispositions or virtues that shape the way they participate.

For some scholars, the most profound challenge to civil society is the co-optation of voluntary associations by the "virtues" of liberal democracy. The enduring influence of liberal individualism on civil society itself raises the question of whether civil society has the independence and capacity to act as a counterbalance to either the state or the market (e.g., Fowler 1999). Liberal theory places a premium on individual freedom, self-reliance, and self-definition. These may be virtues—and, as we suggest in chapter 6, they can be healthy virtues for democratic citizens—but by themselves they do not tend to reinforce an others-centered ethic. To the extent that civil society appropriates these virtues, it is diminished as a corrective to the individualist impulses of both the state and the market. Some intellectuals believe much damage has already been done, especially to the notion that we have duties or obligations that transcend our individual self-interest (e.g., Wolfe 1989).

Religion is not immune from these pressures. As we discuss throughout this book, patterns of religious privatization have increased over time. Many citizens now describe themselves as "spiritual, not religious"; many are alienated from organized religion and therefore do not take part in the public role that religious institutions have always played. But the privatizing effects are not limited to those without religious affiliation. Even those who claim some sort of affiliation with a religious institution may vest that institution with very little authority in their lives. They are religious, but not at the expense of their individual autonomy.

Some cultural observers celebrate that fact. They suggest that we are better off when religion stays safely tucked away in the private sphere, with little to no public "witness." They often advocate a "godless constitution," and claim that the state ought to maintain a secular posture (Kramnick and Moore 2005). This perspective, which reflects a fundamental concern about the potentially harmful influences of religion on the state, has deep roots in American political culture. Some of our most prominent Founding Fathers, including Thomas Jefferson and James Madison, expressed serious reservations about introducing religious influence into the governing process.

Many of the contemporary arguments about religion and the state, however, rest on the assumption that religious tolerance—that is, openness to and legal protection for religious pluralism—is only possible by compartmentalizing religion, that is, by treating it as something less than pervasive in a citizen's life. Consider recent philosophical work on democracy and pluralism in which theorists insist that citizens must come to politics with "public," rather than merely "private" (i.e., religious), reasons (Rawls 1993; Audi 1997). To do otherwise would at best alienate others with different "conceptions of the good," at worst invite violent religious conflict.

Much of this book is devoted to suggesting that such claims about the deleterious effects of religion are overstated. To be sure, religion has been the source of great conflict throughout the sweep of world history, and that role has not subsided. Yet religion is also capable of shaping citizens who are both highly engaged and responsible in their public efforts. The claim that religion ought to be privatized because a "public religion" is a potential threat to democracy is belied by a persistent fact: When religion takes a public role, it often fosters precisely the kinds of norms and behaviors that make democracy thrive.

Notes

1. For example, Edwards (2004) outlines three different schools of thought about the nature of civil society: civil society as associational life, civil society as the good society, and civil society as the public sphere. Of course, other definitions are possible. For example, Lichterman and Potts (2005, 2) suggest that "civic" can mean any relationship(s) not directly dictated by governmental authority in which people communicate with one another and the wider world either as citizens or as members of a community or a society. In so doing, the authors note that they want to "define the civic in terms of communication and relationships, not as a distinct 'sector' of society."

2. Liberal democratic thought varies in the extent to which it advances what might be called correspondence theory, in which associations in civil society are expected to, and if need be required to, incorporate liberal norms and practices within their associational life. This matter will be addressed more thoroughly in chapter 2.

3. Wuthnow (1996, 7) notes that civil society is a preferable concept to that of community. To focus on community is to pay little, if any, attention to the role of government, including law, whereas civil society only has meaning in relation to government. The concept of community, for Wuthnow, suggests that people interact in nearly equal circumstances and govern themselves largely on the basis of moral virtue and altruistic sentiments. On the other hand, civil society is understood to include a variety of organizations that may well be in tension with one another and whose coexistence depends on a framework of shared legal understanding.

4. The notion of character formation naturally raises the issue of which specific virtues should be inculcated.

2

❊

Religion in Contemporary America

In this volume we examine the role of religion in fostering civic responsibility, and we do so primarily by analyzing four forms of religious expression that reflect different ways in which Americans are religious. Because our analytical framework represents a new way to examine religion and because it constitutes a central feature of our analysis, it merits an extended discussion.

Although religious life in America manifests certain distinctive and stable patterns, it also exhibits some important patterns of change. Thus, rather than analyzing specific religious beliefs or religious affiliations, this study begins by examining the way in which people express their religiosity in terms of four different forms (or modes[1]) of religious expression. The second part of the chapter explicates these four forms of religious expression and the theoretical expectations associated with each. We specify the measurement strategy employed to tap such forms of religious expression and examine whether such posited expectations are indeed captured through this strategy. Finally, we examine which types of people tend to exhibit these religious modes and whether the distribution of religious expressions has changed over time.

Stability and Change in American Religious Life

It is somewhat ironic that we seek to analyze the role of religion in fostering American civic responsibility shortly after the turn of the new

41

millennium, as few concepts have occupied a more central position in modern social science than secularization. According to secularization theory, religion is largely a vestige of premodern culture, a human expression that is destined to decline in importance and, perhaps, disappear altogether in an age of science and reason (Hadden 1989, 3; Bruce 2002). From this perspective, as societies modernize, they secularize; religion disappears—or, at the very least, its expression becomes highly privatized (Chaves 1994; Yamane 1997).[2] According to secularization theory, any "impact" that religion may have on contemporary American civic and political life is simply a remnant of some outmoded, and disappearing, facet of social life.

While countervailing evidence to the secularization theory could be examined in great detail, perhaps it is sufficient to note several prominent features of contemporary American life that undermine the theory's contentions. The most obvious of these is the prevalence of religious beliefs and practices in American life even though the United States may be considered among the most modern of societies. In fact, the American people have long been recognized as being highly religious, a characteristic that is particularly distinctive when the religious beliefs and practices of the American people are placed in cross-national perspective.

The distinctly religious character of American life can be seen in table 2.1, which compares the religious beliefs and practices of the American people with those of the residents of Canada and nine largely industrialized and economically developed European countries. Included in this study were residents of historically Protestant countries (Germany, Great Britain, the Netherlands, Norway, and Sweden) and historically Catholic countries (France, Italy, Poland, and Spain). In each, survey respondents were asked questions about their religious behavior, religious beliefs, and their perception of their own religiosity.

These data make evident that Americans are distinctive in terms of their overall religiosity. Americans are much more likely to report weekly church attendance than those who reside in other Western cultural contexts; only those who live in Poland are more likely to attend church weekly than Americans (37 percent versus 32 percent, respectively).[3] Overall, weekly church attendance tends to be somewhat higher in historically Catholic countries. Nevertheless, Americans are much more likely than either Italians or Spaniards to attend weekly. Compared to the populations of

Table 2.1 Distinctiveness of American Religious Life (percent)

Country	Attends weekly	Prays daily	Believes in life after death	Believes in miracles	Considers self very religious
Canada	19	19	70	55	11
France	13	17	52	38	7
Germany	8	10	35	50	8
Great Britain	14	15	14	59	7
Italy	29	32	29	72	14
Netherlands	14	24	60	40	17
Norway	7	14	53	38	9
Poland	37	40	77	64	16
Spain	27	23	56	46	14
Sweden	6	10	51	27	4
United States	32	47	81	79	26

Source: International Social Survey Program: Religion II, 1998. See appendix A for details on surveys analyzed in tables.

Protestant countries that exhibit the highest level of church attendance (Great Britain and the Netherlands), Americans are more than twice as likely to attend church weekly, and they are at least four times more likely to do so than Germans, Norwegians, or Swedes.

Such distinctiveness is not limited to worship attendance; it is also present in terms of private prayer life and religious beliefs. Nearly half of the American people (47 percent) report that they pray daily; only one other country examined comes close to this level (Poland, with 40 percent). In most other comparisons, Americans are more than twice to nearly five times more likely to pray daily. Similarly, the United States ranks first among all eleven countries in terms of religious beliefs, with four out of five Americans reporting that they believe in life after death and that they believe in miracles. Given these patterns, it is probably no surprise that Americans are also the most likely to label themselves as very religious.

Clearly, then, religious life in America has hardly disappeared, and it appears particularly vibrant when compared to the religious life of other Western industrialized countries. Moreover, national surveys over the last half century document the relative stability of various facets of American religious life. For example, over the past fifty years, the percentage of

Americans who report they believe in God has never dropped below 90 percent (Gallup and Lindsay 1999, 23), and in a March 2007 *Newsweek* poll, more than 90 percent of all Americans continued to report such beliefs (Braiker 2007).

Attendance at religious services has also been relatively stable over time. Table 2.2 presents the levels of religious attendance reported by Americans over the past 70 years. Data presented in the first column of table 2.2 are drawn from Gallup surveys gathered since 1937.[4] The second column presents data drawn from Roper surveys collected between 1973 and 1994.[5] Various Roper surveys were conducted each year, and many asked respondents whether they had attended church in the past seven days. The percentages presented in the second column of table 2.2 reflect data

Table 2.2 Reported Weekly Church Attendance of Americans over Time (percent)

	Study			
Year	Gallup	Roper	GSS[a]	NES[b]
1937	41			
1940	37			
1950	39			
1954	46			
1955	49			
1957	47			
1958	49			
1962	46			
1967	43			
1969	42			
1972	40	y	35	26 (37)[c]
1973		y	28	
1974		41	30	
1975	40	44	29	
1976		46	29	26 (38)
1977	41	43	30	
1978	41	42	28	
1979	40	44	y	
1980	40	40	29	25 (37)
1981	41	44	y	
1982	41	39	29	

Table 2.2 *Continued*

Year	Study			
	Gallup	Roper	GSS[a]	NES[b]
1983	40	x	32	
1984	40	43	33	24 (39)
1985		43	33	
1986		x	32	
1987	40	39	29	
1988	41	40	26	28 (40)
1989	43	41	30	
1990		39	30	26 (37)
1991		40	29	
1992		36	y	27 (37)
1993		37	29	
1994	42	39	27	
1996		y	25	26 (38)
1998	40	y	25	
2000		y	25	27 (38)
2002		y	24	
2004		y	28	23 (36)

Sources: Gallup data from Gallup and Castelli 1989, table 2.6, and Gallup and Lindsay 1999, 15; Roper data from Roper Social and Political Trends Data 1973–1994; GSS data from General Social Surveys 1972–2004.

Notes: x = no survey; y = not asked

[a] General Social Surveys
[b] National Election Studies
[c] When "almost every week" option is added

gleaned from across the Roper surveys.[6] The third column presents data gathered through the General Social Surveys, which began in 1972 and were conducted annually until 1994, at which point they became biennial. In these surveys, respondents were asked to indicate their level of attendance at worship services (weekly attendance was one possible response).[7] The fourth column in table 2.2 presents data gathered during presidential election years by the American National Election Studies (NES).[8]

In examining responses to questions on religious attendance conducted by different survey organizations over time, one can draw several conclusions.

First, it appears that the surveys yield somewhat different levels of weekly worship attendance. For example, in 1978 both Gallup and Roper data reveal that slightly more than 40 percent of Americans reported that they attended church on a weekly basis, but data gathered through the General Social Survey (GSS) of that year suggests that slightly less than 30 percent of Americans did so. The same is true in 1980, when data are available for all four survey organizations.

Second, some of the differences may be attributable to the type of response options provided respondents. For example, the NES survey asks the question "Do you ever attend religious services apart from occasional weddings, baptisms, and or funerals?" and provides a response option of "almost every week" that falls between "every week" and "once or twice a month." While respondents who fall in the "almost every week category" are not officially included as weekly attenders in table 2.2, if they are added, the percentage of NES respondents who attend (nearly) weekly would fall between 36 and 40 percent over the past three decades—approximately the percentage reported by Gallup and Roper during the same period of time.[9]

Third, the data suggest some waxing and waning in reported levels of weekly attendance. For example, the Gallup data reveal an increase in weekly religious attendance among the American people during the 1950s, reflecting what some analysts have identified as a "mini-religious revival" in that decade (e.g., Ahlstrom 1960; Hoge and Roozen 1979a; Hoge, Johnson and Luidens 1994, 1–4). However, sociologists have long noted that parents are more likely to attend religious services during those years in which young children are present in the family (Anders 1955; Lazerwitz 1961; Hoge and Roozen 1979b; Stoltzenberg, Blair-Loy, and Waite 1995), so much of the so-called revival during the 1950s can be attributed to the post–World War II baby boom. By the late 1960s and early 1970s, as these baby boomers reached adulthood, the level of weekly church attendance reported by the American people as a whole dropped to a point roughly equivalent to that reported between 1937 and 1950.

Fourth, though levels of weekly church attendance vary across survey organizations, a general pattern of stability is evident in the data collected by each organization over time. Consequently, when taken as a whole the data in table 2.2 suggest that, contrary to the expectations of secularization theory, there has not been a dramatic downturn in reported levels of Americans' church attendance over the past seven decades.[10]

Nevertheless, over the last three decades, weekly church attendance does appear to have slightly eroded. A cursory examination of the Roper data reveals that during the survey's first six years (1974 through 1979), the percentage of Americans reporting that they had attended religious services in the last seven days never dipped below 40 percent. Between 1987 and 1994, however, the percentage dipped below 40 percent in five of eight years. If one combines the data collected for the five years between 1974 and 1978, the percentage of respondents reporting weekly worship attendance is 43.5 percent, while the corresponding percentage for the last five years of data collected (1990–94) is 37.9 percent (data not shown).

Despite a different question format and sampling frame, GSS religious attendance patterns reveal important parallels with the Roper data. Like the Roper data, the GSS data do not reveal any dramatic decline in weekly attendance at religious services. Yet by pooling the data for the first five surveys collected (1972–76) and comparing it to the data collected during the last five surveys (1996–2004), one finds a decline of about 5 percent— from 30.3 percent to 25.0 percent—in reported weekly church attendance over the past three decades (data not shown). Thus, despite the fact that the Roper surveys and the General Social Surveys reveal different levels of weekly church attendance, they both suggest that there has been a small decline in the level of weekly church attendance between 1972 and 2004.[11]

It is unclear, however, whether such a decline in attendance at public worship services is necessarily a function of a decline in the salience of religion among the American people or whether it simply reflects religion becoming more privatized. For example, even if there has been a slight decline in the level of weekly worship attendance, there may not be any similar decline evident in reported levels of religious beliefs or private devotional activity.

Table 2.3 addresses this matter. The various General Social Surveys did not ask respondents how frequently they prayed until 1983, but that question has been asked in many of the subsequent surveys (though sometimes of only one-half or one-quarter of the respondents). As is evident in the first column of table 2.3, the percentage of Americans who report praying on a daily basis exhibits far greater aggregate stability than attendance

Table 2.3 Religious Practices over Time (percent)

Study	Prays daily	Attends church monthly
General Social Surveys		
GSS 1972	x	56
GSS 1973	x	50
GSS 1974	x	53
GSS 1975	x	52
GSS 1976	x	49
GSS 1977	x	52
GSS 1978	x	51
GSS 1980	x	50
GSS 1982	x	49
GSS 1983	55	53
GSS 1984	57	53
GSS 1987	57	52
GSS 1988	54	51
GSS 1996	58 (third sample)	47
GSS 1998	54 (half sample)	48
GSS 2000	56 (half sample)	44
GSS 2004	59 (half sample)	50
National Election Studies		
NES 1988	48	50
NES 1996	52	53
NES 2000	52	51
NES 2004	53	51
Other National Surveys		
Citizen Participation Study, 1990	x	56
Giving and Volunteering, 1996	x	52
God and Society, 1996	57	60
Civic Involvement, 1997	x	52
Arts and Religion, 1999	50	40
Religion and Politics, 2000	63	43
Saguaro, 2000	x	70
Religion and Public Life, 2001	59	60

Note: x = not asked

at religious services. The data reveal that, if anything, the frequency with which Americans report praying on a daily basis has increased over the past two decades. Again, if one combines the data for the years 1983–88 (the first five surveys for which we have data) and compares the result to the data for the last five surveys conducted (1996–2004), the percentage of Americans reporting that they pray on a daily basis has increased slightly from 56.3 percent to 56.9 percent (data not shown).

Despite these patterns of relative stability, there is evidence that American religious life has changed in other ways over the past half century. One school of thought suggests that religion is less bound than previously by social custom, familial tradition, or a sense of communal obligation. It has become more personalized, eclectic, and individualistic, as religionists are increasingly anchoring their faith in the private and subjective spheres of life, eschewing religious authority and replacing it with religious self-definition. A variety of analysts (e.g., Roof and McKinney 1987; Hoge, Johnson, and Luidens 1994) contend that a more "fluid and flexible" religious environment has emerged in American religious life, one that has been labeled the new volunteerism.

As we noted in the introduction, what these different analysts all suggest is that religion is less disappearing than changing, becoming less public and more private in expression. Bellah and his colleagues, for example, identified the archetype of "Sheilaism," named after Sheila Larson, an interviewee who believed in God but couldn't remember the last time she had attended church (1985, 221). Larson held that her faith, which she labeled "Sheilaism—her own little voice" had carried her "a long way." Sheila has come to exemplify the idiosyncratic nature of religious faith for many Americans, a faith that is highly individualized and privatized if for no other reason than because no others can be found who hold similar religious beliefs.

Others have discussed this "fluid and flexible" environment in terms of the phenomenon of "spiritual shoppers" (e.g., Wuthnow 1998a, 2005; Roof 1999; Cimino and Lattin 1998). Reflecting the consumer culture to which many Americans have long been exposed, spiritual shopping connotes "making [spiritual] choices and having the freedom to choose according to one's personal tastes and needs" (Wuthnow 2005, 107). While spiritual shoppers generally believe that God exists, they typically have little interest in religious doctrines or ecclesial authority (Wuthnow 2005, 120). Neither do they see themselves as loyalists—whether in terms of a community, a group, denomination, or a specific house of worship, as they find it necessary "to strike out on their own, searching for the sacred by metaphorically going from place to place" (Wuthnow 2005, 128).

Wuthnow has argued that, as religious beliefs have become more eclectic and religious commitments more private, the character of spirituality in America has been changing. In his words, "a traditional spirituality of inhabiting sacred places has given way to a new spirituality of seeking" (1998a, 1–3). As a result, Wuthnow argues, the basis on which religious identities are shaped is also changing: Whereas religious identity was previously forged through "the holding of predefined social positions within institutions," people today "increasingly create a sense of personal identity through an active sequence of searching and selecting" (Wuthnow 1998a, 10).

Much of the scholarly analysis of spiritual seeking has focused on the baby-boomer generation, but a somewhat similar religious expression has emerged among subsequent generations. In a recent study of spirituality among teenagers, Smith and Denton (2005) found that their subjects were profoundly disconnected from religious institutions and even the most basic tenets of orthodox religion. Many teenagers were instead focused on religion as a therapeutic experience. In echoes of Sheilaism, religion has become a source for psychological satisfaction, which is fairly easily achieved by being good to others and to oneself.

Does the growth in this kind of spiritual seeking and religious individualism suggest secularization? It is noteworthy that Casanova (1994) has argued that secularization may occur in two ways: (1) by way of decline in religious beliefs and practices and (2) by way of marginalization of religion to a privatized sphere. Accordingly, it is possible that religious beliefs and practices might still be widely evident in society (contrary to proposition #1) even as such beliefs and practices become more marginalized and privatized (consistent with secularization proposition #2), until they eventually exercise little bearing on public life.

Thus, one important challenge to religious associational life is the presence of a growing individualism within American religious life, as denominational and congregational life is influenced by the individualistic, sub-jective, and anti-institutional spirit of contemporary American culture. At the same time, there has been a growth in what might be labeled priva-tized faith, reflecting those who are "believers but not belongers" (Davie 1994) and for whom the presence of religious belief is more individual than institutional, more private than public. With the severing of individual spirituality from institutional religion and its collective authority, it is likely that believers will increasingly assert autonomy from religious institutions as individuals become more idiosyncratic and eclectic in forging their re-ligious faith. Thus, privatized religion, as it is used here, indicates a reli-gious faith that is practiced primarily within a personal, rather than an organizational, locus.

Are these changes in American religious life related to the broad changes in American public life discussed earlier? And are those who ex-press a privatized religious faith more inclined to withdraw from public life? As discussed in the conclusion to chapter 1, some analysts hold that it is desirable, given the separation of church and state, that religious be-liefs and values remain private, thus not expressed in the public square. If, however, privatized religion leads to lower levels of public engagement as well, it may work at cross-purposes with the normative democratic value of high levels of public engagement.

Forms of Religious Expression

When considering the link between religion and civic responsibility, what may be important about religion is not so much one's particular religious beliefs or membership in a particular religious tradition, but *the way* in which one is religious (Ammerman 1997). In other words, it may matter less whether one subscribes to particular religious beliefs or is affiliated with a particular religious tradition than how one's religious faith comes to be expressed. If one is religious but chooses to express faith in a privatized fashion, such religious expression may have little public utility. As noted in the introduction, contemporary distrust of organized religion may go hand in hand with contemporary distrust of politics (Elshtain 2002, 24),

Figure 2.1 Forms of religious expression

		Level of public religious practice	
		Low	**High**
Level of private religious practice	**Low**	*Diminished*	*Public*
	High	*Privatized*	*Integrated*

and religious believers who devalue organized religion may express diminished enthusiasm for organizational endeavors within the civic and political spheres of life as well.

Of course, there is no single method of analyzing people in terms of how they are religious; a variety of approaches are possible. Because of our interest in civic and political engagement, we have chosen a method that begins by assessing people in terms of the extent to which their religious behavior exhibits both public and private dimensions of religious life. Obviously, people can express lower or higher levels of religious activity in both dimensions. When each dimension is divided in half, four broad categories of religious expression can be created, as shown in figure 2.1.

As we have noted, this study seeks in part to validate findings across a number of other studies. Hence, we seek to measure the public and private dimensions of religious life using identical operational strategies. Since most surveys ask only a limited number of religious questions, and since we seek to use the widest data array possible, only a minimal number of questions can be used to make such assignments. We chose to operationalize each dimension by employing the most commonly asked question related to each, namely, the respondent's reported level of attendance at public worship activities and the respondent's reported frequency of engaging in private prayer.[12]

First, respondents who reported relatively low levels of religious activity in both the private and public dimensions exhibited what we label a "diminished" form of religious life. While those who fall in this category may vary in terms of their religious beliefs and affiliations—some may be atheists or agnostics; others may believe in God and be members of a religious congregation—they are similar in terms of religious behavior. Seemingly, their religious faith is not particularly important to them, as they report low attendance at public worship and low levels of private religious activity.

Second, some have a "privatized" religious faith. Private religionists exhibit high levels of private and low levels of public expressions of their religious faith. Such individuals are likely to report that their religious faith is salient to them but that their personal beliefs and practices are more important than what is taught by any religious body with which they may or may not be affiliated. While they may engage in public worship occasionally, they do not do so regularly. Nevertheless, they remain relatively religious, at least in terms of their reported levels of private prayer life.

Third, some Americans exhibit their religious faith primarily in a "public" way, reporting high levels of religious attendance but relatively low levels of private religious activity. Some who fall in this category may be associated with religious faiths in which public participation at religious services is emphasized over personal devotional activity. But others in this category may attend public worship for more extrinsic or self-oriented reasons (Edgell 2006, 71–73), in that they choose to attend religious services for utilitarian ends (e.g., as a means to promote their business or professional practice or to socialize with like-minded people). For such individuals, if spiritual growth is a priority at all, it is secondary.

Finally, there are those who exhibit high levels of both private and public religious activity, simply labeled here as an "integrated" form of religious expression. For such respondents, religion is highly salient in their lives. It is likely that these respondents "find their master motive in religion" (Allport and Ross 1967, 434), desiring to internalize their faith and to subordinate all other aspects of life to their religious commitment (Allport and Ross 1967, 441). For such individuals, spiritual growth is a priority, and such growth is intertwined with both private religious activities and active participation in the worship life of a religious community.

To categorize individuals in terms of these modes of religious expression, we needed to determine how to assign respondents to either a high or low category within each dimension. Our approach was to use the point that marked roughly where approximately one-half of the respondents fell on either side of that particular dimension. The "cutting point" utilized in classifying respondents along the public dimension of religiosity was whether or not the respondent reported attending church on a monthly or greater basis; the cutting point for the private dimension was whether or not the respondent reported praying on a daily basis (see table 2.3).[13]

Does the employment of these two simple measures have any validity in terms of capturing the different forms of religious expressions outlined above? Fortunately, several surveys contain a number of questions that permit an initial validation.[14] The analysis presented in table 2.4 supports the conclusion that the differences in religious orientations anticipated theoretically for each form of religious expression are, in fact, captured by this relatively simple measurement.

First, not surprisingly, the God and Society Survey reveals that those who are classified as exhibiting a diminished form of religious expression are, by far, the most likely to report that religion is not important in their life (57 percent), while relatively few (10 percent) report that religion serves to provide them any significant level of guidance in their lives. Likewise, two-thirds (67 percent) of those who fall in this category strongly agree (and nearly all—91 percent—agree; data not shown) that one does not need to attend church to be a good Christian, while a majority strongly agree (50 percent) and an overwhelming majority agree (76 percent; data not shown) that their personal beliefs are more important than the teachings of any religious institution.

More importantly, however, these data reveal that those with a privatized religious faith are much more likely than those with a diminished form of religious expression to indicate that religion does provide guidance in their lives; in fact, a majority (57 percent) of privatized religionists report that religion provides either "quite a bit" or "a great deal" of guidance in their lives (data not shown). Moreover, in accordance with theoretical expectations, those with a privatized faith also overwhelmingly agree that one does not need to attend religious services to be a good person religiously, and they strongly insist that their personal beliefs are much more important than the teachings of any religious institution. In fact, those with a privatized form of religious behavior are the most likely of all the groups examined to strongly agree to these two statements.

One might anticipate that those exhibiting public forms of religious behavior are also inclined to report that religion provides a good deal of guidance in their lives. What distinguishes such religionists from those with privatized faiths, then, is that the former are likely to value public worship and religious institutions more fully. Given the influence of religious individualism within American religious life, however, such differences should be viewed in a relative, rather than an absolute, fashion.

These expectations are also fulfilled in the patterns revealed in table 2.4. First, a majority (52 percent) of those with a public form of religious expression report that religion provides either "quite a bit" or "a great deal" of guidance in their lives (data not shown). And while about a third (30 percent) of public religionists disagree with the statement that one need not go to church to be a good person religiously (data not shown), they were three times more likely to do so than those with a private form of religious expression and nearly four times more likely to do so than those with a diminished form.

Finally, "integrated" religionists are the most likely to report that religion has a great deal of salience in their personal life. They are also the most likely to disagree with the statement that one does not need to attend worship services to be a good person religiously, and are the most likely to disagree that their personal religious beliefs are more important than church teachings.

Several items found in Wuthnow's summary of the 1999 Arts and Religion Survey further confirm that this measurement approach captures theoretical expectations. First, respondents in the survey were asked to express agreement or disagreement with the following statement: "My spirituality does not depend on being involved in a religious organization." If the different forms of religious expression have validity empirically, then those with either a diminished or privatized form of religious life (i.e., those who exhibit low levels of attendance at public worship services) should differ in their responses to this question from those with either a public or integrated form of religious expression (i.e., those who exhibit high

Table 2.4 Validation of Form of Religious Expression Variable (percent)

Survey	Diminished religion	Private religion	Public religion	Integrated religion
God and Society, 1996				
Religious salience				
Religion unimportant	57	24	11	3
Offers great deal of guidance	10	35	27	64
No need to go to church to be a good Christian				
Strongly disagree	4	5	16	32
Strongly agree	67	71	34	23
Personal beliefs more important than teachings of any church				
Strongly disagree	9	8	10	16
Strongly agree	50	61	39	43
Arts and Religion, 1999				
My spirituality does not depend on being involved in a religious organization				
Agree	88	82	57	51
It doesn't matter what you believe, as long as you are a good person				
Disagree	18	34	38	61
How important has attending services at your place of worship been in your efforts to grow spiritually or develop a closer relationship with God?				
Very important	12	34	58	84

levels of attendance at public worship services). Clearly this is the case: Whereas more than four out of five of those with diminished or privatized forms agreed with the statement, only a little more than one in two of those with public or integrated forms did so.

On the other hand, the analytical categories also reveal important differences among those who attend religious services on a regular basis.

Clearly the public and integrated forms of religiosity part ways on the basis of their devotional life, but what does this suggest about the nature of their religious faith? It may reflect different degrees of desire to grow spiritually, but it may also suggest different assessments about the certainty and exclusivity of religious truth.[15] What is central to public religionists is the public aspect of religious expression (not necessarily certainty or exclusivity of religious truth), but public expression is not sufficient for those who exhibit an integrated from of religious expression.

Thus, one might anticipate that public and integrated religionists would respond differently to the statement "It doesn't matter what you believe, as long as you are a good person." As those who exhibit an integrated form of religious expression link participation in the worship life of their religious community to their personal spiritual growth, one might anticipate that they would be less likely to be religious "relativists." For them, adherence to or rejection of particular religious beliefs is likely to have important consequences. This prediction is validated in table 2.4, as integrated religionists tend to stand alone in disagreeing with the statement. More than 60 percent of those with an integrated form of religious expression disagreed, while only 38 percent of public religionists and only 34 percent of privatized religionists did so.

Finally, the Arts and Religion Survey asked respondents "How important has attending services at your place of worship been in your efforts to grow spiritually and develop a closer relationship with God?" Here one might anticipate a gradual increase in the percentage of those responding "very important" as one moves from diminished to privatized, from privatized to public, and from public to integrated forms of religious expression. One would expect those exhibiting diminished religious expression to be the least likely to be concerned about growing spiritually and those with a privatized expression to seek spiritual growth—but largely outside of regular attendance at places of worship. On the other hand, public religionists attend services regularly, but spiritual growth may or may not be a priority. Because they do attend church regularly, however, they might be expected to be more likely than the privatists to state that attending worship services is important in their efforts to grow spiritually. Finally, those with an integrated form of religious expression can be expected to be more likely than those with a public expression to be motivated by a desire for spiritual growth (given their active devotional life). Thus, one would anticipate that integrationists would be more likely than public religionists to agree that attending worship is important in their efforts to grow spiritually.

Once again, these expectations are fulfilled in the data presented in table 2.4, as there is a monotonic pattern in the percentage of respondents reporting that church attendance is very important in terms of their spiritual growth and desire to develop a closer relationship with God. A little more than one in ten (12 percent) of those in the diminished category responded "very important" to the survey question, while a little more than one in three (34 percent) did so among those with a privatized form of religious expression. On the other hand, nearly three of five (58 percent) of those exhibiting a public form of religious expression stated attending worship services was important in their efforts to grow spiritually, and more than four of five (84 percent) of those with an integrated religious form did so.

Overall, it does appear that the theoretical expectations associated with the four forms of religious expression are largely captured empirically by the combined use of the two distinct measures of religious behavior. Therefore, having provided some validation for this measurement strategy, we can now turn our attention to the questions of what kinds of people exhibit these different forms of religious expression and whether such modes of expression have changed over time.

Characteristics of the Four Forms of Religious Expression

Who are the individuals who tend to exhibit these four forms of religious expression? Multiple data files could be employed to present such information, with a different table required for each data file, but such an analysis would be very cumbersome. For simplicity, we have therefore used just one survey, the Religion and Politics Survey of 2000, and we chose this particular survey because it had the largest base of respondents ($n = 5603$), providing a sufficient number of respondents in each of the four categories analyzed. Table 2.5 presents our findings.

Generally speaking, women tend to be more religious than men (Fowler et al. 2004, 269–72). So it is not surprising that men comprise a much larger percentage (58 percent) of those with a diminished form of religious expression. Men are also highly represented among those with a public form of religious expression, accounting for nearly two-thirds of the total. In contrast, women comprise approximately three-fifths of both the privatized form and integrated forms of religious expression. This pattern was evident across all the surveys analyzed (data not shown).

In addition to gender, race influences the composition of the four modes of religious expression. African Americans are three to four times more likely to be found in either the privatized or the integrated categories of religious expression than in the diminished or public categories, while whites are most likely to be located among those with a diminished or a public religious expression. Hispanics and representatives of other racial groups are about equally distributed across all four forms of religious expression.

Age differences are also evident across the four categories. The young generally tend to be less religious, and nearly half of those exhibiting a diminished form of religious expression are under thirty-six years of age. More than three-quarters of those exhibiting an integrated form of religious expression are over thirty-six. The age distribution within the privatized and public categories falls between the younger age distribution of the diminished and the older age distribution of the integrated forms—with about one-third being under the age of thirty-six and about one-quarter being fifty-six or older.

On the other hand, there tends to be little difference in the educational attainment levels displayed by each of the four types of religionists. Perhaps the most distinctive differences among the four categories are that the privatized tend to be somewhat less educated (with 44 percent having attained a high school diploma or less), and the public religionists tend to be the most educated (approximately one-third having attained a college degree). Overall, such differences are rather modest.

Marital status is more markedly varied among the categories of religious expression. Those who are married comprise two-thirds of the public and integrated religionists, while smaller proportions (though still a majority) of married respondents make up the diminished and privatized categories. Those who are currently divorced are particularly evident in the privatized category, while singles are most prevalent in the diminished.

Table 2.5 Demographic Characteristics of Forms of Religious Expression (percent)

Demographic characteristic	Diminished religion (n = 1701)	Private religion (n = 1447)	Public religion (n = 341)	Integrated religion (n = 2114)	eta
Gender					
Male	58	44	66	39	.18
Race					.07
White	80	69	78	73	
Black	4	12	3	13	
Hispanic	11	14	14	10	
Other	5	5	4	4	
Age					.19
Under 36	46	31	35	26	
36–55	37	43	42	39	
56 or older	18	26	23	34	
Marital					.13
Married	52	55	66	67	
Separated	2	2	1	1	
Divorced	9	12	5	7	
Widowed	3	7	4	9	
Single	32	24	24	16	

Education					
Less than high school	13	18	11	15	
High school graduate	31	35	30	32	
Some college	30	29	27	27	
College graduate	16	12	19	16	
Some graduate educ.	10	6	13	9	.10
Religious Tradition					
Evangelical Protestant	15	22	25	38	
Mainline Protestant	12	14	16	13	
Black Protestant	2	6	4	7	
Roman Catholic	22	26	38	26	
Jew	3	1	2	*	.23
Other	15	17	4	2	
Unaffiliated/Secular	31	14	4	2	

Source: Religion and Politics Survey, 2000; *n* = 5603

Finally, different religious affiliations are found within each of the four categories, though their relative proportions shift from one category to the next. Evangelical Protestants are most heavily concentrated among integrated religionists and Roman Catholics among public religionists, as both comprise 38 percent of their respective category. Mainline Protestants tend to be fairly evenly distributed across all four categories, but are somewhat more common in the public category. Black Protestants are more likely to exhibit either the privatized or the integrated form of religious expression, while those who fall in the catchall category of "other" are most common in the diminished and privatized categories. Finally, the religiously unaffiliated are most likely to be found in the diminished category, where they comprise nearly one-third of the total. Overall, these patterns suggest that differences in religious expression are not simply a function of one's religious affiliation. Rather, adherents of all major religious traditions can be found in each expression category.

Religious Forms over Time

Have the relative frequency distributions related to these categories of religious expression changed over time? Table 2.6 addresses this question by examining change in the forms of religious expression among the American people since the early 1980s. The table organizes these distributions over time according to the particular organizations conducting the surveys (e.g., the General Social Surveys and the National Election Studies).

Three important conclusions can be drawn from table 2.6. First, despite the fact that different organizations conducted the surveys and employed different questions, the resulting distributions are roughly similar in that the largest percentages of Americans fall in either the diminished or the integrated religious category. Together, such respondents constitute two-thirds to three-quarters of the American people. About one-third of the respondents in the various surveys fell in the diminished religious category, and one-third to two-fifths of the respondents exhibited an integrated form of religiosity. Only about one-quarter to one-third of the respondents remained within either the private or public category of religious expression.

Table 2.6 Distribution of Forms of Religion over Time (percent)

Study	Diminished religion	Private religion	Public religion	Integrated religion	Total	n
General Social Surveys						
GSS 1984	29	17	13	41	100	1447
GSS 1987	29	18	14	39	100	1819
GSS 1988	32	17	14	37	100	1468
GSS 1996	31	21	12	37	101	948
GSS 1998	34	18	11	37	100	1422
GSS 2000	35	22	9	34	100	778
GSS 2002	33	22	11	35	101	1362
GSS 2004	30	21	11	38	100	1335
National Election Studies						
NES 1988	36	14	17	33	100	2040
NES 1996	34	14	15	38	101	1714
NES 2000	34	15	13	38	100	1807
NES 2004	35	14	12	39	100	1212
Other National Surveys						
CPS, 1990[a]	37	13	11	38	99	2517
God & Society, 1996	27	13	16	43	99	3000
Arts & Religion, 1999	41	19	6	37	101	5603
Saguaro, 2000	31	12	16	41	100	3003
Relig. & Public Life, 2001	27	13	15	46	101	2041

[a] Citizen Participation Study, 1990

Second, the GSS data suggest that a privatized expression of religious life among the American people may have grown over time. Whereas 17 percent of GSS respondents could be classified as exhibiting a private religious life in 1984 and in 1988, the percentage jumped to 21 percent in 1996 and 22 percent in 2000 and 2002. However, the presidential election surveys conducted by NES (as well as the other national surveys examined in the table) do not reveal sustained growth in privatized religion. Thus, if the American people have increasingly chosen to express their religious faith in a more privatized fashion, such growth has been at most modest.

Conclusion

This chapter has documented the continuing high levels of religiosity that characterize Americans, especially when compared to other modern Western countries. In response to secularization theory, the chapter has also examined whether Americans have exhibited any substantial decline in their reported level of religious attendance and daily prayer over the past several decades. On the surface, there is little evidence to support secularization theory's prediction of eroding religiosity; the level of attendance at worship services has fallen only marginally, if at all, and there has been no decline in daily prayer.

We have argued, however, that particularly in relationship to aspects of public life, it may be as or more important to ascertain how people exhibit their religiosity as it is to know what they believe or with whom they affiliate religiously. Building upon two aspects of religiosity (the public act of attendance at worship services and the private act of personal prayer), we have argued that one can discern important differences among people in terms of their religious expression. By combining respondents' reported level of church attendance (public religious involvement) with their reported level of private, devotional prayer (private religious involvement), we created a new measure that yielded a fourfold categorization of the ways in which individuals may express their religious faith: diminished religion (low public and low private religious involvement), private religion (low public religion and high private religion), public religion (high public religion and low private religion), and integrated religion (high public and high private religion).

Efforts at validating this classification scheme revealed that our categories do indeed uncover important facets of religiosity. Respondents in the four categories were distinguished by such measures as the amount of guidance they reported religion plays in their lives, the importance they attach to church attendance and to personal belief, and the extent to which they take a relativistic view of religion. Clearly, the classification scheme differentiates people empirically in ways that are consistent with our theoretical expectations, and as a result, this variable is used extensively throughout the remainder of this book.

The four forms of religious expression are characterized by somewhat different demographic profiles. Women and African Americans are more likely to exhibit privatized and integrated forms of religious expression; males and whites, the more diminished and public forms. Young adults and singles are prone to be found within the ranks of those exhibiting a diminished form. Older adults are more numerous within the integrated category, and those who are divorced, within the privatized. Those with less education are more heavily concentrated in the privatized category, while those who are more educated somewhat disproportionately exhibit the public form of religious expression—though educational differences across the four forms are rather modest. Finally, patterns of affiliation with different religious traditions also show up in the forms of religious expression, with evangelical Protestants being more heavily concentrated in the integrated category, Roman Catholics and to a lesser extent mainline Protestants in the public category, black Protestants within either the integrated or privatized categories, and the unaffiliated within the diminished. But representatives from each of the major religious traditions are found in all categories of religious expression.

Finally, we anticipate that the religious character of the American people is likely to have important consequences for public life in that the religious characteristics of the American people can shape the way they interact socially, how they relate to those outside the boundaries of their religious group, and the particular ends for which they engage in public life. Religion may also shape the ways in which individuals view the role of the state and the responsibilities of public life. Thus, we believe that religion may shape one's motivations for civic and political engagement, the goals of such engagement, and the means by which to accomplish those goals. We now turn our attention to how religion may serve to foster civic responsibility, starting initially with the relationship between religion and associational membership and involvement.

Notes

1. In this volume the terms "forms of religious expression" and "modes of religious expression" will be used interchangeably, primarily for stylistic reasons.

2. Gerard Dekker (1993) identifies three different meanings with regard to the process of secularization: (1) secularization as a decline of religiosity, (2) secularization as the adaptation of religion to modernization through a process of rationalization, and (3) secularization as the restriction of the range of influence of religion. Moreover, each of these facets of secularization can occur at three different levels of analysis: the individual, the organizational, and the societal. Privatization reflects the restriction of the range of religion's influence within an individual's life.

3. For the sake of simplicity, we will use the term "church" to refer to all religious institutions of whatever faith, including mosques, temples, and synagogues.

4. These data were previously reported in Gallup and Castelli (1989, 31) and in Gallup and Lindsay (1999, 15), and they are represented again in table 2.2.

5. These data are made available through the Roper Center as the Roper Social and Political Trends Data, 1973–94. More than 400,000 respondents are contained in this data file, as a number of surveys were conducted each year.

6. Questions related to church attendance were apparently not asked in the Roper surveys conducted during 1973 and 1983.

7. The more numerous response options for the church attendance question in the General Social Surveys may account for the lower reported levels of weekly church attendance. For example, there are nine response options related to church attendance: (1) never, (2) less than once a year, (3) once a year, (4) several times a year, (5) once a month, (6) two or three times a month, (7) nearly every week, (8) every week, and (9) more than once a week.

8. The National Election Studies surveys are conducted in both presidential and congressional election years. Data given in table 2.2 reflect presidential-year surveys only. The NES employs five response options for church attendance: (1) never, (2) a few times a year, (3) once or twice a month, (4) almost every week, and (5) every week. Those who respond "every week" are then asked if they attend more frequently than once a week.

9. The same factors may be at play with the General Social Survey data. As indicated in note 5 above, the General Social Surveys provide several response options between "once a month" and "weekly," including "two to three times a month" and "nearly every week." If "nearly every week" is added to the weekly totals, the GSS data fall much closer to the Gallup and Roper data. For example, in the 2004 General Social Survey, adding the "nearly every week" respondents to the "weekly" respondents results in 33 percent.

10. This is true even though levels of education among the American people have risen over the same course of time; higher levels of education are frequently viewed as being hostile to increased levels of religiosity. Presser and Chaves (2007) also note that there has been stability in religious attendance since 1990, though they claim there was an erosion since the 1950s—the time when parents of the baby-boom generation were taking their children to religious services.

11. Despite this small decline in reported levels of attendance at services, it nevertheless continues to be true that a substantial proportion of the American people engage in public worship. When the American people were asked in the Roper surveys whether they had attended church in the last seven days, roughly 40 percent responded yes each year between 1974 and 1994. In 1974, the first year in which such data are available, 41 percent of the respondents so reported, and in 1994, the last year in which the data are available, 39 percent of the respondents did so. Likewise, among respondents of the General Social Survey data, 28 to 30 percent reported attending church on a weekly basis between 1973 and 1980, and 28 percent did so in 2004. However, even granting a small decline in weekly church attendance over the past seventy years, it may be that the reported decline is less a reflection of change in Americans' worship behavior than a change in cultural expectations related to the social desirability of reporting weekly church attendance. Should any positive response bias be evident, one would expect that such bias would have been much more evident in earlier decades, when weekly church attendance was more expected than it is today.

12. In some surveys, no questions related to private prayer were asked, though a question on religious salience was. As noted earlier, in such cases, religious salience (a subjective assessment) is used as a surrogate measure for the role of religion in the private dimension.

13. The cutting point in each survey partially depended on the number of response options provided with regard to frequency of church attendance.

14. Descriptions of the various surveys that are used in this chapter and throughout the book are presented in appendix A.

15. Wuthnow, for example, analyzes differences between Christian inclusivists and exclusivists, with the former being much more willing to hold that "all major religions contain some truth about God" and that "all religions basically teach the same thing" (2005, 191).

3

❄

Religion and Membership
in Civic Associations

Americans have long shown a propensity to join with others for various collective purposes. Already in the early nineteenth century, Alexis de Tocqueville wrote that "the power of association has reached its uttermost development in America" and noted that the country's citizens hardly despaired of attaining any ends "through the combined power of individuals united in a society" (1969, 199). More than a half century later, Bryce (1910, 281–82) observed that "associations are created, extended, and worked in the United States more quickly and effectively than in any other country."[1]

Such a tendency to form and join associations might represent nothing more than a cultural curiosity were it not for the importance that social theorists have attributed to participation in civic associations. Early empirical studies of associational involvement conducted during the 1950s were generated by various theoretical concerns. Sociologists, for example, were interested in associational membership in the wake of Nazi totalitarianism, in current discussions of mass society, and in the alleged loss of community through social changes such as urbanization. Sociologists also studied the relationship between associational membership and acculturation, assimilation, social stratification, and social mobility (Scott 1957, 316).

Political scientists were interested in associationalism for other reasons. They examined membership in nongovernmental organizations through the lenses of interest-group politics, mass politics, and theories of how cross-pressures shaped human behavior (Verba 1965, 467). And due to Putnam's work (1993, 1995a, 2000), social scientists have more recently focused on associational membership as a means to examine social capital, as "the level of associational membership has become a standard litmus test for the health of a society's social capital" (Stolle and Hooghe 2004, 152).

At a deeper level, all of these theoretical perspectives entail a concern for how democratic government and democratic life might be promoted and protected. In fact, many social theorists have insisted that democracy requires civic associations that are not predominantly political in nature but function for their members as sources of meaning and social engagement. For Tocqueville and his like-minded observers, democracy could not survive unless its citizens participated actively, joining with others of similar mind and interest to address matters of common concern.

Most civic associations are not formed with political goals in mind, as civic engagement denotes "people's connection with the life of their communities, not merely with politics" (Putnam 1995b, 665). Still, these "nonpolitical" associations can have important political consequences. For example, participation in civic associations may help to bridge social cleavages, protect individual liberty, and serve to restrain totalitarian power by keeping the power of governmental coercion at bay. Thus, while much of associational life may not be explicitly political, it is inherently political given its potential for fostering democratic life.

In this chapter we examine the interrelationships of associational membership, politics, and religion. We first discuss the reasons voluntary associations and membership in such organizations are viewed as politically important. Second, we examine the relationship between membership in voluntary associations and religion in terms of different approaches to analyzing religion. Finally, we address whether religion can contribute significantly to membership in voluntary associations.

Associations and Democracy

The past several decades have seen a renewed interest in the relationship between membership in voluntary associations and the health of democratic life. Scholars have once again been raising questions about the role that civil society plays—and, more specifically, that associations play—in fostering democracy. In doing so, discussion of normative assessments and empirical investigations of democracy have been brought together.

Of course, associations take various forms, and discussions of associational involvement do not always differentiate between and among those forms. For example, parent-teacher associations (PTA) and Kiwanis are both voluntary associations, but so are friendship groups and social networks. However, most of the theoretical focus has been on voluntary associations that are usually defined in terms of "a formally organized named group, most of whose members . . . are not financially recompensed for their participation" (Knoke 1986, 2) and social interaction within such groups is "distinguished by virtue of being organized, purposeful, voluntary, and non-remunerative" (Miller 2003, 8).

Broadly speaking, scholars have discussed three distinct ways that involvement in voluntary associational life can enhance democratic life. First, many theorists have long emphasized the capacity of voluntary associations to countervail state power,[2] helping to prevent a concentration and centralization of power (Rose 1954, 50f). When one is a member of a voluntary organization, one is likely to be "less dependent upon and less controlled by" the political system (Almond and Verba 1963, 301). Moreover, organized associations provide their members the capacity to engage in collective action, enabling them to resist what they do not like. This "capacity to resist" provides "incentives for representatives to represent and for state officials to respond" (Warren 2001, 85). Thus one central contribution that voluntary associations can make to democratic life is the mediation of structures between the individual and the state (Almond and Verba 1963, 300), thereby enhancing "resistance to domination and antidemocratic power" (Fung 2003, 522).

A second way in which associational life can enhance democratic life is through the capacity of voluntary associations to represent interests and serve as a medium for public discourse. Through the work of associations, diverse interests can be more fully clarified, more fully articulated, and, at least within the organization itself, more fully harmonized, as associations help to "develop agendas, test ideas, embody deliberations, and provide voice" (Warren 2001, 61). As a result, public officials are better able to discern, represent, and respond to the interests of citizens within a democratic system, and associations serve to enhance the ways in which "interests are represented to lawmakers and translated into law and policy" (Fung 2003, 523).

A third way that associations can foster the health of democratic societies is through their developmental effects on individual members. Voluntary associations can serve as important "schools of democracy," as participation in them may serve to enhance an individual's "sense of efficacy or political agency, information, political skills, capacities for deliberative judgment, and civic virtues" (Warren 2001, 71). It is this alleged effect—namely, that involvement in associational life serves to educate and socialize its members in ways that foster civic responsibility and benefit democracy—that has received the greatest attention among scholars over the past few decades (Fung 2003, 519).

How does involvement in voluntary associations help to achieve this particular effect? It supposedly does so by strengthening the capacity of members to be more informed, skilled, and virtuous citizens. Generally speaking, the argument is structured in the following manner: Participation in voluntary associations fosters interaction among diverse individuals who gather for a common purpose; these relatively structured interactions increase the likelihood that trust between members will be generated and perhaps extended to others outside the group who have similar characteristics. Participation in group activity also serves to increase a member's level of information and broadens the member's scope of interest, making public matters more relevant. Through discussion and the presentation of information, members may become politicized and motivated to protect and enhance joint interests. Moreover, members may develop civic and political skills by serving on committees, by learning to negotiate and compromise in reaching group decisions, or by assuming leadership roles. Finally, participation in voluntary associations may serve to embed members within social networks that increase the likelihood of their being recruited and mobilized for political purposes (Ulzurrun 2002, 498). Overall, associational involvement (1) helps to socialize individuals, teaching members mores necessary for maintaining a healthy society and polity and (2) fosters civic and political engagement through greater public awareness, broadened interests, and enhanced skills.[3] It is little wonder that associations have been viewed as "little schools of democracy."

Measurement and Analytical Issues

Given these alleged effects, the matter of how scholars measure associational participation is an important issue. One of the first problems that confronts analysts researching voluntary membership is whether they are sufficiently capturing the full range of associational memberships they seek to examine. Obviously one cannot provide a list of all existing associations in the country and then ask survey respondents whether they are members of each. So the common practice is to provide a list of associational types (e.g., professional, sport, literary, ethnic) and ask whether the respondent is a member of an association that falls within each category.

While this practice is defensible, several important problems result from it. First, when a respondent answers affirmatively to membership in a general category, most surveys do not follow up by asking for either the number or the names of the organizations claimed. Hence the net result is not a compilation of the total number of voluntary associational memberships to which the respondent belongs, but rather a compilation of the type and range of voluntary associational memberships to which the respondent claims to belong.

Second, different survey organizations utilize different category labels and employ different numbers of categories. In some surveys respondents may be asked whether they belong to any club or organization that fits into the category of "health, fitness, or exercise clubs," but not whether they are members of any "hobby group"; in other surveys the reverse may occur. This variation in categories and item wording is evident in appendix B, which presents the range of voluntary associational categories provided in the surveys analyzed in this chapter. Obviously, these differences mean that surveys capture membership in either a wider or a narrower array of associations, as the more encompassing the list provided, the higher the proportion of respondents who will likely report membership or participation in voluntary associations (Ulzurrun 2002, 501).[4]

Third, survey organizations vary in terms of how they pose questions related to involvement in voluntary associations. Some are less concerned about membership per se and ask simply whether the respondent is involved in a voluntary association; others ask respondents whether they belong to, or are members of, such associations. The former wording probably captures more affirmative responses than the latter.

In addition to these methodological issues is the analytical problem of deciding which organizations should be counted among voluntary associations. For example, one might for good theoretical reasons view church membership as a form of membership in a voluntary association.[5] Yet church membership is customarily not included even though involvement in other forms of religious organizational life (e.g., being a member of the Knights of Columbus) generally qualifies in assessments of organizational involvement.

Union membership raises similar issues. At times, union membership can be compulsory—hardly reflective of voluntary involvement. In addition, given that unions largely address economic concerns, one could view union membership as being linked more to the concerns of the market than to civil society. Nevertheless, union membership frequently qualifies as a form of voluntary associational involvement (Smith 1975, 249–50).

Finally, given the growth of new organizational forms, some analysts (e.g., Verba, Schlozman, and Brady 1995, 59) have treated the act of making a financial contribution to an organization as equivalent to membership. Over the past several decades, one of the most important changes in the voluntary sector has been the growth of tertiary associations at the expense of "classic" secondary associations (Skocpol 1999). Tertiary associations, such as the American Association of Retired People (AARP) or the Sierra Club, are more likely than secondary associations to have salaried staff, exhibit centralized leadership, be less democratically structured, and be supported by members more in the form of money than time. As members in tertiary associations interact less frequently face to face, some analysts contend that membership in tertiary associations does not convey the same benefits as membership in classic secondary associations. Others, however, contend that even membership in tertiary associations has beneficial consequences (Minkoff 1997). Regardless of the merits of either position, the proportion of Americans who can be classified as exhibiting membership in a voluntary association varies depending on whether making a financial contribution counts as membership.

Table 3.1 addresses the proportion of Americans reporting membership in voluntary associations today. Several important conclusions emerge.

Table 3.1 Reported Membership in Voluntary Associations over Time (percent)

Year	GSS[a]	CPS[b]	G&S[c]	NES[d]	CIS[e]	Saguaro[f]
			Study			
1987	67					
1988	70					
1989	69					
1990	72	79				
1991	67					
1992	y					
1993	71					
1994	71					
1995	y					
1996	x		51	80		
1997	y				68	
1998	x					
1999	y					
2000	x					80
2001	y					
2002	x					
2003	y					
2004	62					

Notes: x = not asked; y = no survey

[a] GSS, 1987–2004: Respondents were asked if they were members of an organization in a battery of 16 categories.

[b] Citizen Participation Study, 1990: Respondents were asked if they were a member of or a contributor to an organization within a battery of 17 categories.

[c] God and Society in North America, 1996: Respondents were asked about membership in a battery of 14 categories only if they indicated initially that they were a member of a voluntary organization.

[d] National Election Study, 1996: Only post-election survey respondents were asked questions about membership related to 22 categories.

[e] Citizen Involvement Survey, 1997: Respondents were asked about whether they belong to any club or organization in a battery of 22 categories (percentage does not include belonging to either church or labor union categories).

[f] Saguaro Social Capital, 2000: Respondents were asked if they were involved in groups or associations within a battery of 17 categories (percentage does not include involvement with unions).

First, as one might expect, membership levels depend in part on how survey organizations structure their questions about associational membership. This is evident, for example, by examining the differences between the God and Society in North America survey (G&S) and the 1996 National Election Study (NES), two surveys conducted at approximately the same time. G&S asked an initial filter question, inquiring whether or not the respondent was a member of any voluntary association. Only those who replied in the affirmative were then asked about membership across a battery of fourteen types of voluntary associations. The NES survey presented respondents with a battery of twenty-two types of voluntary associations and asked respondents whether they were members of any voluntary association within each of the twenty-two categories. Not surprisingly, the former approach yielded fewer reported associational membership than the latter (51 percent versus 80 percent).

Second, the manner in which questions are posed also has a significant impact on reported levels of membership. For example, the Saguaro Social Capital Benchmark Survey of 2000 asked respondents whether they were "involved in" particular types of groups or associations, rather than inquiring about membership per se. This approach yields a much higher percentage of "membership" (80 percent) than questions posed in terms of membership itself.[6]

Third, of the various surveys examined in table 3.1, only the General Social Survey (GSS) asked membership questions in a consistent format with some regularity over time (at least until 1994). These surveys reveal that approximately two-thirds of the American people typically report membership in at least one type of voluntary association. For example, between 1987 and 1994 the percentage of Americans affiliated with such associations ranged from 67 percent to 72 percent across the seven national surveys.

Nevertheless, there is growing concern today over what appears to be a declining willingness of Americans to join voluntary associations, as the records of many long-standing but diverse organizations (e.g., the PTA, the Elks, and the League of Women Voters) reveal a decline in membership over the past three decades (Putnam 2000). Not all scholars share the perspective that America is witnessing a decline in civic engagement (e.g., Ladd 1996; Skocpol and Fiorina 1999; Becker and Dhingra 2001),[7] but the GSS data presented in table 3.1 suggest some evidence for a decline in membership within more traditional forms of voluntary associations, as reported membership dropped nearly 10 percentage points between 1994 (71 percent) and 2004 (62 percent).

The analytical and methodological concerns sketched above relate primarily to efforts that seek to ascertain the *absolute level* of organizational membership. That is, one must capture the full range of membership in voluntary associations if one wishes to determine the proportion of Americans joining voluntary associations or whether membership levels have been growing or declining. However, these concerns are less problematic if one seeks simply to ascertain what types of individuals are most likely to report membership in voluntary associations. The characteristics of people who typically join voluntary associations are unlikely to change substantially whether one analyzes membership across sixteen or twenty-two types of voluntary associations, as the effort to determine the correlates of associational membership is less prone than is the effort to discern absolute levels of membership to being affected by the scope and wording of survey questions about membership.

As this chapter seeks to ascertain the relative importance of religion in shaping membership in voluntary associations—rather than the changes in the absolute levels of such reported memberships—it is important to recognize the methodological and analytical limitations of the measures used in the chapter, but these limitations are not likely to undermine substantially the findings and conclusions of the chapter itself. Our analysis now shifts to the demographic factors that are linked to membership in voluntary associations and to their relative importance in shaping that membership.

Church Membership and Associational Involvement

The conventional practice of not counting church membership as a form of membership in voluntary associations does have one particular advantage: It enables a clear examination of the relationship between church membership and membership in other voluntary associations. From the very beginning of survey research, analysts have found a strong relationship between church membership and membership in voluntary associations, with church members being more likely than nonmembers to join secular voluntary associations (e.g., Moberg 1962, 393–94).

This relationship is evident in table 3.2, which clearly shows that church members are much more likely than nonchurch members to report some form of membership in a nonchurch voluntary association; this is true

Table 3.2 Membership in Voluntary Associations by Church Membership (percent)

Church Membership	National Election Study 1996	Civic Involvement 1997	Saguaro Social Capital 2000
Nonmember	75	51	70
Church member	95	80	86
eta[a]	.29	.30	.19

[a] Statistically significant at the .001 level.

regardless of the survey examined. And this relationship is relatively strong, with church members being more than twice as likely as nonchurch members to report such memberships.[8]

A somewhat different approach more fully reveals the pivotal role that church membership plays in associational involvement. Table 3.3 presents an analysis based on merging the three data files found in table 3.2 that contain measures of both church membership and membership in voluntary associations. The first column presents the percentage of the respondents who reported membership in a particular association, the second column the percentage of church members who reported membership in the same associations. The third column reports the percentage of members of a particular voluntary association who also reported that they were church members, and the fourth column presents the percentage of members who also reported that they were members of some other association.

First, it is clear that church membership far surpasses reported membership in other voluntary associations, as 58.4 percent of all respondents report church membership.[9] Moreover, of the thirteen categories of nonchurch membership, the most common is also religious, with 38.7 percent of respondents reporting membership in religious associations other than churches.

The importance of church membership in contributing to membership in other voluntary associations becomes evident when one compares the percentage of the total population who reported membership in nonchurch associations (column 1) with the percentage of church members who reported membership in the same associations (column 2). The percentage

Table 3.3 Relative Importance of Religion in Fostering Membership in Voluntary Associations:
A Multiple Classification Analysis

Associational membership	Percentage of population	Percent of church members who have joined nonchurch orgs.	Percent of non-church org. members who are also church members	Percent of non-church members who are members of another org.
Church member	58.4			
Educational	18.4	21.8	69.4	90.8
Ethnic	5.1	6.0	67.7	96.3
Fraternal	9.3	11.0	69.7	92.6
Hobby/sport	17.0	17.4	59.9	87.5
Literature/arts	9.5	10.9	67.1	90.3
Prof./business	17.6	18.3	60.7	90.4
Political	5.9	6.7	66.4	93.2
Religious	38.7	57.4	86.7	68.6
Self-help	8.4	9.3	64.7	91.0
Service	16.4	18.9	67.3	92.2
Union	11.3	11.7	60.5	83.1
Veterans	7.0	7.7	63.9	89.4
Youth	16.9	20.6	71.0	93.2

Note: Merged data file of NES 1996, Wuthnow CIS 1997, and Saguaro 2000; $n = 6065$

of church members reporting membership in these various types of voluntary associations consistently exceeds the percentage of the total population that reported membership in these same associations. In other words, church members are more likely than members of the public as a whole to indicate that they are members of nonchurch voluntary associations. Moreover, the data reveal that church members did not "boycott" particular types of associations, as there is not a single instance in which the percentage of church members reporting that they are members of a particular type of association is smaller than the percentage found among the population as a whole.

The centrality of church membership is further revealed when one compares the percentage of church members in the population as a whole (58.4 percent) with the percentage of members in nonchurch associations who reported that they were also church members (column 3). The percentages in column 3 consistently exceed the 58.4 percent mark (the "expected" level given distribution of church members in the population as a whole), revealing that church members permeated all types of voluntary associations. Thus, church members are "overrepresented" among members of all types of voluntary associations. While church members comprise, not surprisingly, the overwhelming proportion of those who are members of religious voluntary associations (86.7 percent), church members are also particularly found among members of voluntary associations related to youth (71.0 percent), education (69.4 percent), and service (67.3 percent).

Finally, the last column of table 3.3 reports the percentage of members of nonchurch associations that reported membership in some other type of association. The data clearly reveal that members of one type of association overwhelmingly reported membership in some other type of association as well. For example, more than nine of ten members (90.8 percent) of educational associations, such as parent-teacher associations, reported membership in at least one of the remaining twelve types of voluntary associations.

However, the members who report the lowest level of membership in other organizations are the members of nonchurch religious associations. This finding might be interpreted as counterevidence to the claim that church membership is positively related to membership in voluntary associations outside the church. But it is important to note, first, that this category does not relate directly to church membership itself—only to membership in other types of religious associations. Second, despite reporting lower levels of membership in other organizations, more than two-thirds (68.6 percent) of members of religious associations did report membership in other voluntary associations. Those who reported membership in religious associations were still at the hub of membership in other types of voluntary associations, given that more than one-third of all Americans belong to such religious associations (see column 1). Multiplying the percentages in column 1 by the percentages in column 4 yields the proportion of the population that is involved in each type of voluntary organization as well as some other type of voluntary organization. When one does so for voluntary religious associations, one finds that more than one-quarter (26.6 percent) of the American population reported membership in some kind of religious voluntary association as well as membership in some other type of voluntary association (.387 × .686 = .2655). It is also clear that no other type of associational involvement can match this level (in fact, the next closest figure is 16.7 percent, reflecting those who were jointly involved in educational associations and some other type of voluntary association).

Thus, table 3.3 clearly reveals that members of religious congregations are at the hub for memberships in voluntary associations more generally. While church members are more likely to report membership in religious voluntary associations than in associations located outside of religious life, they nevertheless join other nonreligious voluntary associations at a higher rate than the population as a whole—despite their existing level of engagement in religious life. As a result, church members permeate every type of civic association beyond the proportions that would be anticipated given their proportion of the population as a whole.

Religion and Associational Membership

While it has been long recognized that church membership serves to shape membership in voluntary associations, it is also true that relatively "few studies have specifically examined the impact of religion, other than religious affiliation, on voluntary association memberships" (Lam 2002, 406).

It is unclear why this is the case,[10] but whatever the reason, it is clear that research on determinants of associational membership has not examined religion carefully in terms of either breadth or depth.

Religion is a multifaceted phenomenon, encompassing patterns of belonging, beliefs, and behavior. Each facet of religion might well be tied to the likelihood of joining civic organizations, and it is not readily apparent just what facet of religion might be most highly associated with the likelihood of voluntary membership. Some theological beliefs (e.g., a belief in common grace[11]) might prompt church members to become involved with voluntary associations whose members may not necessarily reflect their own religious understandings, while other theological beliefs (e.g., the notion that the primary task of the religious adherent is to engage in evangelism) might move them to restrict the kinds of activities in which they invest their time. However, the relationship between religious beliefs and the fostering of civic associationalism is not examined in this chapter because relatively few questions on religious belief were asked in the surveys analyzed in this book.[12] Within the surveys examined, the most common such question related to the respondents' views on the nature of biblical authority. Unfortunately, most "Bible" items are plagued by poor response options that put most Americans into just a few categories and suggest most respondents hold very high views of biblical authority.[13] These highly skewed distributions reveal the high regard that many Americans have for the Bible, but they limit the utility of such Bible measures for explanatory purposes.[14] Moreover, it is unclear how views of biblical authority directly relate to choosing to be involved in civic associations.[15] As a result, no religious beliefs are examined in the analysis of the relationship between religion and associational membership.

On the other hand, the analyzed surveys do permit an examination of the relationship between religious tradition affiliation and associational membership.[16] The concept of religious tradition constitutes "a useful and increasingly popular conceptualization of religious belonging" (Layman 2001, 60). A religious tradition comprises a group of religious denominations, movements, and congregations with similar beliefs and behaviors that are interrelated in some historical and organizational fashion (Kellstedt et al. 1996). Religious traditions exhibit several defining characteristics (Smidt 2007), and as a group, members of a religious tradition typically exhibit a characteristic way of interpreting the world, based on common beliefs and practices, though not all members necessarily adhere to the beliefs or practices in question.[17] Religious tradition has proven to be to be a powerful predictor of political attitudes and behavior (Kellstedt and Green 1993; Kellstedt et al. 1996, 1997; Layman and Green 2005; Guth, Green et al. 2006; Guth, Kellstedt et al. 2006; Green et al. 2007; Green 2007).

Previous analyses have shown that certain religious traditions encourage civic engagement more than others do (e.g., Wuthnow 1999a), and table 3.4 confirms that affiliation with different religious traditions is significantly linked to reported levels of associational membership. Mainline Protestant and Jewish respondents were generally the most likely to report memberships, while the religiously unaffiliated or secular respondents were the least likely to do so (except in the 1990 Citizen Participation Study).[18] Evangelical Protestants and Roman Catholics tended to exhibit relatively similar levels of reported membership, though when there are major gaps between the two, evangelical Protestants tended to exhibit higher rates of reported memberships than Catholics. Overall, evangelical Protestants and Roman Catholics tended to trail mainline Protestants, though at times, evangelical Protestants had the same level of organizational involvement as mainline Protestants. Black Protestants have generally trailed evangelical Protestants and Roman Catholics in their level of reported membership in voluntary associations, though in the more recent surveys, the gap between black Protestants and evangelical Protestants has largely disappeared.

On the one hand, we cannot assess just how associational involvement is linked to religious beliefs, although it is clear that membership in civic organizations is tied to both church membership and religious tradition affiliation. On the other hand, we *can* examine religion in terms of *how* people choose to express their religious faith; thus we can ask whether different forms of religious expression are linked to the likelihood that people will report membership in voluntary associations. The data in table 3.5 reveal clearly that they are—and that it is not so much the relative absence of religious life as it is a privatized religious life that is linked to lower levels of reported membership. In five of the six surveys examined,[19] those with a privatized religious faith reported the lowest levels of organizational membership.[20]

Table 3.4 Membership in Voluntary Associations by Religious Tradition (percent)

Religious tradition	Study							
	GSS 1987	CPS 1990	G&S 1996	NES 1996	CIS 1997	Saguaro 2000	GSS 2004[a]
Evangelical Protestant	63	67	57	80	79	81	61
Mainline Protestant	73	77	61	87	78	87	73
Black Protestant	57	61	51	86	78	83	66
Roman Catholic	64	69	54	90	66	75	61
Jewish	95	83	53	90	71	95	80
Secular	54	67	49	60	42	72	60
eta[b]	.15	.11	.08	.26	.29	.13	.17

[a] While a prayer question was available in 2004, it was asked of only half of the sample, while membership in voluntary organization questions were asked in the other half of the sample. Consequently, the religious form variable was created using reported levels of church attendance and strength of religious affiliation as a subjective religious salience question.

[b] Statistically significant at the .001 level.

Table 3.5 Membership in Voluntary Associations by Form of Religious Expression (percent reporting membership)

Form of religious expression	Study						
	GSS 1987	CPS 1990[a]	G&S 1996	NES 1996	Saguaro 2000[a]	GSS 2004[b]
Diminished	64	68	40	75	77	52
Privatized	51	60	37	74	65	58
Public	77	69	56	91	81	60
Integrated	76	74	64	95	86	78
eta[c]	.21	.10	.28	.27	.16	.23

[a] Because no prayer question was asked, the religious form variable was created using religious salience and reported levels of church attendance.

[b] While a prayer question was available in 2004, it was asked for only half of the sample, while membership in voluntary organization questions were asked in the other half of the sample. Consequently, the religious form variable was created using reported levels of church attendance and strength of religious affiliation as a subjective religious salience question.

[c] Statistically significant at the .001 level.

In addition, it was those who regularly attended public religious services who were most likely to engage in civic life through membership in voluntary associations, as respondents exhibiting either a public or an integrated mode of religious expression were much more likely to report membership than those exhibiting a diminished or privatized form. Further, in five of the six surveys examined, respondents with an integrated religious faith were the most likely to report membership in voluntary organizations. It is therefore not simply public attendance at worship services that matters in shaping voluntary associational memberships (because public and integrated religionists attend religious services with the same relative frequency), but rather differences exhibited by public and integrated religionists in the more private dimension of religion within their lives.

Social Factors and Associational Membership

Still, while tables 3.4 and 3.5 reveal that religious variables are clearly and at times strongly related to associational membership, it is also true that religious factors are not the only variables shaping associational involvement. Both membership and involvement take certain kinds of resources: Membership may require money to pay associational dues, physical health and time to attend meetings, and particular skills to engage meaningfully in associational activities. And time, money, and skills are not equally distributed throughout society; certain members of society are more likely to possess these resources than are others.

It is hardly surprising that researchers have long found that membership in voluntary associations is tied to a variety of demographic factors, and a number of these are usually analyzed. If any thread runs through these analyses and the relationships they reveal, it is probably the "dominant status" thread (Lemon, Palisi, and Jacobson 1972)—namely, that rates of membership in voluntary associations tend to be higher among those individuals characterized by a more socioculturally valued or preferred set of social positions, whether ascribed or achieved (Smith 1994, 246).

The dominant status model predicts that men are more likely to be members of voluntary associations than are women, whites are more likely to be members than are minorities, and the more educated are more likely to be members than the less educated. Within the dominant status model, being married is the higher-prestige status, and married people are posited as the most likely to be associational members. Finally, since the middle-aged are more likely than either the young or the old to possess the necessary resources—particularly the combination of money and health—for membership in voluntary association, they are considered more likely to join voluntary associations.

These expectations are examined in table 3.6, which displays the relationship between such demographic characteristics and associational membership across seven surveys conducted over the past two decades. It should be noted that social change occurs and social status shifts; patterns that were evident several decades ago may no longer hold true. Certainly, women's status has changed since World War II in the wake of increased opportunities in both education and the workforce. Thus we might expect gender differences in voluntary membership levels to be less evident today than they were in the past (Verba and Nie 1972), and the data in table 3.6 demonstrate that the relationship between gender and associational membership is, in fact, relatively weak today. Men were clearly more likely than women to report such memberships in the late 1980s and early 1990s, but these differences were erased by the mid-1990s.

Much the same is true with regard to race. Historically, whites were more likely to report associational memberships than nonwhites (Hyman and Wright 1971).[21] But this difference, while evident in the earlier studies presented in table 3.6, tends not to be evident in studies conducted later. Starting with the studies conducted in 1996, whites and blacks shared very similar levels of associational membership, and they both tended to report higher levels of membership than Hispanics and other ethnic minorities.

However, other historical patterns are more persistent. Studies have generally revealed that age is curvilinearly related to associational membership, with the peak time for membership occurring during the middle years of life (i.e., largely in the range of thirty-five to fifty-five years of age) and younger people generally exhibiting the lowest levels of membership (Smith 1975, 1994). This pattern continues to hold true, as does the conventional pattern that married people are the most likely to exhibit associational membership (Wright and Hyman 1958; Hausknecht 1962; Curtis

Table 3.6 Membership in Voluntary Associations by Demographic Characteristics

Demographic characteristic	Study						
	GSS 1987	CPS 1990	G&S 1996	NES 1996	CIS 1997	Saguaro 2000	GSS 2004
Gender							
Male	72	73	48	85	67	82	63
Female	64	67	54	85	70	78	61
eta	.08[c]	.07[c]	.06	.00	.04[a]	.04[a]	.02
Race							
White	71	73	55	86	71	82	63
Black	59	62	54	86	64	83	62
Hispanic	45	42	52	78	49	68	54
Other	*	47	61	82	63	76	57
eta	.15[c]	.17[c]	.02	.06	.13[c]	.14[c]	.06
Age							
Under 36	65	63	45	80	63	74	58
36–55	72	72	58	88	75	83	65
Over 55	66	76	52	87	67	80	64
eta	.07[a]	.12[c]	.11[c]	.10[c]	.11[c]	.09[c]	.08[b]

Education							
Less than 12 years	49	41	33	70	50	60	37
High school	67	62	53	80	63	71	57
Some college	72	78	58	88	74	85	59
College graduate	85	84	65	92	84	89	76
Some post grad	92	95	74	96	**	90	83
eta	.29^c	.37^c	.31^c	.23^c	.25^c	.24^c	.28^c
Family Income							
Lowest level	49	59	31	71	55	70	42
Lower middle	66	79	48	83	68	79	59
Upper middle	76	86	58	91	81	87	73
Highest level	82	87	69	96	89	89	78
eta	.26^c	.26^c	.26^c	.25^c	.25^c	.19^c	.28^c
Never married	66	64	40	79	60	75	53
Widowed	62	65	52	85	61	78	53
Divorced	66	68	50	75	61	82	52
Separated	57	57	41	71	62	75	39
Married	70	73	56	89	75	82	68
eta	.08^a	.09^c	.14^c	.17^c	.15^c	.08^b	.17^c

* = no response option provided beyond white, black, and Hispanic
** = no response option given to respondent beyond college graduate
^{a} Statistically significant at .05 level
^{b} Statistically significant at .01 level
^{c} Statistically significant at .001 level

1971; Auslander and Litwin 1988; Rotolo 2000). Similarly, those with greater financial resources are more likely to report membership in voluntary associations, as increases in family income are monotonically related to an increased likelihood of reporting associational membership. The same is true for education, which has been the strongest and most consistent predictor of voluntary participation (Smith 1975, 1994); this strong relationship is consistently evident within each of the seven surveys examined in table 3.6.

The Unique Contribution of Religion

Having established the relationships between the demographic characteristics of Americans and their membership in voluntary civic associations, the question is whether religion can still be said to play a significant role in shaping membership in voluntary associations. In other words, does the religious character of a respondent add anything to the likelihood of being a member of a voluntary association beyond what one might expect given the gender, race, age, education level, income, and marital status of the respondent?

Table 3.7 begins to address this issue. Rather than analyzing the relative importance of all possible religious variables, just two are examined: religious tradition affiliation and modes of religious expression. These two variables were chosen because both were found to be significantly related to membership in voluntary associations. Therefore, to assess whether modes of religious expression are really shaping involvement in voluntary associations, we have included not only the effects of other demographic variables in the multivariate analysis but religious tradition affiliation also.

To control for the relative effects of various social variables on membership in voluntary associations, a multiple classification analysis (MCA) was performed. MCA accommodates the use of categorical variables in multivariate analysis and avoids the necessity of using dummy variables.[22] Thus a distinct advantage of using MCA is that it can provide a single summary *beta* value for a categorical variable as a whole, rather than a number of scores for each of the categories of that particular variable, with the magnitude of the *beta* value revealing the relative strength of the rela-

Table 3.7 Relative Importance of Religion in Fostering Membership in Voluntary Associations: A Multiple Classification Analysis

Demographic Characteristic	Study					
	GSS 1987	CPS 1990	G&S 1996	NES 1996	Saguaro 2000	GSS 2004
Gender	.07[a]	.04	.05	.01	.06	.04
Race	.09[b]	.15[c]	.06	.06	.06	.05
Age	.05	.16[c]	.04	.10[b]	.02	.01
Education	.21[c]	.27[c]	.24[c]	.16[c]	.14[c]	.18[c]
Family income	.18[c]	.16[c]	.13[c]	.19[c]	.13[c]	.18[c]
Marital status	.07[a]	.07	.10[b]	.06	.05	.10[b]
Religious tradition	.07[a]	.10[b]	.07[a]	.12[c]	.08[a]	.10[b]
Form of religious expression	.19[c]	.07[a]	.25[c]	.19[c]	.12[c]	.19[c]
R square	*.17*	*.19*	*.18*	*.18*	*.08*	*.17*

[a] Statistically significant at .05 level
[b] Statistically significant at .01 level
[c] Statistically significant at .001 level

tionship once the effects of the other variables in the analysis have been taken into account. The *beta* values for each of the independent variables are presented in table 3.7, along with the resulting value of R-square. The R-square value represents the total amount of variance in reported organizational memberships explained by the independent variables contained in table 3.7.

As is evident in the table, one's form of religious expression rivals one's level of education as the most important variable in shaping associational membership. Education ranked first in relative importance in three of the six studies examined, while form of religious expression ranked first in the other three. Moreover, the difference in the magnitude of the *beta* coefficient for these two variables did not exceed .03 in five of the six studies examined. Only in the CPS study of 1990 conducted by Verba and his colleagues (which classified monetary contributions as constituting membership) did one's form of religious expression not rival education as the most important explanatory factor or rank at least second in relative importance. Overall, the data presented in table 3.7 clearly reveal that (1) the relationship between religion and membership in voluntary associations is not spurious and (2) religious variables (specifically, one's form of religious expression and religious tradition affiliation) constitute relatively important explanatory factors in accounting for variation in voluntary associational memberships.[23]

Conclusion

Associational life can potentially contribute to democratic government in several ways, including countervailing state power, serving as a medium for public discourse, and providing venues for socialization and civic education. Thus it is important to understand the origins, nature, and consequences of associational life in the United States. Unfortunately, scholars share no common understanding about the nature of associational life or the proper means of assessing citizen participation in it. Most available survey data provide, at best, a rudimentary assessment of the number of group memberships respondents report rather than the actual associations or the degree of respondents' involvement. Furthermore, there is no scholarly consensus on which groups should be properly labeled as associational groups.

Despite the limitations of existing research, some useful data with which to analyze the relationship between religion and associational membership can be found, and these data form the basis for this chapter. Our analysis of these data first of all clearly supports the conclusions of previous studies that have found a strong relationship between church membership and membership in voluntary associations: Church members do indeed prove considerably more likely than nonchurch members to join "secular" voluntary associations. This is exceedingly important because church membership in the United States far surpasses membership in other types of voluntary organizations.

A second important conclusion of this chapter is that a "joining factor" appears to be at work among the American citizenry. That is, the overwhelming majority of members in one type of voluntary association report membership in some other type of association as well. The result is an "associational matrix" in the United States, a matrix in which members of churches and other religious organizations play key roles. Indeed, over a quarter of the American population reports membership in both some form of religious and some form of secular organization.

But what, specifically, does religion contribute to associational membership and involvement? While data availability limits our ability to answer this question in depth, we are able to draw some important conclusions. In particular, there is a strong connection between respondents' religious tradition and their patterns of associational membership. Mainline Protestant and Jewish respondents tended to be most likely to report memberships in voluntary associations, while the religiously unaffiliated or secular respondents proved least likely to do so. Evangelical Protestants and Roman Catholics tended to fall somewhere in the middle.

A fourth conclusion is that the way in which respondents express their religion is more important than religious tradition in predicting associational membership. Changes in the distribution of various religious traditions may signal changes in the level of civic engagement in the future (Wuthnow 1999a), but what matters more is changing distribution of the forms of religious expression within existing traditions. Not only is the *way* in which respondents express their religion strongly related to associational involvement, but it tends to far outweigh religious affiliation in contributing to the likelihood of membership in voluntary organizations.

A fifth conclusion that can be drawn from the analysis in this chapter is that there may be something in religion itself that encourages associational involvement. Clearly, those respondents who exhibit forms of religiosity that are more public in nature (i.e., the public and integrated modes of religious expression) are more likely to participate in voluntary organizations than those whose religiosity is less public in nature (i.e., the diminished and privatized modes). But involvement in associational life is not simply a function of public religious expression, as important differences in levels of associational membership exist between those who exhibit the two forms of religious expression characterized in part by similarly high levels of attendance at religious worship services—that is, the public and integrated forms of religious expression. Private devotionalism among those who exhibit high levels of worship attendance also shapes (and increases) the likelihood of associational involvement.

The way in which religiosity is expressed has potentially important implications for associational involvement. Calls for the privatization of religious expression in public life are likely to be counterproductive in terms of public involvement more generally. Should religion in America become more individualized and privatized in nature, the prevalence of associational membership and involvement is likely to diminish as well.

Notes

1. In some ways, this propensity of Americans to form and join associations is hardly to be expected. As the noted historian Arthur Schlesinger (1944, 1) has observed: "It seems paradoxical that a country famed for being individualistic should provide the world's greatest example of joiners."

2. However, such alleged contributions can stand in conflict with one another, as different forms of association may be better able to advance some of these contributions than other such associations.

3. These socialization effects yield a collective effect for the organization as well, in that the net result for the association is an "increased capacity for collective action, cooperation, and trust within the group, enabling the collective purposes of the group to be more easily achieved" (Stolle and Rochon 1998, 48).

4. Ulzurrun (2002, 501) notes that this general rule may not apply in all circumstances. To a certain extent, how broadly or narrowly membership categories are constructed may also affect results. Nevertheless, the National Election Studies of 2004 asked just one question—whether the respondent was a member of an organization—and this question yielded a membership rate of only 42 percent, a full 20 percent lower than that obtained through the longer list employed by the General Social Survey of the same year.

5. Some have argued that church membership is largely ascriptive and involuntary in nature (Smith 1975, 249). But given the nature of American religious life, it is hard to understand how religion can be viewed in such a fashion; individuals are relatively free, and frequently choose, to change their religious affiliations (Bibby and Brinkerhoof 1974; Stark and Glock 1968).

6. For example, Wuthnow's Civic Involvement Survey of only three years earlier inquired about actual membership and revealed a much lower level of reported membership (60 percent).

7. For example, some observers contend that examining the historical trends in membership found in long-standing organizations obscures the rise of membership in newly forged organizations, a rise that may well offset the decline of memberships in longer-standing organizations. Other analysts sometimes point to the explosive growth in interest groups represented in Washington, D.C.; they note the establishment of and the rise of membership in what might be labeled "mailing list" organizations (e.g., the American Association of Retired People or the Sierra Club) as counterevidence to the contention that there has been a decline in civic engagement within American public life over the course of the past several decades.

8. However, such an analysis also reveals that not all church members claim that they are members of a voluntary association (data not shown). Additional analysis revealed that the same is true with regard to union membership; not all members of unions necessarily claim that they are members of a voluntary association. If church membership (and/or union membership) were counted as a form of membership in a voluntary association, the percentage of Americans reporting membership in at least one voluntary association would substantially increase.

9. Cnaan et al. (2006, 124) cite more recent surveys that find two-thirds of adults in the United States report belonging to a congregation of some religious faith.

10. This is not simply a function of the limited number of surveys examined in this volume. All surveys on associational involvement of which the authors are aware contain relatively few religious belief questions, and the few questions that are asked in such surveys tend to be generic rather than directed specifically toward religious beliefs related to social and political engagement.

11. Common grace is that grace afforded to all people regardless of religious belief. As Jesus declares in Matthew 5:45: "[God] makes his sun rise on the evil and the good, and sends rain on the righteous and the unrighteous." The common grace of God is experienced in the ordering of nature, the restraint of evil, and the ability of unbelievers to reason and perform acts of civic good. The doctrine of common grace holds that God bestows on humanity a grace that, while not "saving," enables unbelievers to develop many virtues and express many truths.

12. During the latter half of the twentieth century, there was a widespread acceptance among scholars of the thesis of secularization. This thesis asserts that, with modernization, religion becomes much less socially relevant. It is not surprising that the prevalence of this thesis might have also discouraged an examination of the relationship between religion and membership in civic associations.

13. For example, the Bible question in the National Election Studies provides the response options: "The Bible is the actual word of God and is to be taken literally word for word," "The Bible is the word of God but not everything in it should be taken literally," and "The Bible is a book written by men . . ." In 1964, only 15 percent of the American people chose the last option; in 2004, 16 percent did so.

14. Variance in any dependent variable can only be explained by variance in the independent variable. Consequently, limited variance in the independent variable cannot account for whatever variance may exist in the dependent variable.

15. Such views of biblical authority may be correlated with associational involvement, but such correlations are likely to be spurious in nature, reflecting the influence of some third factor associated with both views of biblical authority and associational involvement (e.g., membership in particular religious traditions).

16. As noted earlier, not all the surveys examined here contained a question related to church membership, but each contained a question related to religious affiliation—a form of association that is less formal than membership per se.

17. For example, while evangelical Protestants are more prone than members of other Christian traditions to hold that Christians should share their religious faith with others, not all evangelicals hold such a position.

18. It should be recalled that the Citizen Participation Study of 1990 considered those who simply contributed money to an organization to be members of the organization.

19. Wuthnow's Civic Involvement Survey of 1997 is not examined here because the survey did not ask either a question on frequency of personal prayer or questions related to the salience of religion in the life of the individual.

20. It should be noted that the religious form variable for the 1990 Citizen Participation Study, the Saguaro Social Capital Survey of 2000, and the General Social Survey of 2004 could not be constructed using a private prayer variable. As a result, a measure of religious salience (a subjective measure of the importance of religion in one's life) was used as a surrogate measure for constructing the religious form variable.

21. This pattern holds true when socioeconomic status (SES) is not controlled; when SES is taken into account, such differences disappear (e.g., Olsen 1970).

22. Multiple Classification Analysis first provides the mean score on the dependent variable for each category of the independent variable. This procedure yields a bivariate measure of association (*eta*) between the independent and dependent variable; these *eta* values have already been presented in the two previous tables. In addition, MCA provides deviations from the mean score on the dependent variable for each category of the independent variables after controls for each of the other independent variables have been entered in the analysis, with the statistic *beta* being the multivariate equivalent of *eta*—revealing the relative strength of the relationship once the effects of the other variables in the analysis have been taken into account.

23. A relationship is labeled as spurious when some third factor accounts for the initial relationship observed between two variables.

4

❖

Religion, Volunteering,
and Philanthropic Giving

Civic responsibility is not limited to associational involvement. Two other kinds of civic behavior have attracted a considerable amount of scholarly attention: the act of volunteering and the act of charitable giving. Cultural expectations related to volunteering and giving charitable donations are deeply embedded in the American civic tradition (Putnam 2000; Verba, Schlozman, and Brady 1995), and both volunteering and giving are widely prevalent in American life. While exact estimates vary, due partly to the nature and timing of survey questions, somewhere between 45 and 55 percent of Americans usually report that they volunteer at some point over the course of a year (e.g., Greeley 1997; Independent Sector 1999, 2001), while even larger numbers (89 percent of American households) report donating portions of their income to charitable causes (Independent Sector 2001).

This chapter addresses the role of religion in fostering volunteering and philanthropic giving. It is true that volunteering and giving tend to go together (Putnam 2000, 118; Hodgkinson, Weitzman, and Kirsch 1990, 102–14). Despite this relationship, the specific role that religion plays with regard to each behavior may differ for a number of reasons. First, volunteering is largely a public activity, and giving is more private. Moreover, volunteers frequently have a direct personal stake in the public good toward which their volunteering is directed, while donors are less likely to have a personal stake in the particular cause to which they are contributing.[1] Finally, volunteering is related more to one's patterns of social interaction and the extent of one's social networks, while giving is associated more with one's level of personal resources. Thus it is worthwhile to examine the role of religion in fostering volunteering separately from its role in generating charitable giving.

Religion and Volunteering

Volunteering can be viewed as any activity that is freely given to benefit another person, group, or organization (Wilson 2000, 215).[2] Some contend that it is solely the desire to help others that forms the basis for volunteering, while others hold that volunteering means acting to produce a public good without reference to particular motive(s) (Wilson 2000, 216). For purposes of the analyses presented here, volunteering constitutes any action to aid others that is freely given, regardless of its particular motivation(s).[3]

Previous research has shown that members of religious congregations volunteer their time more frequently (and volunteer more hours) than those who are not members of religious congregations (e.g., Hodgkinson, Weitzman, and Kirsch 1990, 102). Most studies of religion and volunteering, however, look beyond membership in religious congregations to attendance at religious worship services and the relationship between attendance and volunteering. Here too there is near-unanimous agreement: More frequent patterns of attendance at religious services are related to higher levels of volunteering (e.g., Hodgkinson et al. 1996; Brooks 2003; Campbell and Yonish 2003). For example, Brooks (2003, 43) reports that regular church attendees "volunteer an average of 12 times per year, while secular people volunteer an average of 5.8 times," a difference that persists even after controlling for a number of demographic characteristics. Many other studies have produced similar findings (e.g., Wuthnow 1999a, 351; Wuthnow 2004, 103; Campbell and Yonish 2003; Park and Smith 2000).

These relationships are clearly evident in the top portion of table 4.1, which examines the relationship between volunteering and church membership and church attendance across twelve national surveys conducted between 1996 and 2004.[4] Because the specific wording of questions about

Table 4.1 Volunteering by Church Membership and Church Attendance (percent reporting that they have volunteered)

Study	Church Membership			Church Attendance				
	Nonmember	Member	eta[a]	Rarely	Occasionally	Regularly	Weekly	eta[a]
NES, 1996	31	50	.17	29	35	44	59	.21
God & Society, 1996	x	x	x	28	37	50	61	.26
Giving & Volunteering, 1996	38	53	.14	32	41	48	64	.26
CIS, 1997	39	60	.21	29	46	54	73	.32
GSS, 1998	x	x	x	39	50	66	82	.34
Arts & Religion, 1999	36	61	.24	29	39	53	73	.33
Religion & Politics, 2000	47	77	.31	41	49	68	81	.33
Saguaro, 2000	37	61	.24	29	44	54	64	.24
Religion & Public Life, 2001	x	x	x	45	55	73	84	.35
GSS, 2002	30	54	.23	25	42	55	63	.28
NES, 2004	x	x	x	28	41	47	56	.22
GSS, 2004	x	x	x	35	46	57	61	.20

Note: x = not asked

[a] Statistically significant at .001 level

volunteering differs across the surveys,[5] it should be noted that it is inappropriate to assess changing levels of volunteering over time from the data. Rather, what is important is the pattern of relationship—and its consistency across the various surveys—regardless of how the question of volunteering was asked.

Clearly church members are much more likely to engage in volunteering than nonmembers. The patterns are consistent, and the relationship is strong: Members of religious congregations reported volunteering at much higher rates than those who were not members. The pattern between church attendance and volunteering is even stronger and consistently monotonic in nature, with the proportion reporting that it volunteered consistently increasing as one moves from those who rarely or never attended religious services to those who reported that they attend such services weekly.

Despite the consistency of these patterns, previous research produced conflicting answers to the following questions related to religion's role in fostering volunteering: Do more highly religious people volunteer for nonreligious, secular organizations at higher rates than less religious people? Why is it that religiously involved people tend to volunteer more than those who are less religiously engaged? Does religion contribute anything distinctive in nature in patterns of volunteering? Each of these questions is addressed below.

Secular Volunteering

The first issue that has generated discrepant findings is the relationship between religious involvement and volunteering for secular charitable programs. Some patterns are clear: Those who are religious volunteer more than those who are nonreligious, and those who are religious, not surprisingly, volunteer more for religious organizations.

Ambiguities arise, however, when one tries to determine whether those who are religious volunteer more for nonreligious, or secular, organizations than those who are not religious. On the one hand, some research suggests that they do. For example, Brooks (2003, 43) found that 60 percent of the highly religious volunteered for nonreligious causes, while only 39 percent of the less religious did so, even when controlling for basic demographic variables. Likewise, Campbell and Yonish (2003, 102) found that those who did not attend church averaged only 2.56 hours of volunteering a month for nonreligious causes, while those who attended church weekly averaged 5.33 hours of volunteering for nonreligious causes.

On the other hand, some studies have revealed slightly different patterns. For example, Park and Smith (2000) found that regular church attendance decreased volunteering for nonchurch-related causes, although they found that other forms of church activity increased volunteering for the same causes. Park and Smith's analysis was limited to Protestants, however, so it is unclear just how church attendance may relate to secular volunteering when other religious faiths are included in the analysis.

Lam (2002) also found that regular church attendance decreased volunteering for nonreligious causes, albeit only slightly, but this particular finding must also be viewed cautiously. Lam's analysis employed data from the Religion and Society survey of 1996. In that study, only those respondents who reported that they were a member of a voluntary association were asked questions related to volunteering—specifically, whether they had volunteered for the organization for which they claimed to be a member. But as is evident in table 4.3 below, people who are not members of voluntary associations do engage in volunteer activity. As a result, the data employed do not permit an assessment of whether increased church attendance has a negative effect on volunteering generally or simply a negative effect on volunteering within the associations of which one is a part.

Various analysts have theorized that church involvement diminishes the time available for active church members to participate in activities outside the church. As a member spends time in church activities—as indicated by weekly church attendance—less time is available to volunteer in extra-church causes. This is certainly true in the abstract—there are only 24 hours in a day—yet it may not be true empirically, as those who give of their time to church activities may also give of their time for activities outside the church itself. Consequently, the relationship between religious involvement and volunteering for nonreligious organizations remains somewhat murky.

To address this issue, surveys must ask separate questions about religious volunteering and secular volunteering. Of the twelve surveys examined in table 4.1, only six contained questions that permitted a differentiation between the two kinds of volunteering. These studies are examined in table 4.2, which analyzes the specific type(s) of volunteering reported by those exhibiting different levels of church attendance.

The six surveys reveal several consistent patterns. First, those who rarely or never attend church were the least likely to report any kind of volunteer activity, whether religious or secular. Second, those who attend church occasionally were much more likely to report that they engage in nonreligious than in religious volunteering. Third, among regular as well as weekly church attenders, the most common pattern was volunteering in both religious and nonreligious activities.[6]

The patterns evident in table 4.2 also clarify certain other disputed facets of the relationship between church attendance and volunteering. It is true that weekly church attenders were the most likely of all respondents to report that they engage only in religious volunteering. However, such weekly church attenders were far more likely to report that they engage in both religious and secular volunteering than in religious volunteering only, usually by rather substantial margins. Most regular church attenders also reported that they engage in both forms of volunteering, but those who engage in only one form of volunteering were generally far more likely to report volunteering for nonreligious rather than religious activities (true in five of the six surveys examined).

Finally, table 4.2 may actually underestimate the extent to which church attenders engage in secular volunteering. Most, if not all, studies have failed to clearly distinguish between volunteering for one's local congregation in its core ritualistic activities and volunteering for one's own congregation in programs that offer services to the broader community. Whereas the former includes activities such as teaching Sunday school, singing in a church choir, or ushering at religious services, the latter entails working at a congregation's food bank, tutoring children at a church-sponsored after-school program, or preparing meals at a faith-based spouse-abuse shelter. This is a crucial differentiation; in its absence, researchers are likely to underestimate the extent to which religious people volunteer for endeavors that reach beyond the life of the congregation to which they belong.

Table 4.2 Form of Volunteering by Church Attendance (percent)

Survey	Level of Church Attendance				
	Rarely	Occasionally	Regularly	Weekly	eta[a]
Giving and Volunteering, 1996					
Did not volunteer	70	62	52	38	
Secular volunteering only	26	30	20	13	
Religious volunteering only	1	2	4	15	.40
Both secular and religious vol.	3	7	24	34	
Civic Involvement Survey, 1997					
Did not volunteer	71	53	46	28	
Secular volunteering only	28	39	19	14	
Religious volunteering only	1	2	6	9	.50
Both secular and religious vol.	*	6	30	50	
General Social Survey, 1998					
Did not volunteer	61	47	32	18	
Secular volunteering only	33	29	18	10	
Religious volunteering only	*	3	7	14	.51
Both secular and religious vol.	6	21	42	58	

Religion and Politics Survey, 2000					
Did not volunteer	60	52	33	19	
Secular volunteering only	29	25	15	6	
Religious volunteering only	4	8	20	32	
Both secular and religious vol.	7	15	32	43	.44
Saguaro, 2000					
Did not volunteer	71	57	46	36	
Secular volunteering only	27	36	22	10	
Religious volunteering only	*	1	2	4	
Both secular and religious vol.	2	7	30	50	.39
Religion and Public Life, 2001					
Did not volunteer	55	45	27	16	
Secular volunteering only	40	41	41	13	
Religious volunteering only	1	3	8	19	
Both secular and religious vol.	3	11	25	53	.55

* Less than 1 percent

[a] Statistically significant at .001 level

Social Networks and Volunteering

Scholars have offered two competing explanations for why religiously involved persons tend to volunteer more than nonreligious persons: social
networks and religious convictions.

Some research suggests that social networks linked to churches' organizational life contribute to differences between the two groups (e.g.,
Becker and Dhingra 2001, 316; Wilson and Janoski 1995, 138). Churches
can serve as a recruiting ground for volunteers, provide increased exposure to community needs, and command "valuable resources for mobilizing people, turning the good intentions of worshippers into concrete
actions so that the needy are actually helped" (Wuthnow 1991, 284).
Simply stated, involvement in a religious congregation places one in social
networks outside of one's immediate family and circle of friends. As one's
experience extends into the broader community, one is drawn into a wider
social network—whether rooted in religious or secular involvements.

Social networks increase volunteering in two ways: by exposing one to
the needs of larger communities and by increasing the likelihood one will
be exposed to recruitment efforts. Accordingly, differences in levels of social
interaction serve as an important predictor of volunteering (Wilson and
Musick 1998), more so than differences in holding particular cultural
values about the duty to help others (Wilson and Musick 1997).

However, if higher levels of volunteer activity on the part of church
members and frequent church attenders are simply a function of the social
networks associated with congregational life, then one should anticipate
that "ties to service clubs and other voluntary associations should promote
helping" in much the same way that religious involvement does (Jackson
et al. 1995, 61). These expectations are examined in table 4.3, which presents the percentage of respondents who report volunteering by whether
or not they report membership in some kind of voluntary association. In
the six surveys that ask questions about membership in voluntary associations and volunteering, the patterns are once again consistent and the relationships strong: Those who claim associational membership reported
volunteering at much higher rates than do those who were not members
of voluntary associations. Nonmembers have opportunities to volunteer,
and many reported doing so, but they consistently reported volunteering

Table 4.3 Volunteering by Voluntary Associational Membership and Attendance (percent)

Study	Voluntary Association Membership			Voluntary Association Attendance				
	Non-member	Member	eta[a]	Never	Few times/year	Monthly	Weekly	eta[a]
NES, 1996	15	47	.23	x	x	x	x	x
Giving & Volunteering, 1996	31	71	.41	54	61	75	83	.33
CIS, 1997	13	69	.52	x	x	x	x	x
Saguaro, 2000	17	60	.34	34	68	79	81	.40
GSS, 2002	25	54	.27	x	x	x	x	x
NES, 2004	30	58	.29	x	x	x	x	x

Note: x = question not asked

[a] Statistically significant at .001 level

at lower—and usually markedly lower—rates than did those who reported membership of some kind.

Moreover, if the theory of social networks holds, then regular attendance at meetings of voluntary associations should function similarly to regular church attendance, with reports of volunteering rising as the frequency of attendance at such meetings increases. This too is evident in table 4.3. Only two studies, the Giving and Volunteering Study of 1996 and the Saguaro Social Capital Benchmark Survey of 2000, asked respondents how frequently they attended meetings of the associations in which they were members, but the pattern is clear: Reports of volunteering increase as the frequency of attendance at associational meetings increases.

Other scholars have reported a similar relationship. For example, when Campbell and Yonish (2003, 103–5) compared those who attend church weekly with those who attend secular organizations weekly, they found that both attendance patterns were significantly related to volunteering in both religious and nonreligious organizations. As one would expect, church attendance was more strongly related to religious volunteering, and attending secular organizations was more strongly related to nonreligious volunteering. But both types of attendance were significantly related to both forms of volunteering, leading the authors to conclude that being part of a church community "does not have appreciably different effects from that found within secular voluntary associations, at least in regards to voluntarism."[7]

While data examining the frequency with which members of voluntary organizations attend and participate in associational meetings is quite limited, one can construct an alternative test to determine whether social networks function as an important means of fostering voluntary activity. If membership in a voluntary association enmeshes people in an expanded social network, then it stands to reason that membership in multiple associations should expand social networks accordingly. If the social network explanation holds, one should find that rates of volunteering increase as respondents report an increased number of memberships in voluntary associations.

This expectation is addressed in table 4.4. It is clear from the data there that a strong monotonic relationship exists between volunteering and the extent to which respondents report membership in voluntary associations.

Table 4.4 Volunteering by Extent of Voluntary Associational Membership (percent)

Study	Number of Voluntary Associational Memberships				
	None	One	Two or three	Four or more	*eta*[a]
NES, 1996	14	22	46	71	.41
Giving and Volunteering, 1996	32	64	77	91	.43
CIS, 1997	13	47	71	93	.59
Saguaro, 2000	18	32	53	77	.46
GSS, 2002	25	35	58	74	.37
NES, 2004	30	43	69	79	.34

[a] Statistically significant at .001 level

As the number of memberships increases,[8] so too does the likelihood of volunteering. Whereas less than one-third of those with no associational membership respond that they have volunteered during the past year, nearly three-quarters or more of those who are members of four or more kinds of associations indicate that they have done so.

Overall, the data examined to this point suggest that members of religious congregations and members of voluntary associations exhibit similar patterns in terms of volunteering: Both are more likely to volunteer than are nonmembers. Likewise, attendance at religious services and attendance at meetings of voluntary associations are similarly related to volunteering: Reports of volunteering increase as the frequency of attendance increases. These data patterns suggest that patterns of social interaction and the extent of one's social networks significantly influence voluntary activity. The patterns further indicate that religion may serve to shape volunteer behavior less through religious beliefs than through the enforcement of social norms that transpire through interacting in groups (White 1969).

Despite all of the similarities between volunteering in religious and secular organizations, some important differences should be noted. These differences stem from the different rates at which Americans report church membership and attendance at worship services and the rates at which they report membership in voluntary associations and attendance at associational meetings. These differences are easily seen when one examines table 4.5. This table first displays the percentage of Americans who reported membership in a particular type of voluntary association, along with their associated level of attendance at associational meetings; it then compares such levels to reported levels of church membership and church attendance. The data are drawn from the Giving and Volunteering Survey of 1996, the only survey examined that provides reports of relative frequency of attendance at meetings across different types of voluntary associations.

Note first that more Americans report church membership than report membership in all other kinds of voluntary associations combined! Approximately two in five Americans (41.4 percent) reported membership in some type of voluntary association, but nearly three in five (57.8 percent) reported that they were members of some religious body.

Moreover, a higher percentage of church members reported weekly church attendance (44.2 percent) than members of voluntary associations reported attending associational meetings on a weekly basis (33.1 percent).[9] Consequently, whereas about one in seven Americans (13.7 percent) were members of a voluntary association and participated weekly in their associations, more than one in four Americans (25.5 percent) reported that they were church members who attended church weekly.[10] Thus, the extent to which Americans are actively engaged in congregational life far exceeds the extent to which Americans are engaged in *all* other voluntary associations combined!

Even these initial data can be viewed as overestimating the contribution of membership in voluntary associations, as many church members and frequent church attenders are found within the ranks of those reporting membership in, and attendance at, voluntary associations. What then is the relative proportion of Americans who report an active engagement in voluntary organizational life apart from any active involvement in American religious life?

This is addressed in the last two rows of table 4.5, which present the percentages of voluntary association members that result when: (1) those who report church membership are removed from the analysis or (2) those who report weekly church attendance are so removed. Doing so clarifies just how central congregational life is within American civic life. Only

Table 4.5 Frequency of Organizational Attendance by Members (percent)

Voluntary Organizations	Reporting membership	Reported Level of Attendance		
		Monthly or more	Nearly every week or weekly	Members attending weekly
Service clubs	4.8	66.1	22.3	1.1
Fraternal associations	3.2	39.8	8.0	*
Greek organizations	7.4	22.9	0.5	*
Civic associations	7.2	53.3	13.2	1.0
School groups	10.6	55.1	16.7	1.8
Professional associations	8.1	39.8	8.6	*
Voluntary associations	6.7	58.4	26.2	1.8
Religious groups	5.4	71.9	44.5	2.4
Political groups	5.7	19.9	6.4	*
Veterans groups	4.9	37.9	10.6	*
Labor unions	6.5	36.0	10.7	*
Other	11.4	71.8	45.6	5.2
Member of any vol. assoc.	41.4	65.3	33.1	13.7
Church member	57.8	72.3	44.2	25.5
Members of assoc. minus:				
Church members	15.7	62.8	30.9	4.9
Weekly church attenders	23.1	63.3	31.3	7.2

Source: Giving and Volunteering Survey, 1996

* Less than 1 percent

about one in seven Americans (15.7 percent) reports membership in some voluntary association but not in a church. Moreover, when one takes into account participation in these associations, fewer than one in twenty Americans (4.9 percent) are nonchurch members who, as members of some voluntary association, participate in its activities on a weekly basis. The corresponding figure for the percentage of Americans who are church members and attend worship service on a weekly basis is more than five times greater (25.5 percent).[11]

Clearly, religious participation is at the heart of social networks associated with organizational life within the American context. Even if it is the social interaction that transpires in congregational life that fosters civic responsibility (as demonstrated by volunteering) rather than religious faith per se, the fact remains that religious organizational life extends far more broadly and deeply than other forms of voluntary organizational life within the American context.

The Unique Contribution of Religion to Volunteering

A second theory that seeks to explain higher levels of volunteer activity by religious persons focuses on the content of an individual's religious beliefs and holds that there is something distinctive in religion that fosters volunteering. Since Christianity, Judaism, and Islam all teach the responsibility of the believer to help those in need, one could argue that religious faith itself leads to increased volunteering, an argument contained in what Wuthnow (1990, 7–9) calls the religious belief theory.

There is some empirical evidence to support this theory. Hodgkinson and her colleagues found that persons who had a personal goal of "making a strong commitment to a religious life" gave and volunteered in a much higher proportion than persons who had other types of personal goals (Hodgkinson, Weitzman, and Kirsch 1990, 109).[12]

Also, a number of studies suggest that private devotional activities—religious activities that are noteworthy because they do not involve persons in social networks—may increase volunteering. Some of this evidence is indirect. For example, Loveland and his fellow researchers (2005) found that those who more frequently engaged in private prayer were more likely to report that they were members of voluntary associations (and, as was evident in table 4.3, those who are members of voluntary associations are much more likely than those who are not members to report that they volunteer). Other evidence is more direct. Wuthnow (2004, 103), for example, found that persons who reported daily Bible reading, prayer, or meditation also volunteered for charity or social service programs to a greater extent than those who did not; while 31 percent of those who read the Bible "nearly every day" volunteered, only 13 percent of those who read the Bible less often had done so (Wuthnow 2004, 103). Lam (2002, 420) also found that "the devotional dimension of religiosity, measured by frequency of prayer and religious reading, does have a significant positive influence on voluntary association participation." These studies suggest that private devotional activities—even though they do not involve people in social networks—increase volunteering.

It will be recalled that the modes of religious expression differentiate between public and private forms of religious expression—with the public and integrated forms being separated on the basis of whether those who attend church regularly report engaging in daily private prayer. In other words, those with public and integrated forms of religiosity display similar levels of worship attendance; what differentiates them is their level of devotional activity. Consequently, the volunteer rates reported by those who exhibit different forms of religious expression can be examined as an initial step to ascertain the extent to which religious faith, as opposed to social networks, may contribute to volunteer activity. If the religious belief theory has any merit, then one would anticipate distinct differences in the reported levels of volunteering by the two categories of regular church attenders—those who exhibit the public form of religious expression and those who exhibit the integrated form.

This expectation is examined in table 4.6. The table presents the percentage of respondents who report having volunteered according to their form of religious expression, as revealed across ten different national surveys conducted between 1996 and 2004. Clearly, those who exhibit integrated forms of religious expression were much more likely to report that they had volunteered than were those who exhibit public forms. These differences in levels of volunteering are consistent in nature and fairly large in magnitude: (1) In all ten surveys, integrated religionists were more likely

Table 4.6 Volunteering by Form of Religion Expression (percent)

Study	Diminished	Privatized	Public	Integrated	eta[a]
NES, 1996	32	30	43	54	.21
God and Society, 1996	33	36	51	62	.26
GSS, 1998	42	46	72	75	.32
Arts and Religion, 1999	36	43	58	72	.31
Religion and Politics, 2000	49	52	79	81	.31
Saguaro, 2000	43	32	50	64	.23
Religion and Public Life, 2001	49	49	73	84	.35
GSS, 2002	32	36	48	61	.26
NES, 2004	32	31	44	53	.20
GSS, 2004	42	40	51	59	.17

[a] Statistically significant at .001 level

to have volunteered than public religionists, and (2) in seven of the ten surveys, the magnitude of the difference in volunteering between these high church-attenders exceeded 10 percentage points.

The question then arises whether religion continues to be significantly related to the likelihood of volunteering once controls are introduced for other variables related to volunteer activity. In other words, does the religious character of the respondent influence the likelihood of volunteering beyond what one might expect once a respondent's educational attainment, age, and even voluntary organizational membership are taken into account?

Table 4.7 addresses this issue by examining the relative strength of the relationship between specific independent variables and volunteering once the effects of other variables have been taken into account. This multivariate analysis was conducted by means of a multiple classification analysis (MCA) in which we examined the relative effects of nine variables on the likelihood of volunteering[13]: membership in a voluntary association, gender, race, age, education, family income, marital status, religious tradition affiliation, and form of religious expression. Previous research has established that voluntary-association participation is related

Table 4.7 Relative Importance of Religion in Fostering Volunteering:
A Multiple Classification Analysis

Demographic Characteristic	Study			
	NES 1996	Saguaro 2000	GSS 2002	NES 2004
Membership in voluntary organization	.13ᶜ	.27ᶜ	.22ᶜ	.23ᶜ
Gender	.03	.08ᵃ	.03	.08ᵃ
Race	.13ᶜ	.05	.12ᶜ	.04
Age	.13ᶜ	.07ᵃ	.06	.09ᵇ
Education	.15ᶜ	.12ᶜ	.13ᶜ	.17ᶜ
Family income	.05	.10ᵇ	.10ᵇ	.03
Marital status	.07	.04	.09ᵇ	.08ᵃ
Religious tradition	.13ᶜ	.07ᵃ	.09ᵇ	.11ᵇ
Form of religious expression	.19ᶜ	.16ᶜ	.28ᶜ	.21ᶜ
R square	*.16*	*.19*	*.21*	*.20*

ᵃ Statistically significant at .05 level
ᵇ Statistically significant at .01 level
ᶜ Statistically significant at .001 level

to a number of demographic characteristics, including gender, marital status, age, education, and income (for a review of previous research, see Knoke 1986 and D. H. Smith 1994). But given our desire to analyze the effects of membership in voluntary associations and forms of religious expression as well, our analysis is limited to the four surveys that contain all the requisite variables.[14]

As table 4.7 suggests, a number of variables help to explain the likelihood of volunteering. Membership in a voluntary organization is clearly related to formal volunteering, and such memberships tend, overall, to be one of the two most important variables shaping the likelihood of reporting that one has volunteered within the past twelve months. Membership in a voluntary organization ranked first in relative importance in half of the studies examined—specifically, the Saguaro 2000 and the NES 2004 studies. However, even in this latter survey, where membership in a voluntary organization exhibited the largest *beta* value, the *beta* value for the form of religious expression was virtually identical to the beta value for membership in a voluntary organization.

In fact, one's form of religious expression tends to rival associational membership as the most important variable in shaping volunteering. The form of religious expression ranked first in the remaining two studies (the NES 1996 and the GSS 2002 studies), but as just noted, it nearly equaled the *beta* weight for organizational membership in the NES 2004 study as well. Overall, one's form of religious expression ranked as important as, if not more important than, one's membership in voluntary associations in shaping the likelihood of volunteering in some capacity.

One's level of education also serves as an important factor in volunteer activity. In one survey (the NES 1996 survey), the *beta* value for education actually exceeded that for membership in a voluntary organization. In the remaining three surveys, however, the *beta* value for education consistently ranked third. On the other hand, family income consistently trails education in its relative importance for shaping volunteer activity; of the nine variables contained in the MCA, family income ranks no higher than fourth in any of the surveys.

The remaining variables (gender, race, age, marital status, and religious tradition affiliation) consistently stand toward the bottom in terms of relative importance. In the NES 1996 survey, race, age, religious tradition affiliation, and membership in voluntary organizations all exhibited identical *beta* values, with each tied for third place in terms of relative ranking. However, these sociodemographic variables usually rank among the least important variables, though their relative unimportance varies by survey.

Taken together, the data presented in table 4.7 demonstrate that the relationship between religion and volunteering is not spurious, as one's form of religious expression serves as an important factor in explaining variation in volunteering.[15] Moreover, in terms of volunteering, the nature of one's religious tradition is less important than the mode of one's religious expression, as the magnitude of the *beta* associated with the latter variable exceeds that for religious tradition affiliation across all four surveys analyzed. Finally, the mean score for volunteering after controlling for the other variables was less for public religionists than for integrated religionists (data not shown); consequently, it cannot be inferred that it is simply the social networks linked to religious worship attendance that foster volunteering. Rather, it would appear that there is something in religious faith itself that contributes to volunteering.

Religion and Charitable Giving

Earlier in the chapter we noted that while giving of one's time and giving of one's money are related, the two activities differ in some important ways. The old adage states that "time is money," but many people apparently find it easier to contribute money than time to causes they support: A higher percentage of Americans report that they have made some kind of charitable contribution than report that they have volunteered in the past year.[16]

Americans have historically been generous contributors to charities and charitable causes. In recent years, nearly 80 percent of Americans reported that they made a donation to some kind of charitable cause.[17] However, because charitable contributions can serve as a tax deduction (and given that many married couples file jointly), survey questions about charitable giving are frequently asked in terms of household, rather than individual, giving. When analyzed in these terms, nearly three out of every four families report having made some kind of charitable donation each year (Brooks 2006, 3), with nearly nine in ten reporting a donation in 2001 (Independent Sector 2001).

It is true that making a financial donation to a formal charity does not represent all types of generosity. One may drop coins in the coffee cup of a homeless person begging on the street, donate blood, or pay for a friend's dinner at a restaurant. Nevertheless, an examination of giving patterns represents "an excellent way to flag the people who are truly charitable in American society—and those who are not" (Brooks 2006, 6).

To this end, one might expect that there would be a relationship between religion and charitable giving. Most, if not all, major religious faiths stipulate that followers should exhibit compassion for those who are less fortunate. And normative expectations related to religious giving (tithing) are often an important part of religious belief (Park and Smith 2000). One of the major reasons people donate is out of a sense of duty. For example, about 80 percent of givers in 2000 indicated that they gave because "those who have more should give to those who have less" (Brooks 2006, 7). Similarly, Jones (2006, 259) reports that "the more someone believed that helping was important, the more they donated to charity."

Given these considerations, it is hardly surprising to learn that one of the most consistently reported findings regarding religion and giving is that persons who are religious are more likely to donate money to charitable organizations and give more money than those who are not religious. Among the religious, those who are more religious are more likely to give and to give more than those who are less religious; this pattern holds whether one considers financial gifts to all charitable organizations, only to religious organizations, or only to secular organizations. And it holds true whether religion is measured in terms of religious belonging (e.g., Hodgkinson, Weitzman, and Kirsch 1990, 103 and 107; Nemeth and Luidens 2003) or in terms of church attendance (e.g., Hodgkinson et al. 1996, 4–93; Brooks 2003; Regnerus, Smith, and Sikkink 1998).

Membership and Charitable Giving

The relationship between church membership and charitable giving is examined in table 4.8,[18] along with the relationship between membership in a voluntary association and charitable giving.[19] The data support strong relationships between charitable giving and both church membership and associational membership: The percentage of church members who report having made a donation in the past year generally reflects the percentage of associational members who report doing the same (around 80 percent or higher). The proportions claiming to have donated varies by survey and the nature of the question(s) asked, but the patterns within each survey are basically identical.

The final four columns in table 4.8 reveal the effects of membership in voluntary associations on reporting a donation in the past twelve months, while controlling for church membership. Clearly, both forms of membership shape patterns of giving. Nonchurch members who are members of voluntary associations were much more likely to report having made a charitable contribution than those who reported neither kind of membership. Likewise, among church members, those who were also members of voluntary associations were more likely to give than those who did not hold voluntary associational memberships.

On the other hand, a higher percentage of nonchurch members who were members of voluntary associations reported having made a donation than did those who were church members but not members of any other

Table 4.8 Donating within the Last Year by Form of Organizational Membership (percent)

Study	Church Member			Voluntary Orginization Member			Nonchurch Member Vol. Mem.		Church Member Vol. Mem.	
	No	Yes	eta[a]	No	Yes	eta[a]	No	Yes	No	Yes
NES, 1996	71	88	.22	37	85	.41	40	81	50	91
Giving and Vol., 1996	55	78	.25	56	87	.33	41	78	67	92
Saguaro, 2000	45	70	.24	33	66	.27	22	55	50	73
GSS, 2002	70	84	.17	64	86	.26	61	78	67	90

[a] Statistically significant at .001 level

kind of voluntary association. This pattern is consistent with Putnam's report (2000, 120) that members of religious congregations are more likely to give and to give more than nonmembers, but that an even higher percentage of members of secular organizations donate to charities than members of religious organizations (and that they tend to give larger amounts). Still, church membership adds to the likelihood of contributing beyond that linked to membership in voluntary associations per se. Church members who were also members of other voluntary associations were far more likely to make charitable contributions than were nonchurch members who reported membership in voluntary associations.

Ways of Being Religious and Charitable Giving

The ways in which individuals are religious also shape patterns of charitable giving. We will first examine the frequency of reported giving and then, second, the level of reported giving among those exhibiting different forms of religious expression.

Frequency of Giving

Of the twelve surveys analyzed in this chapter, eight contain questions that permit an examination of the relationship between one's form of religious expression and charitable donations. As shown in table 4.9, there is a consistent pattern across all eight surveys in the relationship between one's form of religiosity and likelihood of giving. Each survey demonstrates a consistent increase of those reporting that they have made a charitable contribution as one moves from respondents exhibiting a diminished form of religious expression to those exhibiting an integrated form. Privatized religionists are more likely to give than those whose religious expression is diminished, those with a public form of religious expression are more likely to have donated than those with a privatized expression, and those with an integrated form of religiosity were the most likely to have reported some kind of charitable contribution in the past year.

Table 4.9 Donating by Form of Religion Expression (percent)

Study	Diminished	Privatized	Public	Integrated	eta[a]
National Election Study, 1996	63	66	88	91	.32
God and Society Society, 1996	43	45	55	57	.13
General Social Survey, 1998	54	62	76	81	.26
Arts and Religion, 1999	54	66	77	80	.25
Saguaro, 2000	49	43	62	72	.23
General Social Survey, 2002	70	75	79	87	.17
National Election Study, 2004	63	69	88	93	.34
General Social Survey, 2004	72	75	83	86	.15

[a] Statistically significant at .001 level

Level of Charitable Giving

However, giving can be assessed not only in terms of whether one has made a contribution but also in terms of the amount donated. Most people are able to afford a donation of several dollars for some worthy cause and thereby cross the threshold of having made a charitable contribution in the past year. Yet the significance of religion's effect on charitable giving may be far greater when measured in terms of the level of financial sacrifice rather than in terms of simply having made a contribution. Consequently, it is important that one examine not only the frequency with which giving is reported but also the level of such giving.

Several of the surveys analyzed in this chapter asked respondents to estimate the amount of money they had contributed over the past twelve months to their congregation and various religious causes, as well as the amount that they had donated to secular charitable causes. Three of these surveys also contained questions that permitted an analysis of giving levels in terms of the forms of religious expression. The results are presented in table 4.10.

Table 4.10 Average Dollars Contributed by Form of Religious Expression

	Mean $		
Study	Religious	Secular	Total
General Social Survey, 1998			
Diminished	120.12	223.17	343.29
Privatized	254.25	250.36	504.61
Public	2113.26	642.02	2755.28
Integrated	2181.52	373.28	2554.80
Arts and Religion, 1999			
Diminished	142.84	35.98	278.82
Privatized	298.86	195.26	494.12
Public	890.05	152.22	1042.27
Integrated	1933.62	160.13	2093.75
Saguaro, 2000			
Diminished	282.44	473.16	755.60
Privatized	320.50	285.99	606.49
Public	961.31	504.94	1466.25
Integrated	1676.78	481.24	2158.02

Several important patterns emerge from the table. First, and not surprisingly, those with a diminished form of religiosity contributed far more money, on average, to secular than to religious causes. In two of the three surveys examined, the ratio of the dollars given by those with a diminished religious expression to secular, as opposed to religious, causes is almost two to one.

On the other hand, those with a privatized religious expression tended to split the level of their charitable contributions more evenly between religious and secular causes. In two of the surveys, the mean level of dollars contributed to religious causes is roughly equivalent to that contributed to secular causes, though in the Arts and Religion Survey of 1999, such respondents reported far higher levels of contribution to religious (mean = $298.86) than to secular (mean = $195.26) causes.

Those who attend worship services on some regular basis exhibited the highest levels of charitable contributions. In fact, the average total amount of dollars contributed to charitable causes on the part of those with public or integrated forms of religious expression range anywhere between twice the amount (when comparing public versus privatized forms of expression in the Arts and Religion Survey of 1999) to eight times the amount of total dollars contributed (when comparing integrated versus diminished forms of expression in the General Social Survey of 1998).

These differences raise the question of how best to explain the relationship between religion and charitable giving. Can the differences be explained simply by self-interest? For example, are the differences simply the result of members giving to their own churches and their own church programs? A critic might argue that contributions to religious causes on the part of regular worship attenders are no more than acts of self-interest. If public worship is important enough to be maintained, then financial costs will be incurred to support worship services: Pastors and other religious leaders must be paid and edifices maintained for worship services to transpire. Thus, it is in the self-interest of regular worshippers to contribute to religious causes, particularly those related to their local congregation.

However, the data presented in table 4.10 suggest that the different giving levels exhibited by people with different forms of religious expression cannot be attributed simply to self-interest. First, while contributions to one's own religious group might be linked to some notion of self-interest, it is much harder to make the same case when addressing contributions to nonreligious causes. Here, contributions are much more likely to be based on internalized social or religious values, because donations to secular causes are more strongly rooted in social values such as responsibility for the common good than are donations to religious causes. Notions of who constitutes one's neighbor tend to benefit strangers, as religion expands definitions of neighbors who deserve one's help to include more "distant others" (Bekkers and Schuyt 2007).

Second, the level of giving to secular causes by regular church attenders is generally equivalent to, and sometimes even exceeds, the level of donations to such causes by those who attend religious worship services only occasionally. In both the General Social Survey of 1998 and the Saguaro Social Capital Survey of 2000, the average contribution to secular causes on the part of those with a public or integrated form of religious expression exceeded the average level of contributions made to secular causes on the part of those who were less religiously engaged. Moreover, what makes this level of giving to secular causes so remarkable is that the contributions to secular causes were made in addition to the substantial contributions that these regular church attenders were already making to religious causes. Giving at such levels to secular causes on the part of those exhibiting public and integrated forms of religious expression is, relatively speaking, likely to be far more costly for them than for the diminished and privatized givers.

Finally, even among those who attend church regularly, there appear to be some important differences in their reported levels of charitable donations. While the mean level of total dollars contributed by those with public and integrated forms of religious expression was roughly equivalent in the General Social Survey of 1998, integrated religionists gave considerably more dollars than did public religionists in the other two surveys (approximately 50 percent more in the one and more than double in the other).

One might argue that differences in giving across the different modes of religious expression are nothing more than a reflection of variation in the distribution of family income across these four different categories. However, when one controls for level of family income, these differences in giving patterns across the four forms of religious expression remain consistent. This is shown in table 4.11, which analyzes the relationship between total reported giving by one's form of religious expression, when the distribution of family income is divided in terms of quartiles, with roughly one-quarter of the respondents falling within each of the income categories.

As is evident across all three surveys, those with a privatized form of religious expression tended, as a whole, to give slightly more total dollars to charitable causes than those with a diminished form. This pattern holds true until one reaches the upper quartile of family income, when those with a diminished form outpace private religionists in charitable contributions. But it is those holding public and integrated modes of religiosity who particularly gave, donating far more than those who exhibit either a diminished or privatized form of religious expression. In fact, except for the lowest quartile, those with public and integrated modes contributed nearly twice as much, if not more, as those with either a privatized or a diminished form. Finally, those who exhibit an integrated mode generally contributed the most, regardless of the level of family income (the sole exception being the upper-middle quartile in the GSS 1998 data).

Table 4.11 Average Dollars Contributed by Form of Religious Expression, Controlling for Level of Family Income

Level of Family Income	GSS 1998	Arts & Religion 1999	Saguaro 2000
Lowest Quartile			
Diminished	40.98	87.70	273.41
Privatized	436.06	448.71	280.33
Public	391.83	282.13	503.47
Integrated	1020.21	499.69	1107.88
Lower-Middle Quartile			
Diminished	144.92	206.70	319.52
Privatized	425.83	383.42	622.96
Public	2208.13	729.11	1268.69
Integrated	1595.54	1532.44	1153.80
Upper-Middle Quartile			
Diminished	346.81	443.17	627.02
Privatized	437.21	598.61	629.27
Public	3357.57	1805.04	1531.10
Integrated	3123.20	3479.61	2517.05
Highest Quartile			
Diminished	1357.31	1940.78	1811.79
Privatized	1165.00	1129.43	1744.44
Public	6202.00	2471.06	3670.59
Integrated	7676.74	8300.03	3919.73

Thus differences in levels of family income cannot account for the variation in giving patterns across the different forms of religious expression. Moreover, from similarly limited financial resources, public and integrated religionists simply gave more to others. This pattern exists despite the fact that there is nothing that precludes those who are less engaged in corporate religious life to give more generously to secular charities and nonprofits.

The Unique Contribution of Religion to Giving

One might conclude that something about religion itself fosters greater charitable contributions on the part of the religious, particularly those who attend church with some regularity (i.e., those with either a public or integrated form of religious expression). There are competing factors, however, that might explain such differences. For example, it is possible that differences in charitable giving stem from demographic characteristics of those who are religious. The question can then be raised whether religion continues to influence the likelihood of making donations once controls have been introduced for such factors as family income, educational attainment, age, or voluntary organizational membership.

Table 4.12 addresses this issue, examining the relative strength of the relationship between one's form of religious expression and giving, once the effects of the other independent variables have been taken into account. This analysis was once again conducted by means of multiple classification analysis, and the variables examined are the same variables included in the chapter's earlier MCA analysis on the likelihood of volunteering.

Table 4.12 Relative Importance of Religion in Fostering Charitable Giving: A Multiple Classification Analysis

Demographic Characteristic	Study				
	NES 1996	Saguaro 2000 A*	Saguaro 2000 B**	GSS 2002	NES 2004
Membership in voluntary organization	.25[c]	.18[c]	.11[b]	.15[c]	.12[c]
Gender	.03	.02	.08[a]	.08[a]	.05
Race	.03	.08[a]	.07	.01	.17[c]
Age	.10[b]	.02	.08[a]	.18[c]	.15[c]
Education	.08[a]	.12[c]	.16[c]	.17[c]	.13[c]
Family income	.19[c]	.17[c]	.30[c]	.23[c]	.18[c]
Marital status	.07	.07	.05	.05	.04
Religious tradition	.11[b]	.05	.09[b]	.06	.18[c]
Form of religious expression	.19[c]	.21[c]	.32[c]	.12[c]	.25[c]
R-square	*.29*	*.19*	*.35*	*.24*	*.26*

* This *beta* reflects whether one reported having donated.
** This *beta* reflects the level of total giving reported.

[a] Statistically significant at .05 level
[b] Statistically significant at .01 level
[c] Statistically significant at .001 level

Given the desire to include variables related to membership in voluntary associations and forms of religious expression, only the same four surveys analyzed in table 4.7 could be included, as they contain the requisite questions to permit such an analysis.[20] It should be noted, however, that the dependent variable examined is not the level of financial contributions made but whether or not the respondent made a donation.

A number of variables help to explain the likelihood of giving. Overall, one's form of religious expression tends either to be the most important variable or among the most important accounting for differences in the likelihood of making a charitable contribution. It ranked as the most important variable in the Saguaro 2000 and the NES 2004 surveys, and trailed only membership in voluntary associations in the 1996 National Election Study. Only in the General Social Survey of 2002 did it fail to be among the top two variables accounting for variation in giving.

Membership in voluntary organizations is also clearly related to giving, but it is not as central in accounting for differences in the likelihood of making a charitable contribution as it is in accounting for differences in the likelihood of volunteering. Associational membership ranked first in relative importance in one of the four studies examined (NES 1996), and it ranked second in the Saguaro 2000 survey when the dependent variable was constructed in terms of whether or not the respondent reported making a charitable contribution. However, in the remaining two studies, associational membership failed to rank even as high as third.

As anticipated, family income is much more important in shaping the likelihood of making charitable contributions than it is in fostering volunteering. Higher levels of family income are clearly linked to the likelihood of making a charitable donation. Family income ranked as the most important variable fostering giving in the General Social Survey of 2002, and it was tied for second in relative importance in both the NES 1996 and NES 2004 surveys. In addition, in the Saguaro study, when the dependent variable is constructed in terms of the reported total amount of dollars contributed to charity, the *beta* value for family income also ranked second in magnitude, nearly matching one's form of religious expression. Thus, while social ties also influence giving, philanthropy appears to be more strongly related to personal resources such as wealth than does volunteering.

One's level of education also contributes to explaining differences in charitable giving, but it trails family income in relative importance, a reversal of the pattern found with regard to volunteering. Age, race, marital status, and gender generally trail substantially in relative importance, as the variables tend consistently to be among the least important factors explaining charitable giving. On the other hand, religious tradition affiliation reveals a somewhat mixed pattern, ranking as high as second in relative importance in the NES 2004 survey and third in the NES 1996 survey, but falling in the bottom half of the other two surveys.

The Saguaro data enable one to examine whether the same independent variables can account for the total amount of money contributed, rather than only for whether a contribution was made, and these data are also presented in table 4.12. Given that there is greater variation in the dependent variable, the *beta* coefficients generally increase in their magnitude (as well as the amount of variance explained—the R-square value—which also increases in magnitude). When one focuses on the level of giving rather than simply on the act of giving, age and gender become much more important in shaping philanthropy, while membership in voluntary organizations declines in significance. The *beta* values for both family income and form of religious expression also increase, with both variables being substantially important in the level of giving. Nevertheless, even when one focuses on the size of charitable gifts made, the *beta* value for form of religious expression still exceeds that for family income.

Overall, the data presented in table 4.12 demonstrate that the relationship between religion and giving is not spurious and that the form of one's religious expression constitutes a relatively important explanatory factor in accounting for variation in charitable giving. Moreover, in terms of giving of one's financial resources, the nature of one's religious tradition is once again less important than the mode of one's religious expression because the magnitude of the *beta* associated with the latter variable always exceeded that for religious tradition affiliation regardless of survey analyzed. In addition, the expected mean scores for donating after controlling for the other variables was less for those with a public mode of religious expression than it was for those manifesting an integrated mode (data not shown). As a result, these patterns suggest that it is improper to infer that it is the social networks linked to religious worship attendance alone that fosters these forms of behavior. Rather, given that public religionists and integrated religionists attend worship services at equal rates but differ in their levels of charitable contributions, it would appear that something in religious faith itself contributes to charitable endeavors, beyond what may result from the social networks generated by worship attendance.

Conclusion

This chapter has examined the role religion plays in contributing to civic life through volunteering and charitable giving. We found religion to be an important factor in both types of civic engagement. First, with regard to volunteering, church members and those who attend church regularly tend to volunteer more than nonmembers and those who rarely attend. Those who attend religious services only rarely or occasionally choose to volunteer for secular causes more than those who attend worship services regularly, but those who attend religious services regularly tend to volunteer more frequently overall, as they volunteer not only for religious causes but for secular causes as well.

Church-based social networks help to recruit and mobilize volunteers. But religious faith itself also leads people to volunteer, as those with an integrated form of religious expression are more likely to volunteer than those who exhibit a public form of religious expression—despite the fact that both attend worship services at the same relative level of frequency.

Involvement in voluntary associations also tends to increase volunteering. However, since many more Americans are involved in religious congregations than in voluntary associations, houses of worship play a far more important role than nonreligious voluntary associations in contributing to the absolute level of volunteering in the United States. Moreover, multivariate analysis reveals that form of religious expression is one of the most important factors shaping whether or not someone reports having volunteered in some capacity.

The levels at which people make charitable contributions are also closely linked to form of religious expression, as the likelihood of having made a charitable contribution generally increases as one moves from diminished to privatized, from privatized to public, and from public to integrated forms of religious expression. Moreover, not only do those who exhibit a public or integrated form of religiosity tend to give far more to religious causes than those with diminished or privatized modes of expression, but they tend to give more to secular causes as well. When compared to a variety of other sociodemographic factors linked to whether or not one reports having made a charitable contribution, a person's form of religious expression is either the most important or one of the most important variables.

Taken together, our findings in this chapter emphasize the importance of religion in explaining patterns of volunteering and charitable giving. To ignore religion while trying to explain either behavior would be to ignore a crucial variable. Religion's important role is not merely a function of the social networks linked to religious involvement but it is also a function of the form of one's religious beliefs and practice. A person's form of religious expression is consistently related to patterns of volunteering and giving, revealing that the presence or absence of private, personal religious exercises—and not simply involvement in public acts of worship and related religious social networks—also contributes to explaining the civic acts of both volunteering and giving.

Notes

1. For example, parents of school-age children are likely to participate more frequently in parent-teacher associations than parents who have no children in school, while one may choose to donate to the American Cancer Society even though one does not have cancer.

2. Such a definition, however, does not preclude volunteers from benefiting from their work. While some scholars contend that voluntary endeavors cannot by definition be work that is remunerated, others hold that those who choose to work in poorly paid positions, because they wish to do good, should be considered "quasi-volunteers" (Wilson 2000, 216).

3. Even if one wished to take into account the motivation(s) for volunteering, it would be difficult to do so. Most surveys that inquire about volunteering do not include questions about motivation for such work. Some analysts distinguish between "informal" volunteering (e.g., minding the children of a neighbor

while a parent is briefly away from the home) and "formal" volunteering (activities that further the interests of various organizations). This chapter focuses only on the more "formal" expressions of volunteering that are the more conventionally examined aspects of volunteering.

4. All analyses of volunteering found in this chapter focus on whether or not a respondent has volunteered. No effort was made to take into account the amount of time volunteered.

5. For exact wording of these questions tapping volunteering, see appendix C.

6. Regular attenders are operationally defined as those who report that they attend monthly or more but less than weekly.

7. Putnam (2000, 119) reports that when one compares those who attended church at least monthly with those who attended club meetings at least monthly, club attendees actually volunteered more than did church attendees. Moreover, these two types of involvements reinforced each other: those who attended both church and clubs volunteered the most, and those who attended neither volunteered the least.

8. As discussed in chapter 3, technically speaking what is being measured is the number of memberships across different types of voluntary associations rather than purely the specific number of such memberships.

9. The response options to the church attendance question in the Giving and Volunteering Survey of 1996 specified (a) every week or nearly every week, (b) once or twice a month, (c) only a few times a year, or (d) not at all.

10. These figures are obtained by multiplying the percentage who report membership by the percentage of those reporting weekly attendance. Thus the percentage of Americans who are church members (57.8 percent) who reported attending worship services on a weekly basis (44.2 percent) is 25.5 percent (.578 × .442 = .255). The same process can be followed to obtain the various percentages reported in the final column of table 4.5.

11. Were the calculations based on eliminating weekly church attenders rather than church members, the percentage of Americans who are members of a voluntary association and participate in such associations weekly increases to 7.2 percent, but even this larger percentage is still less than one-third the proportion who are members of a church and attend church weekly (see bottom portion of table 4.5).

12. Similarly, Wuthnow (2004, 103) found that those respondents who indicated spiritual growth as being extremely or very important were more than twice as likely to volunteer as those who indicated it was less important.

13. For more information on multiple classification analysis, see the discussion related to table 3.7 in chapter 3.

14. Two surveys had to be eliminated from the analysis for different reasons. As noted in note 7 above, the God and Society Survey of 1996 asked volunteering questions only of those who were members of voluntary associations. Because more than 90 percent of those who were members reported that they volunteered, analysis basically indicates, not surprisingly, that volunteering is explained by membership in voluntary associations, with an R-square of .859. On the other hand, the General Social Survey frequently employs what is known as a split-half technique, in which some survey questions are asked of all respondents and other questions are asked only of segments of respondents (frequently one-half of those sampled). While the General Social Survey of 2004 asked questions about both volunteering and organizational membership, the questions were asked of two different groups. As a result, one cannot examine the relationship between the two variables.

15. It should be recalled that forms of religious expression are an important variable shaping the likelihood of joining voluntary associations in the first place. From a "path analysis" perspective, this variable (one's form of religious expression) has both a direct and an indirect effect on volunteering. Not only must its direct effect (a straight line from religious expression to volunteering) be taken into account, but so too must its indirect effects (i.e., the path that runs from religious expression to membership in volunteer organizations to volunteering).

16. In the eight surveys examined in this chapter that contain questions related to both volunteering and donating, the percentage of those who reported donating was always higher than the percentage who reported volunteering. Depending on the way the questions were asked, these differences in percentages ranged between ten and thirty points. In the three most recent surveys examined (the GSS 2002, NES 2004, and GSS 2004), the percentage difference was greater than thirty points with volunteer activities falling in the 40 percent range and donating in the upper 70 percent range.

17. The percentage of Americans who reported making a charitable contribution in the first half of this decade was between 77 percent and 79 percent.

18. For the exact wording of the questions that tap making a charitable contribution, see appendix D.

19. Brooks (2006, 5) reports that "people who give away their time and money to established charities are far more likely than nongivers to behave generously in informal ways as well." He cites various data patterns that confirm this assertion.

20. The God and Society survey simply asked whether or not respondents were going to claim an income tax credit for charitable contributions made in the past year. Many people may make a donation without claiming credit for doing so on their income taxes. Hence these data are not analyzed in table 4.12.

5

❊

Religion and Civic Capacities

Responsible citizens willingly share with others through activities such as volunteering, giving, and donating time and resources as needed in their search for "a reasonable balance between their own interests and the common good" ("The Civic Mission of Schools" 2003, 10). But exhibiting civic responsibility does not stop there; it also entails being competent and informed citizens, as responsible citizens exhibit the requisite *skills* and *knowledge* needed to accomplish public purposes.

Not all civic engagement is necessarily of equal value. Some people may engage in civic life and yet possess relatively little awareness and understanding of the matters at hand; others may demonstrate a depth of knowledge and understanding. Citizens need not be scholars or skilled managers to fulfill their civic responsibilities, but there is a minimal level of knowledge below which reasoned judgments related to civic life become impaired (Galston 2001, 218). Yet even if all members of society possessed such knowledge and skills, the net result would not necessarily be a consensus about the proper course of public action. Rather, the presence of civic skills and knowledge on the part of the public would work primarily to enhance the quality of civic discussion and deliberation, perhaps resulting in a broader consensus but, if not, certainly in more fully informed and thoughtful decisions.

In this chapter we focus on how religion shapes the civic capacities of the American people. Broadly speaking, we examine whether religion promotes the development and exercise of civic skills, attention to public affairs, and knowledge related to public life. Of course, civic capacities and civic engagement are interrelated, as civic knowledge promotes participation in public affairs (Galston 2001, 225). Likewise, without some minimal level of knowledge and skills, individuals are not as likely either to aspire to or to become involved in public life. Thus the relationship between capacities and engagement is likely to be reciprocal,[1] and in this chapter we focus on religion and civic capacities based on the assumption that exercising these capacities enhances and fosters civic engagement. More specifically, we examine (1) the relationship between religion and the practice of civic skills and (2) the relationship between religion and cognitive engagement in public life, particularly attention to public affairs and political knowledge.

The Practice of Civic Skills

Civic skills denote the capacity of individuals to engage in activities by which they are able to "express voice in the political process—such as running meetings or giving speeches" (Campbell 2006, 156). While such skills are developed through a range of experiences and endeavors in civic life, they can also serve as resources for participation in politics because they are easily transferred and applied to the political arena.

Although the possession of civic skills may be an important foundation for public engagement, it is not necessarily sufficient to produce such engagement.[2] Nor does the absence of civic skills necessarily preclude engagement in public life; even those who possess few, if any, civic skills may be engaged in public matters. Nevertheless, civic skills enhance the capacity of individuals to engage in public affairs in a more responsible fashion.

How, specifically, are civic skills generated and developed among American citizens? Some civic skills may be acquired in the work setting, and certain occupations are more likely than others to provide opportunities for their acquisition. For example, white-collar positions are more likely than blue-collar to offer opportunities to practice such skills as chairing a meeting, participating in a meeting where a decision is made, or coordinating activities—activities that "spill over" into political life (Peterson 1992; Schlozman, Verba, and Brady 1999).

Following Tocqueville, many scholars (e.g., Verba, Schlozman, and Brady 1995; Wuthnow 1999a; Putnam 2000) postulate that voluntary associations also serve as a training ground for the acquisition of civic skills. By participating in these associations, citizens are able to acquire and hone such skills as serving on committees, learning to compromise, raising funds, writing letters, generating publicity, and mobilizing support. For example, Putnam (2000, 290) has argued that voluntary associations such as parent-teacher associations help citizens to develop civic skills, asserting that "belonging to the PTA almost certainly inculcates civic skills in parents" in that "people who might never have designed a project, given a presentation, lobbied a public official, or even spoken up at a meeting are pressed to do so." Similarly, Verba, Schlozman, and Brady (1995, 309) contend that voluntary associations "offer many opportunities to acquire, or improve, organizational or communications skills in the context of activities that have nothing to do with politics." Such statements mirror the contentions of Tocqueville (1969, 252), who asserted more than 150 years ago that "one may think of (civic) associations as great free schools."

The Building of Civic Skills within Religious Institutions

There are a variety of arenas in which civic skills might be acquired, and some of these skills may be derived through participation in religious life. But as noted in chapter 3, the battery of questions conventionally employed to tap membership in voluntary associations usually does not include church membership, though it includes religious or church-related groups as options among voluntary associations. Yet participation in congregational life undoubtedly offers citizens opportunities to generate civic skills. The various organizational activities found with the weekly life of a religious congregation, such as working in a soup kitchen, singing in a choir, or serving on a church council, provide opportunities to become involved beyond attendance at worship services. By chairing church committees, working together on mission projects, teaching church school, or writing articles for church newsletters, congregants learn skills that are readily transferable to other civic and political activities. Thus, through their various committees and other organizational activities, churches provide members with opportunities to develop and exercise leadership and communications skills (Verba, Schlozman, and Brady 1995).

In fact, both Verba and his colleagues and Putnam acknowledge that churches, synagogues, and other houses of worship are among the most important vehicles by which people learn and develop civic skills. However, from their perspective, any prominence in developing civic skills that houses of worship may exhibit does not stem from any unique ability that they possess; rather, their efficacy is deemed simply to be a function of their ubiquity and rather large membership levels.

To what extent, then, do churches serve as sites for the acquisition of civic skills? Although relatively few surveys inquire about these matters, several surveys do contain a couple of relevant questions, though each of these surveys utilizes different wording. To address this matter, data were drawn from three national surveys that asked respondents specifically about their practice of civic skills within the context of congregational life.

These data are presented in table 5.1. The first column presents the percentage of those involved in church life who reported they had engaged in the noted activities; the second column presents the same responses as

Table 5.1 Practicing Political Skills within a Church Setting (percent)

Survey and Type of Civic Skill Practiced	Group Reporting	Population
Citizen Participation Study, 1990		
Served on a board past five years	28	20
Attended a meeting past six months	64	18
Given a presentation past six months	36	10
Planned a meeting past six months	32	9
Wrote to a newspaper past six months	22	6
Contacted a public official past six months	5	1
Civic Involvement Survey, 1997		
Served on church board or committee (past year)	19	12
Religion and Politics, 2000		
Currently holds leadership position	26	15

the percentage of the total population. Thus the first figure in each row provides an assessment of the likelihood of engaging in such opportunities within congregational life, and the second figure provides an estimate of the extent to which such participation is found within the broader public.

The first conclusion that can be drawn from the data is that civic skills are widely and frequently exercised within the context of church life. The study that provides the richest source of relevant data is the Citizen Participation Study, in which those who gave time to educational, charitable, or social activities in their churches beyond simple attendance at services were asked about their experiences and activities within the life of the congregation. Among this subset of the church or synagogue population, more than one-quarter (28 percent) indicated that they had served on some kind of board within their house of worship within the past five years. When questioned whether they had, as part of their church or synagogue activities, attended a meeting within the past six months in which decisions were made, nearly two-thirds (64 percent) of the respondents reported they had done so. Lower, but still notable, percentages of these congregants also reported they had within the past half year engaged in a number of more active roles as part of their religious activities, including giving a presentation (36 percent), planning a church meeting (32 percent), writing a letter (22 percent) or contacting a public official (5 percent). In general, these data suggest that participation in congregational life provides ample opportunities for those involved to develop a variety of different civic skills.

Other surveys tend to confirm this general assessment. The Civic Involvement Survey of 1997 asked whether respondents had served on a board or committee related to their house of worship over the course of the past year. Among those who reported that they attended church a few times a year or more, nearly one in five (19 percent) indicated that they had served on a church board or committee during the past twelve months. A similar pattern of skill acquisition through serving in lay leadership positions emerges from the Religion and Politics Study of 2000. Slightly more than one in four (26 percent) of those respondents who attended religious services at least a few times a year and who were members of a place of worship reported that they currently held some sort of leadership position at their place of worship.

A second general conclusion that emerges from the data in table 5.1 is that, even when considered as a proportion of the total population, the number of Americans who exercise civic skills within the church setting is quite substantial. These figures become even more impressive when one considers them in light of the turnout rate for most congressional and presidential elections over the past couple of decades (generally in the range of 40 to 55 percent). Turning out to vote on election day requires only a brief investment of time once every two or four years, whereas serving on boards and committees requires blocks of time, frequently on a regular basis. Realizing that only about one-half of all Americans choose to take the time to cast their ballot on one day every four years, one is better able to appreciate the time commitment reflected in participating in periodic activities (e.g., committee meetings) that foster the development of civic skills, and the proportion of Americans who are so involved begins to look much more impressive.

Religious congregations do indeed offer a variety of opportunities for civic skill development, and many Americans report that they take advantage of these opportunities. Through attending congregational decision-making meetings, serving on committees, organizing youth activities, and other opportunities, churches provide members with opportunities to develop and exercise leadership and communications skills. And a substantial proportion of Americans appear to acquire and develop certain civic skills within the context of their religious activities. In fact, as Lichterman and Potts (2005, 2) point out: "Religious congregations may be the most widespread and egalitarian sites of civic engagement in the United States."

However, opportunities to acquire civic skills within religious life are not equally present across all religious congregations. Smaller congregations provide more opportunities for certain kinds of skill acquisition than larger houses of worship. This can be seen in table 5.2, where the data reveal a clear monotonic decline in the percentage of respondents who report holding leadership positions at their places of worship as one moves from smaller to larger congregations. For example, whereas 37 percent of those associated with houses of worship of less than one hundred members

Table 5.2 Relationship between Building Leadership Skills
and Congregation Size (percent)

Study and Type of Civic Skill Practiced	Congregation Size			
	Less than 100	100–499	500–1999	2000+
Civic Involvement Survey, 1997 Served on church board or committee during past year	24	21	19	18
Religion and Politics, 2000 Hold leadership position at place of worship	37	26	22	17

reported that they held some kind of leadership position within the congregation, only 17 percent of those in congregations of more than two thousand members did so. Clearly, opportunities to acquire and exercise certain civic skills diminish as the size of the congregation increases.

In this regard, it is important to note that churches with weekly attendance over two thousand have nearly doubled in number over the past five years (Thumma, Travis, and Bird 2007). Many American congregations continue to be relatively small, but the growth of such megachurches undoubtedly holds some important implications for American civic life. Efforts to achieve greater economies of scale in congregational life, for example, can work at cross-purposes with having members of such congregations develop important core skills.

Nevertheless, is important to point out that larger congregations may provide other opportunities for the development of civic skills. For example, Wuthnow (2002, 171–72) notes that "members of large churches are somewhat more likely than members of medium-sized or small churches to have done some volunteering during the previous year." And the same study revealed that nearly two-thirds of those who reported that they had volunteered in the past year indicated that they had developed some new skills as a result (data not shown). Thus the acquisition of civic skills can also be simply a byproduct of having been willing to volunteer.

Certain denominations and religious traditions also appear to be better able than others to encourage congregant participation in church affairs and to foster civic skills. Some researchers doubt this link (e.g., Djupe and

Grant 2001; Warren 2003), but other studies suggest that important links do exist between religious tradition and the propensity to develop civic skills within such religious settings (e.g., Verba, Schlozman, and Brady 1995; Burns, Schlozman, and Verba 2001). In particular, it is generally argued that denominations and religious traditions that are more hierarchically structured provide less hospitable environments for civic skill development than more decentralized denominations and traditions. Burns and colleagues (2001, 237–38) found that "although Catholics are as likely as Protestants to receive requests for political activity, they are much less likely to develop civic skills in conjunction with church activity—which, presumably, reflects the hierarchical structure of the Catholic church, the larger size of Catholic parishes, and the more limited role for the laity in the liturgy and in church governance." Verba, Schlozman, and Brady (1995, 321–22) also found "a dramatic difference between Catholic and Protestant respondents in terms of both opportunities to exercise politically relevant skills in church and time devoted to church-related educational, social, or charitable activity." Moreover, such differences appeared to be related more to the characteristics of the two religious traditions rather than to the personal characteristics of individual congregants (Verba, Schlozman, and Brady 1995, 324–25).

In this regard, however, the Protestant tradition itself is not uniform. Some denominations, particularly those within the evangelical and black Protestant traditions, tend to be more congregationally based than those within mainline Protestant denominations. Likewise, evangelical and black Protestants tend to differ from mainline Protestants in terms of the extent to which their religious commitment shapes their personal lives, as evangelical and black Protestants are more likely to report greater investments of time and resources (at least as a proportion of their total resources) than mainline Protestants (Wald, Kellstedt, and Leege 1993; Kellstedt et al. 1996).

The one survey that provides some data on the number of hours invested in church activity per week, as well as the extent to which civic skills are practiced within the congregational setting, is the Citizen Participation Study of 1990. Table 5.3 analyzes these reports for four religious traditions: evangelical Protestants, mainline Protestants, black Protestants, and Roman Catholics.

Table 5.3 Time Invested and Practice of Civic Skills
in Church by Religious Tradition

Religious Tradition	Time Invested in Church Activities (hours per week)	Percent of Church Members Practicing Civic Skills at Church
Evangelical Protestant	1.92	28
Mainline Protestant	1.28	20
Black Protestant	1.77	32
Roman Catholic	0.73	10

Source: Citizen Participation Study, 1990

These data make clear that Protestants, regardless of their particular tradition, are more likely than Roman Catholics to contribute time to church activities outside the worship service. For each of the three Protestant traditions, the mean number of hours per week contributed beyond attending weekly services exceeds the mean number of hours contributed by Roman Catholics. Evangelical Protestants rank first in terms of the number of hours per week contributed, with nearly two hours (1.92 hours) reported per week. Black Protestants are not far behind, with 1.77 hours contributed per week. In fact, the amount of time that both evangelical Protestants and black Protestants contribute is more than double the time reported by Roman Catholics (0.73 hours). The mainline Protestants trailed evangelical and black Protestants by a fairly wide margin, though they also contributed, as a whole, more time to church activities than did Roman Catholics.

Clearly, members of different religious traditions devote differing amounts of time to congregational activities beyond attending weekly worship services, and one would anticipate that these differences would lead to variation in the extent that these groups report having practiced civic skills within their congregational settings. This expectation is confirmed by the data found in the second column of table 5.3. Moreover, the number of hours invested in congregational life is significantly related to practicing civic skills within congregations—though not perfectly so. Black Protestants are the most likely to report practicing civic skills within the church, as nearly one in three (32 percent) did so. Evangelical Protestants trail black Protestants but lead mainline Protestants in the extent to which they practiced civic skills within the congregational setting (28 percent versus 20 percent, respectively), but all Protestants were more than twice as likely as Roman Catholics to do so, as only 10 percent of Catholics indicated that they had engaged in civic-skill-building activities in their local church.

The practice of such skills within the setting of religious congregations has important, though unintended, benefits. Religious institutions play a special role in providing opportunities for the development of civic skills. And because congregations provide many opportunities for the exercise of civic skills in a relatively democratic fashion, religious institutions possess "a powerful potential for enhancing the political resources available to citizens who would, otherwise, be resource-poor" (Verba, Schlozman, and Brady 1995, 320). Thus, religious associations have the potential to narrow the opportunity gap enjoyed by more privileged groups when it comes to civic skill-building activities.

The Building of Civic Skills within Voluntary Organizations

While churches provide considerable opportunities for the acquisition and development of civic skills, can the same be said with regard to participation in religious or church-related voluntary associations? And how do religious or church-based organizations, not necessarily directly related to congregational life, compare with other types of organizations in terms of their civic skill development?

Unfortunately, surveys have not asked respondents questions about the types of civic skill-building opportunities they have encountered within specific types of voluntary associations. As a result, it is not possible to ascertain whether people are more likely to serve on committees or to be officers within cultural or literary groups than within religious or church-related voluntary organizations.

Even without such information, it is possible to classify respondents more broadly in terms of whether they report memberships solely in secular organizations, solely in religious or church-based organizations, or in some combination of religious and secular organizations. In so doing, it becomes possible to determine whether the likelihood of exercising certain civic skills is greater within religious organizations or organizations that are more secular.

Two studies, the General Social Survey of 1987 and the Citizen Participation Study of 1990, have batteries of questions related to the practice of civic skills within voluntary associational life, while several other surveys contain one or two items that address this issue. These data are presented in table 5.4, which examines reports of practicing skills by membership in solely religious, solely secular, and combinations of religious and secular voluntary associations.

These data reveal both mixed and some consistent patterns. First, as is the case with the relationship between congregational life and civic skills, it is clear that those who participate solely in religious voluntary associations

Table 5.4 Acquisition of Civic Skills by Type of Organization (percent)

Study and Type of Civic Skill Practiced	Secular Only	Religious Only	Both
General Social Survey, 1987			
Served on committees	49	62	75
Served as officer of group	38	43	58
Attended group conferences	55	51	72
Wrote to newspaper	16	7	20
Contacted government officials	20	7	23
Civic Participation Study, 1990			
Attended a meeting	52	62	69
Gave a presentation	25	14	41
Planned a meeting	23	14	44
Wrote to newspaper	26	14	42
Contacted government officials	13	0	15
God and Society, 1996			
Served on committee/officer of group	54	21	74
Saguaro, 2000			
Served as officer or on committee for local club or org. in past 12 months	49	34	62
Attended public meeting in past 12 months in which school or town affairs were discussed	19	13	36

enjoy important opportunities to acquire and develop civic skills. Sometimes these opportunities appear to be more common within religious than secular organizations (e.g., in terms of serving on a committee or attending meetings in which decisions are made). At other times, the data are more mixed (e.g., serving as an officer within the association): One study may suggest one pattern, while another study may reveal a different pattern.

Second, those who participate solely in secular voluntary organizations are more likely than those who participate solely in religious organizations to practice certain types of civic skills, namely, writing to a newspaper and contacting government officials as part of their activities within the voluntary association. These particular civic skill-building activities were, however, among the least likely to be reported, regardless of organizational type. Nevertheless, in both surveys those who were solely members of secular voluntary associations were two to three times more likely to have engaged in such activities than those who were solely members of religious voluntary associations.

Third, the one consistent pattern found throughout table 5.4 is that those who participate in *both* secular and religious voluntary associations reported the highest levels of practicing civic skills. This is true regardless of the civic skill-building activity analyzed. Whether these skill-building opportunities are primarily a function of their participation in secular or religious associations cannot be ascertained from these data. But what is clear is that those involved in both kinds of organizations not only enjoy ample opportunity to build and practice civic skills but frequently avail themselves of these opportunities by attending decision-making meetings, serving as officers or members of committees, planning meetings, and making presentations.

Comparing Religious Institutions and Voluntary Organizations

The data examined in table 5.4 do not reveal how civic skills practiced within religious congregations relate to civic skills acquired within voluntary associations. Some people may acquire and develop civic skills only within congregational life, others only within voluntary associations, and some within both congregational and associational contexts. To compare the two settings as loci of civic skill acquisition and practice, it is necessary to have data that enable one to differentiate the practicing of civic skills within congregational settings from that within other types of voluntary associational settings.

To date, the only study that enables such a comparison is the Citizen Participation Study of 1990. Hence its data are used for the analysis found in table 5.5. First, civic skills are examined in terms of the four most common skill-building activities analyzed in the previous table, with responses differentiated in terms of four categories: those who reported not performing the skill-building activities, those who reported performing them within a congregational setting only, those who reported performing them within a voluntary associational setting only, and those who reported performing them in both kinds of settings. Finally, the practice of these skills within the different settings is examined in terms of four distinct kinds of respondents: those who were a member of a religious congregation only, those who were members of voluntary associations only, those who were a member of neither a church nor a voluntary association, and those who were members of both.

The first pattern that emerges from table 5.5 is that some respondents were unlikely to report having exercised any civic skills, at least within the contexts of congregational or associational life. Those who were not members of either religious congregations or voluntary associations usually reported that they had not practiced civic skills in either setting, though a few such respondents indicated having done so within the congregational context. For such respondents, the opportunities to practice civic skills were largely limited to their work setting.[4]

One might expect that those who are solely church members would be somewhat more likely than nonmembers to report practicing civic skills within the congregational setting. This pattern is evident in table 5.5, but what is more noteworthy is that those who were members only of voluntary organizations were more likely to report having practiced civic skills than those who were members solely of religious congregations. This pattern holds true by a ratio of 2:1, except for writing to a newspaper, an activity that members of voluntary associations are more than five times more likely to perform.[5]

However, it is those who are members of churches as well as voluntary associations who are by far the most likely to report exercising civic skills.

Table 5.5 Locus of Civic Skills Acquisition by Form of Organizational Membership (percent)

Locus of Skill Acquisition	Non-member both church & sec. org.	Church member only	Non-church but sec. org. member	Both church and sec. org. member
Attended a meeting where decisions were made				
No	95	83	62	42
Church only	5	17	0	12
Vol. organization only	0	0	38	25
Both church and org.	0	0	*	20
Planned a meeting where decisions were made				
No	98	94	85	68
Church only	2	6	*	9
Vol. organization only	0	0	15	15
Both church and org.	0	0	0	8
Made a speech at a meeting where decisions were made				
No	97	90	81	67
Church only	3	10	*	11
Vol. organization only	0	0	19	14
Both church and org.	0	0	*	8
Wrote to newspaper				
No	99	96	78	71
Church only	1	4	0	6
Vol. organization only	0	0	22	17
Both church and org.	0	0	0	6

Source: Citizen Participation Study, 1990

* Less than 1 percent

Those with combined church and voluntary associational memberships were the most likely to indicate that they had attended a meeting where decisions were made, planned a meeting where decisions were made, made a speech at such a meeting, and written to a newspaper as part of their church or voluntary associational activities. Moreover, when one examines the percentages of those reporting "no" to each of the four questions examined in table 5.5, the percentages found in the first three columns fall relatively close together, while the percentages reporting no such activity in the final column are substantially lower than in the first three columns.

Among those who are members of both churches and voluntary associations, the acquisition of civic skills is more likely to occur within the voluntary organization setting than in the church setting. This finding lies in the fact that the percentages related to practicing skills in voluntary organizations only consistently exceed the percentages associated with practicing those skills in the congregational setting (and the percentage of those who report both, when added to each, would result in the same margin of difference between the two different sites).

Clearly, the overall distribution of membership in religious congregations and voluntary associations has important implications for American public life, particularly in terms of building civic skills. America is still a nation of joiners, as a plurality of Americans (44 percent) report membership in both religious congregations and voluntary associations, while less than one in six (16 percent) report that they are members of neither (data not shown).[6] Slightly less than one in five (17 percent) report being a member of a religious congregation but not a voluntary association, while the reverse is true for nearly one in four (23 percent) Americans (data not shown).[7] Given the relative frequency with which civic skills are practiced in these sites, this distribution of membership patterns tends to work to increase, rather than decrease, opportunities for civic skill development.

Religion and the Number of Civic Skills Practiced

To this point, the focus has been on the nature and locus of civic skills practiced by Americans. Another issue worth investigating is the range of such skills and how it relates to religious factors. Only two surveys contain a sufficient number of questions related to the practice of different kinds of civic skills: the General Social Survey of 1987 and the Citizen Participation Study of 1990. As was shown in table 5.4, each survey asked respondents about five distinct kinds of civic skill-building activities. The GSS only asked members of voluntary organizations whether they had practiced skills within the context of those associations, while the CPS asked respondents about the practice of civic skills within both congregational and voluntary associational settings.

As was demonstrated, Roman Catholics and mainline Protestants were less likely than evangelical Protestants and black Protestants to report that they practiced civic skills in the context of their congregations. However, as table 5.6 reveals, this apparent disadvantage is offset by the greater extent to which both mainline Protestants and Roman Catholics practice civic skills within the context of voluntary organizations.

First, as can be seen from table 5.6, Jews are the most likely to report practicing a civic skill, whether within the context of voluntary associations only (GSS 1987) or within the context of both voluntary associations and religious congregations (CPS 1990). Following Jews, mainline Protestants and Roman Catholics are the most likely to report practicing civic skills within the context of voluntary associations (GSS 1987), though this advantage within voluntary associations largely dissipates when one combines voluntary associational and congregational contexts (CPS 1990). In fact, when the two settings are combined, Roman Catholics trail those of other religious faiths in the extent to which they report practicing civic skills. Finally, table 5.6 reveals that those in the secular category tend to be among the least likely to practice civic skills, even when limited to the context of voluntary associations only (GSS 1987).

While religious tradition is related to the practice of civic skills, the form of religious expression is even more strongly related to civic skill-building practices, as is evident by the higher *eta* values associated with forms of religious expression. This finding is also evident in table 5.6.

Those with a privatized religious expression were the least likely to report, across surveys, that they had practiced a civic skill, and they were the least likely to report having practiced three or more civic skills. Those with a diminished form of religious expression were more likely than the

Table 5.6 Practice of Civic Skills by Religious Tradition and Form of Religious Expression (percent)

Religious Tradition	None	One or Two	Three or More	Total	eta[a]
General Social Survey, 1987					
Evangelical Protestant	51	25	23	99	
Mainline Protestant	38	28	35	101	
Black Protestant	53	25	23	101	
Roman Catholic	43	30	27	100	.15
Jewish	21	26	53	100	
Secular	57	22	22	101	
Citizen Participation Study, 1990					
Evangelical Protestant	56	22	23	101	
Mainline Protestant	54	24	22	100	
Black Protestant	52	30	18	100	
Roman Catholic	65	19	15	99	.10
Jewish	45	29	26	100	
Secular	62	21	17	100	

Form of Religious Expression				
General Social Survey, 1987				
Diminished	52	25	23	100
Privatized	64	20	17	101
Public	42	31	27	100	.22
Integrated	36	29	36	101
Citizen Participation Study, 1990				
Diminished	69	19	13	101
Privatized	75	15	11	101
Public	52	23	25	100	.28
Integrated	41	28	31	100

[a] Statistically significant at .001 level

privatized to report having practiced a civic skill, but the extent to which they did so never exceeds the percentages found among those who exhibit a public form of religious expression. When examined in terms of the practice of three or more civic skills, public religionists were far more likely than those with a diminished form to report having practiced three or more skills.

Those with an integrated form of religious expression were the most likely, regardless of the survey examined, to report having practiced a civic skill. This pattern holds true regardless of whether the survey assesses practicing civic skills within voluntary associations only (GSS 1987), within congregations only, or within congregational contexts combined (CPS 1990). Moreover, it is those with an integrated form of religious expression who most frequently reported that they had practiced a variety of civic skills.

The Unique Contribution of Religion to Practicing Civic Skills

Having examined civic skills in terms of the types of skills practiced within religious contexts, the relative frequency with which they are practiced within religious settings and more secular contexts, and the extent to which those exhibiting different religious characteristics are more likely to practice one or more such skills, the question now becomes whether religion continues to significantly shape the likelihood of practicing civic skills once controls have been introduced for other pertinent variables. For example, Verba and colleagues (1995) have revealed that the exercise of civic skills is positively correlated with income and job status, and other social variables (e.g., education, race, and gender) may shape the practice of such skills as well.

Table 5.7 displays the relative strength of the relationship between various independent variables and the practice of civic skills once the effects of the other independent variables have been taken into account. This multivariate analysis was conducted once again by means of multiple classification analysis. Because we wanted to examine the practice of civic skills more generally, rather than the practice of a certain civic skill (e.g., serving on a committee), we are limited to using the only two surveys that

Table 5.7   Relative Importance of Religion in the Practice of Civic Skills: A Multiple Classification Analysis

Demographic Characteristic	Study			
	GSS 1987	GSS 1987	CPS 1990	CPS 1990
Membership in a voluntary organization	(.56)[c]	x	.20[c]	.20[c]
Membership in a religious congregation	x	x	.08[a]	x
Gender	(.03)	(.00)	.06	.05
Race	(.03)	(.08)[b]	.02	.02
Age	(.10)[b]	(.13)[c]	.15[c]	.15[c]
Education	(.16)[c]	(.28)[c]	.24[c]	.24[c]
Family income	(.04)	(.10)[b]	.12[c]	.13[c]
Marital status	(.06)	(.06)	.05	.05
Religion tradition	(.05)	(.07)[a]	.12[c]	.11[c]
Form of religious expression	(.10)[b]	(.20)[c]	.07[a]	.11[c]
R-square	*(.45)*	*(.19)*	.28	.27

Notes: In the GSS 1987 survey, civic skills questions asked only of members of voluntary organization; x = not asked.

[a] Statistically significant at .05 level
[b] Statistically significant at .01 level
[c] Statistically significant at .001 level

asked respondents a range of questions related to the practice of civic skills: the General Social Survey of 1987 and the Citizen Participation Study of 1990.[8] It is once again important to recognize that these two surveys utilized different question formats to probe the practice of civic skills. In the 1987 survey, only respondents who reported membership in some kind of voluntary association were asked about activities related to the practice of civic skills; in the 1990 survey, those affiliated with church life as well as those who indicated membership in a voluntary association were asked such questions.

The assessment examines the relative effects of ten variables on whether respondents reported having practiced a civic skill: membership in a voluntary association, church membership, gender, race, age, education, family income, marital status, religious tradition affiliation, and form of religious expression.[9] Because the General Social Survey of 1987 asked only those who were members of voluntary associations about different kinds of civic skill activities, the *beta* coefficients for the GSS are placed in parentheses to designate that they should not be directly compared to the *beta* coefficients for the Citizen Participation Study of 1990.

The data reveal that several variables help to explain the likelihood of practicing some kind of civic skill. Examining first the data from the General Social Survey of 1987,[10] one notes that membership in a voluntary association strongly relates to reports of practicing a civic skill; this is hardly surprising given that only those who were members of such associations were asked about civic skills. When included in the analysis, the *beta* coefficient for membership in voluntary organizations (.56) clearly overwhelms all other explanatory variables, with education ranking second (.16), and form of religious expression and age ranking third (.10).

Of course, given the question format, this is hardly a fair assessment of the relative importance of other independent variables. The second column for the General Social Survey of 1987 provides the results of a similar MCA when the voluntary organizational membership variable is excluded. In this second analysis, the *beta* coefficients for the remaining variables increase substantially, and their relative rank orderings shift somewhat. Education, which previously ranked second, now ranks first in relative importance (.28), while form of religious expression, which previously ranked third, now ranks second (.20).

The Citizen Participation Study of 1990, meanwhile, asked questions about the practice of civic skills in both voluntary organizations and religious congregations. In addition, this study asked respondents whether they were a member of a church or religious congregation. The data from the survey are analyzed here to see if church membership may account for any variation in the opportunities to practice civic skills once the relative effects of membership in voluntary associations and form of religious expression, as well as the effects of the other remaining independent variables, are taken into account.

In this broadened context, level of education (*beta* = .24) ranks as the most important variable accounting for variation in the dependent variable, with membership in voluntary associations (*beta* = .20) and age (*beta* = .15) ranking second and third in importance, respectively. Given that analytical and organizational skills are likely to be more closely linked to the practice of civic skills than are financial resources, it is not surprising that education far outstrips family income (*beta* = .12) in terms of relative importance, as the *beta* for the former variable is twice the size of that of the latter variable.

However, while religious tradition affiliation served only a minor role in accounting for variation in volunteering and giving (see chapter 4), it ranks far higher in terms of accounting for differences in the practice of civic skills. As noted earlier in this chapter, religious traditions vary in terms of the opportunities they offer to practice civic skills, and these differences are evident by the magnitude of the beta for religious tradition affiliation (*beta* = .12). The difference between the relative importance of religious tradition in the CPS survey of 1990 and in the GSS 1987 survey is likely due to the inclusion of the practice of civic skills in both voluntary organizational and religious congregational contexts in the former survey but only voluntary organization contexts in the latter.

Church membership also contributes to greater opportunities to practice civic skills (*beta* = .08), and it ranks as roughly equivalent in importance to form of religious expression (*beta* = .07) in accounting for differences in the level of civic skill-building activities. But when church membership is dropped from the analysis (the last column of the table), making the CPS analysis more comparable to the first column of the table, the *beta* for form of religious expression jumps to .11—equivalent to the *beta* for religious tradition affiliation.

In the end, form of religious expression does not match either educational attainment or associational membership as the most important variables accounting for differences in the likelihood of practicing some form of civic skills. Nor does it necessarily match the importance of age. Nevertheless, the religious variables examined generally outweigh most of the other sociodemographic factors. Overall, the data presented in table 5.7 reveal once again that the relationship between religion and the practice of civic skills is not spurious, as both one's religious tradition affiliation and one's form of religious expression serve as relatively important explanatory factors in accounting for variation in such practices.

Religion and Cognitive Engagement in Public Life

Another way in which responsible citizens demonstrate civic capacity for public life is cognitive engagement with civic and political matters. Cognitive engagement may be manifested whether or not someone exercises certain civic skills. Even someone who does not practice any civic skills may still be interested in or attentive to public matters. And cognitive engagement is likely tied to exhibiting greater levels of political knowledge, another form of civic capacity.

That the practice of civic skills and interest in politics are interrelated can be seen from table 5.8.[11] Examining the data from the two surveys that permit an analysis comparing the practice of civic skills and level of political interest,[12] it becomes clear that the two variables are related. Those who reported having practiced the most civic skills were also the most likely to report the highest level of interest in politics, regardless of survey analyzed.[13] Conversely, those not exercising any civic skills were the most likely to report a low level of interest in politics.

Table 5.8 Cognitive Engagement in Politics by Practice of Civic Skills (percent)

| | Civic Skills Practiced | | |
Cognitive Engagement	None	Low	High
Citizen Participation Study, 1990			
Level of Political Interest			
Low	48	32	21
Medium	27	33	25
High	25	35	55
(n)	(1436)	(558)	(515)
		$r = .27^a$	
Saguaro Social Capital, 2000			
Level of Political Interest			
Low	43	28	16
Medium	32	41	38
High	25	31	45
(n)	(1546)	(1060)	(396)
		$r = .21^a$	

[a] Statistically significant at .001 level

On the other hand, while they are related, these variables are clearly empirically distinct. For example, in the Citizen Participation Study of 1990, a quarter of those who had not practiced any skills nevertheless reported that they had a high level of interest in politics, while more than one-fifth of those who practiced a high level of civic skills reported a low level of political interest. Because civic skills and interest in politics are analytically and empirically distinct, the role of religion in contributing to one may differ from the role religion plays in contributing to the other. We first turn our attention to the role of religion in fostering a cognitive engagement in public life.

Religion and Attention to Politics

When they attend religious services or religious meetings, congregants enjoy a variety of opportunities that can enhance their civic capacities. Some of these opportunities are a byproduct of engaging in activities related to church programs, including teaching Sunday school, organizing church picnics, and recruiting volunteers for driving the church van. On other occasions, the opportunities of congregants to enhance their civic capacities may be more direct. For example, clergy frequently engage in cue-giving, both on and off the pulpit, in an effort to impart knowledge and values to their congregants (Quinley 1974; Guth et al. 1997; Crawford and Olson 2001; Djupe and Grant 2001; Smidt 2004).

Religious congregations are first and foremost places of worship. Those who attend worship services come to engage in activities connected to worship, including praying, offering praise, reciting confessions of faith, hearing sermons, and celebrating the sacraments. But at the center of many worship services is the sermon—particularly within the Protestant tradition where preaching has historically been at the heart of the worship service—and sermons can be vehicles by which to remind worshippers of the commands found in the sacred texts of the faith. All of the Abrahamic faith traditions emphasize care for the poor, the outcast, and the downtrodden, and sermons can easily become a means "for exhorting congregants to express concern for the needy in their personal lives and through their congregations" (Wuthnow 2004, 66).

Previous research has shown that many, if not most, clergy across almost all denominations report that their sermons frequently address issues such as hunger and poverty, with those clergy who address such topics varying little in terms of theological orientation, denominational affiliation, or personal background (Guth et al. 1997). Given the prevalence of this practice, attendance at worship services may well serve to foster attention to public matters generally and political interest more specifically.[14]

This expectation is confirmed, in part, by data drawn from the Religion and Politics Survey of 2000. This survey asked respondents whether they had heard sermons that addressed certain matters related to public life and inquired about the level of attention respondents gave to government and public affairs. Table 5.9 examines the relationship between these two variables.

While far from conclusive, the data presented in table 5.9 reveal that those who report hearing sermons addressing matters related to public life are more likely to report a high level of attention to politics. This is true for four of the six topics examined (government policies toward the poor, race relations, the social responsibilities of corporations, and being more

Table 5.9 Attention Given to Public Affairs by Whether Heard Sermon on Public Matters (percent reporting most of time)

		Attends Church		
	Does not attend church	Did not hear sermon on	Heard sermon on	eta[a]
Government policies toward poor	35	43	46	.15
Race relations	35	40	47	.15
Social responsibilities of corporations	35	43	49	.14
Gap between rich and poor	35	44	43	.13
Protecting the environment	35	44	44	.13
Being more supportive of homosexuals	35	43	48	.13

Source: Religion and Politics Survey, 2000

[a] Statistically significant at .001 level

supportive of homosexuals), though such increased levels of attention given to such matters are not associated with reports of hearing sermons on the two remaining topics (the environment and the gap between the rich and the poor). In addition, it should be noted that those who attend church, regardless of whether they hear sermons on such matters, are more likely to report a high level of attention to politics than those who do not attend church at all.

Other evidence could possibly be marshaled, but it is probably not needed to make the case that those who attend church are likely to hear messages about serving those in need. Of course, sermons that address matters related to specific public policies are less likely to be preached than sermons that discuss the moral obligations of parishioners to address social ills. Even in the latter type of sermons, community problems may be brought to the attention of congregants, and thereby contribute to enhanced interest in public affairs among listening congregants.

Those who exhibit public and integrated forms of religious expression attend worship services with similar levels of regularity; seemingly, these two groups would be then equally exposed to sermons on matters of public life. Can one therefore discern varying levels of attention to public affairs among those displaying different forms of religious expression? Or, is there little, if any, relationship between such forms and interest in public affairs? This question is addressed in the upper half of table 5.10.

Six surveys contain questions that permit an analysis of the relationship between forms of religious expression and level of political interest. Questions related to political interest were worded differently across the surveys, sometimes asking about interest in politics, sometimes about whether respondents followed politics, and sometimes about whether they paid attention to politics. Response options also varied from survey to survey. What is reported in table 5.10 is the percentage of those expressing the highest level of interest or attention possible.

What is initially evident after examining the data is that the rank ordering of the various forms of religious expression in terms of interest in politics varies from survey to survey. However, upon closer inspection it is clear that those with an integrated form of religiosity exhibit the greatest consistency in terms of their level of political interest. Not only do they have the highest level of attention to public affairs in five out of the six

Table 5.10 Political Interest by Form of Religious Expression
(percent reporting highest level of interest)

Study	Diminished	Privatized	Public	Integrated	eta[a]
Citizen Participation Study	28	38	31	38	.12
National Election Study, 1996	24	21	18	26	.11
National Election Study, 2000	17	15	23	22	.15
Saguaro, 2000	25	27	32	34	.14
Religion and Politics, 2000	35	40	38	45	.08
National Election Study, 2004	26	26	28	31	.12

[a] Statistically significant at .001 level

surveys examined, but even in the National Election Study of 2000, the sole exception to this pattern, those with an integrated mode trail those with a public expression (i.e., those exhibiting the highest level of attention) by only one percentage point.

Generally speaking, those with a diminished form of religious expression exhibit the lowest level of political interest. This pattern prevails in four of the six surveys examined. The relative rank ordering of those with a privatized and a public form of religious expression varies from survey to survey, but the differences in the two groups' percentages is not, at times, very substantial.

Overall, it appears that religion may foster an interest in political affairs. This interest is not simply a function of attendance at religious services, as those with public and integrated forms of religious expression do not express similar levels of political interest despite their equivalent levels of attendance at worship services. And while hearing sermons on topics related to public affairs may stimulate some attention to such matters, it appears that the increased attention may be tied more to the content of the sermons heard. Still, those for whom religion seemingly serves as a "master motive" remain the most likely to indicate that they devoted a good deal of attention to public matters. The added dimension of private devotionalism among integrated religionists appears to increase their likelihood of attending to public matters, compared to public religionists, whose private religious life is less robust.

While the data presented in table 5.10 suggest that forms of religious expression relate to levels of attention given to public affairs, it remains unclear just how much variance in such attentiveness can be explained by form of religious expression once other relevant variables are taken into account. To make such an assessment, another multiple classification analysis was conducted, using the same variables employed in previous MCA analyses. This analysis is presented in table 5.11.

The data make clear that level of educational attainment and age are the two most powerful variables in explaining variance in attention to public matters, as the two variables rank either first or second in the magnitude of their *beta* coefficients across each of the five surveys examined, with higher educated and older respondents being more attentive to politics than lower educated and younger respondents. Of the two variables, age appears to be somewhat more important than education. Overall,

Table 5.11 Relative Importance of Religion in Fostering Political Interest: A Multiple Classification Analysis

Demographic Characteristic	Study				
	CPS 1990	NES 1996	Sag. 2000	NES 2000	NES 2004
Membership in voluntary organization	.16[c]	.10[b]	.10[b]	.11[b]	.12[c]
Gender	.07[a]	.19[c]	.09[b]	.20[c]	.13[c]
Race	.04	.09[b]	.03	.13[c]	.11[b]
Age	.16[c]	.21[c]	.25[c]	.23[c]	.25[c]
Education	.24[c]	.19[c]	.21[c]	.24[c]	.23[c]
Family income	.09[b]	.01	.07[a]	.06	.03
Marital status	.04	.02	.04	.06	.07[a]
Religious tradition	.07[a]	.05	.03	.14[c]	.12[c]
Form of religious expression	.12[c]	.10[b]	.07[a]	.11[b]	.09[b]
R square	*.19*	*.15*	*.16*	*.21*	*.16*

[a] Statistically significant at .05 level
[b] Statistically significant at .01 level
[c] Statistically significant at .001 level

gender ranks somewhat below age and educational attainment, with men exhibiting higher attention levels than women.

Membership in voluntary associations and form of religious expression tend to fall in the middle in terms of their explanatory power. The *beta* coefficients for the two variables are roughly equivalent, though the *beta* coefficient for membership in voluntary organizations tends to be slightly larger.

Form of religious expression tends to be relatively more important than religious tradition affiliation in accounting for variation in expression of interest in politics. In three of the surveys, the *beta* for form of religious expression is nearly double that for religious tradition. In the NES 2000 and the NES 2004, however, religious tradition exhibits a larger *beta*, though the differences are more marginal. The greater relative importance of religious tradition in accounting for variation in levels of political interest in these two surveys may reflect simply increased interest among various religious groups during the 2000 and 2004 presidential elections.

Overall, the multivariate analysis reveals that the presence of other explanatory factors reduces, but does not eliminate, the contribution that religion makes to increased civic capacities. Those who exhibit more public forms of religious expression, particularly those who exhibit an integrated form, tend to be more attentive to public life. It appears that religion not only contributes to greater civic capacities through fostering and developing civic skills, but it also does so, at least in part, through fostering greater attention to public affairs.

Religion and Political Knowledge

An individual's level of political knowledge is another important element in one's cognitive engagement in politics, as political knowledge serves as an important basis for making informed political decisions. It is a fundamental premise of representative democracy that elections are means by which citizens hold public officials accountable for their behavior in office. But for representative governments to function in such a fashion, citizens must be sufficiently politically knowledgeable (e.g., aware of which public officials and political parties are currently in power). Everything else being equal, "the more informed people are, the better able they are to perform as citizens" (Delli Carpini and Keeter 1996, 219).

However, the opportunities to learn and acquire information about politics vary. These differences reveal themselves in various ways: in differing levels of political information made available through work environments, in different kinds of people with whom one regularly interacts, in the kinds of mass media one uses and for what purposes. Naturally, interest in politics is related to political knowledge,[15] as those who are the more interested exhibit higher levels of knowledge (Delli Carpini and Keeter 1996, 184). How citizens choose to attend to freely available information also varies, thereby affecting the extent to which different individuals who are similarly situated exhibit political knowledge. It is also true that "the amount and type of information available also affects how much they learn" (Delli Carpini and Keeter 1996, 210).

Political knowledge is influenced by a number of variables, including education, race, gender, and age. Of all sociodemographic variables, the one most strongly correlated with political knowledge is level of educational attainment. Yet even though a higher proportion of Americans are college educated today compared to a half century ago, the overall levels of political knowledge have hardly changed (Delli Carpini and Keeter 1996). Differences in levels of political knowledge across demographic groups also continue to remain fairly stable, despite increased educational attainment. For example, despite educational advances, the political knowledge levels of women and minorities are about the same as they were in the 1950s and 1960s (Delli Carpini and Keeter 1996, 162–63).

Despite the significant body of research on political knowledge, the relationship between it and religion has rarely, if ever, been probed. In some ways, this lack of attention is understandable, as other sociodemographic factors (e.g., education) are generally assumed to be much more directly related to differences in political knowledge. Yet religious factors have been shown to foster both giving and volunteering, as well as the practice of civic skills. If involvement in public life and political knowledge are reciprocally related, one might also anticipate that religious factors are related to political knowledge.

Political knowledge can be considered an important precursor to political action.[16] Some would even argue that political knowledge constitutes a form of political participation in its own right (Milbrath 1965, 64–72). For the analysis presented here, political knowledge simply reflects what might be labeled "externally verifiable descriptive beliefs about what 'is' (politically)" (Lambert et al. 1988, 361). However, depending on the particular study examined, assessments of political knowledge may combine factual knowledge about such matters as the names of political office holders or which party holds a majority of seats in a legislative body with conceptual knowledge about differences between a democracy and a dictatorship, or the meaning of civic liberties.[17]

One religious factor that may relate to political knowledge is the extent to which one's form of religious expression is private or public. Hence, the relationship between forms of religious expression and political knowledge are examined in table 5.12. Rather than percentages, the table presents the mean number of correct answers provided for a series of questions designed to tap the respondent's level of political knowledge, with the data being drawn from six surveys that contain the requisite questions to permit the analysis. These six surveys employ different questions, and different numbers of questions, to tap political knowledge.[18]

Clearly there is a relationship between form of religious expression and level of political knowledge. Respondents with higher levels of church attendance (i.e., the public and integrated forms) exhibit higher mean scores than those whose religious expression is less public (i.e., the diminished and privatized forms). Those with a public form of religious expression ranked first in their level of political knowledge in four of the six surveys analyzed, while in the remaining two surveys they ranked second. Those with an integrated form of religious expression ranked second in five of the six surveys, while in the other survey they ranked first. On the other hand, those with a privatized form of religious expression ranked last in political knowledge in each of the six surveys examined. Thus, there are relatively consistent differences between and among the four forms of religious expression in terms of the level of political knowledge that they exhibit. These differences prevail regardless of the number of questions asked, the specific questions asked, or the format employed.

Table 5.12 Political Knowledge by Form of Religious Expression
(mean score on index of political knowledge)

Study	Diminished	Privatized	Public	Integrated	*eta*
General Social Survey, 1987	1.43	1.24	1.72	1.51	.14[b]
Citizen Participation Study, 1990	4.10	3.90	4.22	4.31	.08[a]
National Election Study, 1996	3.88	3.31	3.72	3.72	.11[b]
National Election Study, 2000	3.93	3.09	4.42	4.05	.15[b]
Saguaro, 2000	1.58	1.43	1.70	1.62	.09[b]
National Election Study, 2004	2.83	2.77	3.04	2.88	.04

[a] Statistically significant at .01 level
[b] Statistically significant at .001 level

One anomaly present in tables 5.10 and 5.12 is that the privatized tend to rank relatively high in expressed political interest (table 5.10), but consistently low in terms of their relative level of political knowledge (table 5.12). In contrast, those with a public form of religious expression were not among those who reported the highest level of attention to politics, but overall they were the most knowledgeable politically.

It is unclear from table 5.12 just how much of the total variance in political knowledge can be explained by form of religious expression once controls are introduced for other variables known to relate to levels of political knowledge. To assess the relative importance of religion in shaping political knowledge, a multiple classification analysis was conducted on political knowledge, utilizing the same variables employed in previous MCA analyses in this volume. This analysis examines the relative influence of various independent variables across the six national surveys for which there are the requisite variables, and this analysis is presented in table 5.13.

Given the variables examined, it is clear that those sociodemographic factors previously found to be related to variation in political knowledge continue to be important factors, as they tend to overwhelm the relative effects of both membership in voluntary associations and form of religious expression in accounting for differences in political knowledge. Age and education are the variables most strongly related to political knowledge, with higher-educated and older respondents being more politically informed than lower-educated and younger respondents. In some surveys, the magnitude of the *beta* coefficients for age and education are virtually the same; in other surveys, education clearly surpasses age. However, in four of the six surveys, education and age rank either first or second in importance (with the exceptions being the National Election Study of 1996 and 2000).

Gender and race generally constitute important secondary variables in explaining differences in levels of political knowledge, with men and whites exhibiting higher levels of political knowledge than women and non-whites.[19] In some surveys, gender ranked ahead of race as an explanatory variable; in others, the converse was true. Both variables, however, exhibited general consistency in terms of their relative importance; beginning with the 1996 survey, these two variables always ranked in the top half in terms of relative importance. While marital status and family income also shape levels of political knowledge, the magnitude of their *beta* coefficients tended to fall in the bottom half of explanatory variables.

Even after controls have been introduced, those who are members of voluntary associations and those who exhibit a more integrated form of religious expression are somewhat more likely to exhibit higher levels of political knowledge.[20] However, after accounting for sociodemographic characteristics of respondents, relatively little of the remaining variance in political knowledge is explained by either membership in voluntary associations or form of religious expression. Moreover, the *beta* coefficients for both variables tend to be relatively equivalent within each of the six surveys analyzed, with each adding some explanatory power but neither serving as a major explanatory variable.

It appears, then, that religion's contribution to civic capacities is to be found more in its contribution to the development and refinement of civic skills than in its fostering of attention to public affairs.[21] It also appears that religion's contribution to increased attention to public affairs is greater than its contribution to increased levels of political knowledge, as religion appears to have rather weak effects on levels of political knowledge.

Table 5.13 Relative Importance of Religion in Fostering Political Knowledge: A Multiple Classification Analysis

Demographic Characteristic	Study					
	GSS 1987	CPS 1990	NES 1996	Sag. 2000	NES 2000	NES 2004
Membership in voluntary organization	.11[c]	.14[c]	.05	.06	.10[b]	.06
Gender	.04	.11[b]	.13[c]	.12[b]	.24[c]	.16[c]
Race	.02	.09[b]	.23[c]	.14[c]	.13[c]	.12[c]
Age	.16[c]	.18[c]	.18[c]	.22[c]	.12[b]	.19[c]
Education	.16[c]	.26[c]	.33[c]	.21[c]	.32[c]	.35[c]
Family income	.07[a]	.08[a]	.13[c]	.08[a]	.07[a]	.12[c]
Marital status	.06	.09[b]	.09[b]	.08[a]	.11[b]	.05
Religious tradition	.12[c]	.08[a]	.08[a]	.04	.13[c]	.10[b]
Form of religious expression	.09[b]	.05	.05	.04	.07[a]	.04
R-square	*.14*	*.24*	*.30*	*.18*	*.23*	*.33*

[a] Statistically significant at .05 level
[b] Statistically significant at .01 level
[c] Statistically significant at .001 level

However, while religious tradition affiliation was relatively unimportant in accounting for behavioral facets of civic responsibility (i.e., joining voluntary associations, volunteering, making charitable contributions), it exhibited enhanced importance when cognitive facets of civic capacities were examined (interest in public affairs and political knowledge). In contrast, forms of religious expression were far more important than religious tradition in accounting for differences in behavioral facets of civic responsibility. Finally, forms of religious expression more substantially affect the exercise of civic skills and attention to public affairs than they do levels of political knowledge.

Conclusion

We have sought in chapter 5 to examine more fully the relationship between religion and civic capacities. We have done so by examining the role that religion plays in the acquisition and development of civic skills as well by analyzing the ways in which religion fosters greater levels of attention given to public affairs and higher levels of political knowledge. A variety of findings enhance our understanding of the role religion plays in the development of civic capacities.

To begin, houses of worship constitute an important arena in which attendees have ample opportunities to learn and exercise civic skills, and many church members report that they have, in fact, engaged in congregational activities that enable practical civic skills to be acquired, practiced, and enhanced. While not conclusive, the evidence suggests that this is particularly true in smaller and less hierarchically organized churches.

However, churches are not the only arena in which people can acquire and develop civic skills; voluntary organizations are also important sites for learning and practicing such skills. Those who participate in secular voluntary associations but not in churches tend to exercise more civic skills than do those who participate in churches but not in voluntary associations. Those who participate in both churches and secular voluntary associations exercise more civic skills by far than do those who participate in only one setting or the other.

One's form of religious expression is also related to the practice of civic skills, as those with an integrated form are the most likely to have practiced civic skills and those with diminished and privatized forms are the least likely to have done so. Moreover, even when one takes into account differences in education and membership in voluntary associations, this relationship between form of religious expression and practice of civic skills continues to hold true.

Religion also serves to foster greater cognitive engagement in public life, in terms of both increasing levels of attention given to public affairs and increasing levels of political knowledge. Persons with an integrated form of religious expression are more likely than those marked by public, privatized, or diminished forms to report higher levels of interest in public affairs. Other factors, particularly age and education, are more important in explaining such interest, but even when these factors are taken into account, religion continues to play a role in explaining political interest.

Both forms of religious expression and membership in voluntary associations are related to political knowledge, but when factors such as age and education are taken into account, much of the apparent relationship to political knowledge dissipates. Thus, the contribution of religion to the development of civic capacities appears to be found largely in terms of fostering civic skills and interest in political affairs rather than fostering political knowledge. These contributions of religion ought not to be underestimated. As noted earlier, churches and other religious organizations comprise the most ubiquitous voluntary organization in the American context. As a result, more persons learn and practice civic skills within religious contexts than in any other type of voluntary organization. This fact is especially noteworthy because houses of worship may be the only place where many persons with limited educational attainments and non-professional careers are encouraged to develop and practice civic skills, as those with higher educational attainments and professional careers often have other civic skill-building opportunities. In terms of civic skills, churches act as a leveling force.

As in previous chapters, we have seen that those who fall into the integrated form of religious expression—that is, those who are most deeply religious, marked by both private and public expressions of religion—are also the respondents most marked by the development of civic skills and the most likely to be politically interested. Nevertheless, religion is not always the most powerful force in the civic education realm; in the case of political knowledge, religion has a positive, but relatively weak, effect, as it tends to be overshadowed by other forces such as education and age.

Notes

1. Civic engagement can also serve as a means by which those who are involved become more informed about matters under discussion and learn the requisite skills in addressing such matters. The possession of other resources (e.g., time and money) as well as differing opportunity structures and varying recruitment patterns are also likely to play important roles in shaping levels of civic engagement.

2. Obviously, not all who possess civic skills choose to engage in civic or political activity.

3. Verba, Schlozman, and Brady (1995) also found that religiosity did not have the same salutary effect for Latinos, possibly because of the relatively high percentage of Latinos who are members of the Roman Catholic Church.

4. Verba, Schlozman, and Brady examined three spheres in which civic skills might be practiced: churches, voluntary organizations, and work. They found that the workplace is "especially rich in opportunities for the exercise of skills," though work, voluntary organizations, and churches are all "places where citizens can learn how to be active citizens" (1995, 312–13).

5. Perhaps the difference in rates of civic skill practice is a function of differences in the presence of paid or full-time staff within these two kinds of organizations, as churches frequently have staff who are paid and full-time, while voluntary associations (particularly "classic" voluntary associations such as book clubs or parent-teacher associations) generally do not. The lack of paid or full-time staff may enhance opportunities for members of such voluntary associations to become involved in order to move forward the goals of the association, resulting in more skill-building opportunities.

6. These percentages are based on data from the Citizen Participation Study of 1990.

7. These percentages are also based on data from the Citizen Participation Study of 1990.

8. As is evident in table 5.4, neither the God and Society Study of 1996 nor the Saguaro Study of 2000 included two or more questions related to the practice of civic skills, and, as a result, these two surveys are not analyzed in table 5.7.

9. Since, as evident in table 5.6, form of religious expression is more strongly related to the practice of civic skills than is religious tradition. We will once again employ the religious-form variable in our multivariate analysis.

10. The General Social Survey of 1987 did not include a question on church membership; the Citizen Participation Study of 1990 did. The variable is included in the MCA to assess in the latter survey the relative importance of church membership and voluntary organizational membership.

11. Interest in politics is treated here as a form of cognitive engagement in politics. However, it might be noted that some differentiate between political interest and political awareness, treating only the latter as a cognitive engagement, while viewing interest in politics as a form of affective involvement. See Zaller (1992, 43).

12. The General Social Survey of 1987 did not include a question related to the respondent's level of interest in or attention to politics. Hence, these data could not be analyzed in table 5.8.

13. This analysis is simply intended to reveal the interrelationship between these two variables. More than likely, the two variables are reciprocally related, with the practice of civic skills enhancing interest in politics, and interest in politics increasing the likelihood of practicing civic skills.

14. It may also be true that those who are interested in politics seek out pastors who speak on political issues. However, since attendance at worship services is more a function of religious, rather than political, interests, it is more likely that one chooses to worship with a congregation based primarily on religious considerations.

15. The field of study related to the concept of political knowledge employs a variety of different but related terms. For example, sometimes a study will employ the term "political sophistication" (e.g., Neuman 1986; Luskin 1987); at other times, it will use a term such as "political literacy" (e.g., Cassel and Lo 1997). Some may choose to differentiate "factual knowledge" from "conceptual knowledge" (Lambert et al. 1988), while others may differentiate among "knowledge of principles of democracy," "knowledge of leaders," and "knowledge of other current political facts" (Nie, Junn, and Stehlik-Barry 1996, 22–25).

16. However, it is true that political knowledge and political participation are also reciprocally related (Delli Carpini and Keeter 1996, 186).

17. It should be noted that "the public's knowledge of institutions and processes is significantly higher than its knowledge of people and policies, perhaps because the former are more stable over time and require less regular monitoring" (Galston 2001, 221).

18. For example, the political-knowledge item in the 1987 General Social Survey is composed of three questions asking whether respondents could correctly name the local head of the public school, the governor of the state, and the representative from their congressional district. Five questions were employed to measure political knowledge in the Citizen Participation Study of 1990: whether respondents could name one U.S. Senator from their state, name the second U.S. Senator as well, name the representative from their congressional district, identify whether bosses or reformers were behind the move to primary elections, and explain the meaning of civil liberties. The political-knowledge item for the Saguaro 2000 survey tested respondents' ability to name both U.S. Senators from their state, and the political-knowledge measure for the National Election Studies tests whether respondents can correctly identify certain public figures (e.g., Gore, Rehnquist, Yeltsin, and Gingrich in 1996) and, in addition at times, correctly identify which party controlled Congress prior to the election and which party controlled Congress following the election. The practice of civic skills is also related to political knowledge, with those who practice increased levels of civic skills exhibiting higher levels of political knowledge. These relationships hold across the surveys even though each employs somewhat different questions to tap civic skills, political interest, and political knowledge.

19. These specific patterns are not evident from the data presented in the table itself. Rather, these patterns were determined by an examination of the specific "corrected" mean scores associated with each category of the independent variables, information not presented in the table for purposes of simplicity.

20. This particular pattern is not evident in the table itself. Rather, this pattern was determined by an examination of the specific "corrected" mean scores associated with the religious-form variable, information not presented in the table for purposes of simplicity.

21. This chapter focuses on the role of religion in relationship to the development of civic capacities within individuals. However, there are other ways in which religion may serve to enhance civic capacities—for example, the use of religious facilities as sites for public discussion and the delivery of community social services. Particularly in urban areas, congregational properties serve

as important centers of community life, as "numerous activities take place on congregational properties, most often free of charge" (Cnaan et al. 2006, 111). Congregational facilities are used for various kinds of community meetings, as places in which to sponsor after-school programs, as locations for community health clinics and immunizations, as home for different kinds of scout troops, and frequently as polling places on election day.

6

❖

Religion and Civic Virtues

To be civically responsible, a citizen must possess capacities such as civic skills and knowledge. By themselves, such capacities are morally neutral; they reveal nothing about the citizen's specific purposes or motivations for acting in public life. The concept of civic virtue brings a moral dimension to the exercise of civic responsibility. To possess civic virtue suggests that a citizen has a disposition to use civic skills and knowledge for socially beneficial purposes and with morally appropriate motivations.

To speak of morality in this way, especially in a pluralistic society, is inevitably controversial. Some, fearing that such language would produce insoluble and dangerous political conflict, would prefer to avoid it altogether. After all, to say that an action is moral is to make a normative claim that entails expectations about behavior; it suggests that one *ought* to engage in some act and/or refrain from doing its opposite. One exhibits civic virtue, contends theorist Richard Dagger (1997, 13), "when he or she does what a citizen is supposed to do."

The problem is that morality is a heavily contested concept, as citizens can and do disagree about what they ought to do. Many of the great policy conflicts of our day—abortion, the definition of marriage, the war on terror, or even taxation and Social Security—reflect fundamentally different normative expectations of right and wrong conduct (that is, morality) found among the American people. These differences in moral perspectives, which can be rooted in social identity itself, may lead to political conflicts that have little hope for resolution through compromise (Mooney 2001). Even believers within the same religious tradition can have intractable disagreements about what morality recommends for actual behavior.

More formally, civic virtue is a set of internal dispositions or orientations that reflects a particular kind of role or moral "character," namely, a citizen who sees it as his or her duty to foster the public or the "common" good.[1] But the nature of these dispositions, let alone the "common good," is not self-evident. Reasonable people can and do disagree about whether characteristics such as obedience, thrift, or tolerance are truly "civic" virtues and, if they are, what they actually require in terms of behavior. Thus our examination of religion and civic virtue, which has clear moral overtones, is controversial from the start.

Nonetheless, disagreements about what the specific virtues are and what they entail have not stopped many prominent voices from declaring that civic virtue is an integral feature of the healthy polity. As discussed below, commentators from the ancient Greeks to the American founders to contemporary theorists of democratic citizenship have suggested that good citizens are defined, in part, by their civic virtue. Ordinary citizens, too, place importance on civic virtue in their own thinking about good citizenship and public life (Wuthnow 1998b, 157), even when they do not use the term or have a well-developed understanding of its philosophical underpinnings.

As a general matter, we argue that civic virtue is a necessary (though not sufficient) ingredient in responsible democratic citizenship.[2] Consequently, this chapter examines Americans' attitudes about civically virtuous behavior, seeking to ascertain the extent to which religion shapes virtuous dispositions. Drawing from a range of contemporary theorists and social scientists, we identify and then empirically examine several manifestations of civic virtue. While our understanding of civic virtue is capacious, our examination of specific virtues is not comprehensive because of the confines of space. Rather, we focus on selected factors that serve to illustrate some broader patterns in the relationship between religion and civic virtue.

The first part of the chapter discusses the relationship between and among civic virtue, civic responsibility, and civil society. The second part of the chapter consists of an empirical examination of the relationship between religion and specific civic virtues. This examination focuses on three distinct manifestations of civic virtue: law-abidingness, respect for others and the rights of others, and work ethic. While this examination is not exhaustive, it is nevertheless quite wide-ranging and suggestive of the ways in which religion may contribute to civic virtues.

Civic Virtue, Civic Responsibility, and Civil Society

The concept of virtue has a history as long as political theory itself. The ancient Greeks argued that virtue (*arete*) reflects the excellence of something, and excellence is defined in relation to the end (*telos*) of that thing. As Macintyre (1984, 172) explains, virtuous persons possess "a quality the exercise of which leads to the achievement of the human *telos*." Many ancients described that telos as a profound state of happiness or a well-ordered soul. Aristotle, perhaps the greatest ancient scholar of virtue, argued that human beings could not achieve such happiness outside of a social and political context. We are, as he put it, "political animals." To be reared and to live outside of society is to be "a beast" without developed language skills, social manners, artistic talent, or other indicators of human excellence. An isolated person is still a human being (as opposed to another kind of animal), but only in a superficial sense, because outside of a broader social context no person can fully realize the potential of what it means to be human. Social and political activity, Aristotle believed, is formative of "moral virtue" that helps us achieve our potential as human beings.

Other ancients insisted that duty to the republic was a key aspect of virtue. While the Roman statesman Cicero and other classical republicans celebrated the value of human liberty, they insisted that virtue provided necessary limitations to citizens' unbridled use of liberty and had the salutary effect of keeping their attention focused on the *res publica*. These classical modes of thinking about civic virtue were appropriated by later Christian thinkers such as Augustine and Aquinas, who argued that human law, when properly calibrated to reflect the natural law (as epitomized particularly in Roman Catholic teachings), can habituate civic virtue and supply healthy boundaries to human freedom.[3]

Centuries later, it was precisely those boundaries that troubled the French liberal Alexis de Tocqueville as he took stock of American political culture. In the absence of European aristocratic norms, Tocqueville feared that citizens in the United States would be tempted to use their liberty without regard to duty. The American emphasis on equality of condition, he contended, meant that citizens were uniquely liberated to pursue their self-interests and, without some kind of counterforce to mitigate against this tendency, would likely pursue those interests at the expense of others. However, Tocqueville perceived a peculiar form of "democratic" virtue that diminished this temptation, namely, "self-interest properly understood," which he viewed to be "enlightened self-love [that] continually leads [Americans] to help one another and disposes them freely to give part of their time and wealth for the good of the state" (1969, 526).

It is hardly surprising that Tocqueville spoke of the importance of civic virtue within the life of the American republic; it had been a key tenet of American public philosophy since the founding. Echoing statements made by many of the other founders, John Adams was quite forceful about the need for virtue: "The only foundation of a free Constitution, is pure Virtue, and if this cannot be inspired into our People, in a greater Measure, than they have it now, They may change their Rulers, and the forms of Government, but they will not obtain a lasting Liberty" (as quoted in Smith 2000, 279). Even James Madison, who placed enormous trust in the institutional arrangements of separation of powers and federalism as mechanisms to counter the tendencies of factions to seek enhanced power, believed that those arrangements presuppose "sufficient virtue" among the citizenry.

As we discussed in chapter 1, both contemporary republicans and liberal virtue theorists lay claim to the tradition of relating the moral dispositions of the citizenry to a healthy polity. Each does so in at least two ways. First, they tend to suggest that good character is inseparable from good government. Whatever institutional structures may be in place—and sometimes despite them—there is *public* value in citizens who are honest in their dealings with government and respectful of the rights of others. Indeed, the robust participation of the citizenry in a democracy relies on these moral dispositions (Colby et al. 2000). Second, many modern advocates of civic virtue point to another key assumption of democratic theory: the role of the individual citizen in pursuing collective goals. While such goals are difficult to discern in pluralistic and individualistic societies, most democratic theorists suggest that individual citizens have a responsibility to seek out the good of others (as well as their own) in their own political decision-making.

The literature is voluminous on the link between the networks of civil society and "virtuous" citizenship. Civil society can act as a "seedbed" for civic virtue by "train[ing] our moral sensibilities" in ways the state and market simply fail to accomplish (Glendon 1991, 109; Streeter 2002, x; see also Glendon and Blankenhorn 2005), or it can serve a "mediating" role between the individual and the state or the market (Berger and Neuhaus 1977), even to the point of providing a "site of resistance against tyranny and oppression" (Galston 2000, 69). In its various roles, civil society becomes a mechanism for developing healthy citizenship (Eberly 1998, 142).

Recent scholarship on social capital seems to confirm the role civil society can play in generating civic virtue. Putnam's work on American civic culture, for example, has linked the networks of civil society, with their norms such as trust and reciprocity, and the concept of virtue. Social capital, he argues, "refers to connections among individuals—social networks and the norms of reciprocity and trustworthiness that arise from them. In that sense social capital is closely related to what some have called 'civic virtue'" (Putnam 2000, 19). The difference between the two concepts, however, is that "'social capital' calls attention to the fact that civic virtue is most powerful when embedded in a dense network of reciprocal social relations." Those social relations include a host of voluntary associations within civil society, from sports leagues to religious groups.

Indeed, many commentators view civil society as so important in developing civic virtue that it deserves intensive cultivation by the state itself, usually through formal education. In taking on this task, the state acknowledges that it cannot pursue the common good simply through institutional mechanisms such as separation of powers, elections, or federalism. Rather, the state must rely on civil society to help define and pursue the common good, which means that the state has a stake in fostering a robust civil society. In a tradition that traces back to Jefferson and other early advocates of public education, countless government agencies, nonprofits, and other associations today recommend civic education initiatives to address perceived erosion in civic knowledge and commitment (see, e.g., Macedo et al. 2005; National Commission on Civic Renewal 1998; Ackerman and Fishkin 2004; Ostrom 1997). While these advocates disagree about how best to promote civic education among students from elementary school to college, they appear to share a general consensus that educational institutions can serve as incubators of civic virtue (Andolina et al. 2003).

Another potential source for civic virtue is religion (Smidt 2003). Religion, among other aspects of civil society, can form an "unconventional partnership" with democracy in which religion relies on democracy for its own freedom, while democracy uses religion to overcome its own excesses (e.g., see Fowler 1989). Unlike state-sponsored education, religion maintains its power because the state generally stays out of its business. Disestablishment creates the environment for religion to flourish, and religion, in turn, shapes morality and individual character in socially beneficial ways. Indeed, Tocqueville not only identified religion as a source of citizen attitudes and orientations—mores or "habits of the heart" that mitigate against the baneful effects of American individualism—but he also suggested that religious institutions acted as mediating structures that helped Americans develop the capacity and confidence to act as citizens.

Civic Virtues

Given these insights, one might expect different religious beliefs and practices to be linked to different manifestations of civic virtues. Our question is how religious beliefs and practices might affect civic virtue. To answer that question, however, we need to be more specific about the kinds of virtues that might illustrate the connection between religion and civic virtue. There are, of course, many different types of virtues. Ancient ethicists, for example, identified temperance, justice, courage, and wisdom as cardinal virtues. The Christian tradition often hails the theological virtues of faith, hope, and love. However, the strategy employed in this chapter for identifying virtues draws as much from contemporary social science as from these ancient sources.

Our focus, first of all, is on virtues that have a *civic* nature, that is, dispositions that define our roles as citizens in public life. As Galston (1991) notes, some civic virtues are generally applicable regardless of form of government; nearly every political community honors and even requires loyalty, courage, and obedience. There is, however, a set of unique virtues that serves to sustain democracies, especially in their liberal form. The liberal economy, for example, demands a work ethic and adaptability in the market; the liberal polity entails respect for the rights of others, tolerance of political differences, the ability to evaluate the performance of elected officials, and a willingness to engage in public discourse. In addition to these general economic and political virtues, social virtues such as independence, trust in others, and open-mindedness are important to public life within democracies.

This chapter examines several different kinds of virtues. We first address law-abidingness, an example of a general virtue (Galston 1995, 43). Next, several political virtues are examined: political efficacy, interpersonal trust, respect for the rights of others, and political tolerance. Finally, we examine an economic virtue that is important to public life—namely, one's work ethic, a virtue that Galston (1991) identifies as a key virtue of liberal economy.

As was the case in other facets of civic responsibility (e.g., associational membership, philanthropy, development of civic knowledge), we anticipate that religion is linked to the development of civic virtue, particularly in terms of the form that religiosity takes. If many observers of civil society and social capital are correct, citizens who actively participate in the public worship life of a congregation (along with its social networks) are the most likely to develop and exhibit such virtues as honesty in their dealings with government, respect for the rights of others and tolerance, and a work ethic. Overall, therefore, we anticipate that those citizens who have little connection to the social networks embedded in religious institutions are less likely to have these virtues reinforced in their lives, despite the fact that some of these same citizens may have an active "private" spiritual life (e.g., regular meditation or prayer).

Law-Abidingness

The first virtue we examine is law-abidingness. While recent work on social capital has reoriented attention on the role of social or interpersonal trust in enabling collective action (a type of trust addressed in the next section), one might also consider obedience to the law as reflecting trust in or acceptance of *institutions*. This is not to suggest that such acceptance is blind or unconsidered. Rather, civic responsibility requires some basic level of support for the legitimacy of institutions and rules of government. Even the greatest advocates of targeted civil disobedience in our time (e.g., Martin Luther King and Mahatma Gandhi) were not anarchists; they respected the legitimacy of the state to the point of accepting the consequences for their own disobedience.

When asked simply whether it is an imperative always to obey the law, the vast majority of American citizens say that it is. For example, in the 2004 General Social Survey, respondents were asked on a seven-point scale about the importance of always obeying the law. Nearly 70 percent chose the highest response, denoting "very important," while less than 5 percent of Americans choose any one of the four points on the scale ascribing the least importance to obedience (data not shown). When citizens were asked whether it is important never to evade taxes, a similar pattern emerges (data not shown).

However, as table 6.1 demonstrates, significant differences emerge among respondents once they are categorized by forms of religious expression. Those respondents with diminished religiosity were nearly eight percentage points less likely than integrated respondents to choose the highest response on the question on tax evasion. These differences are even more pronounced in responses to the question about obedience, with integrated respondents being far more likely to offer the highest response than those within the other categories. Indeed, the difference between an integrated and diminished respondent is over fifteen percentage points.

A second way to analyze law-abidingness is to move from abstract questions about obedience to specific acts of compliance that honest citizens would display in their practical interactions with institutions of government (e.g., paying taxes or filling out applications for state assistance truthfully). Letki (2006, 306) describes this kind of honesty as part of "civic

Table 6.1 Law-abidingness by Form of Religious Expression
(percent giving highest possible responsive)

Law-abidingness	Diminished	Privatized	Public	Integrated	eta
How important is it never to evade paying one's taxes?[a]	69	72	74	76	.09[b]
How important is it to always obey the laws?[a]	59	66	69	75	.15[c]

Source: General Social Survey, 2004

[a] Respondents provided with a 1–7 scale, with 1 representing "not at all important" and 7 representing "very important."
[b] Statistically significant at .05 level
[c] Statistically significant at .001 level

morality," as it "represents honesty in the context of the public good" by maximizing public, rather than private, gain. Moreover, citizens who exhibit such honesty help to reduce the costs incurred by the state to ensure compliance with the law. Unlike interpersonal trust, relatively little is known about the origins of honesty as a distinctively civic virtue, and particularly whether religion plays a role in its development.

The analysis conducted here largely follows the lead of Letki (2006) in her cross-national study of civic morality and honesty. While Letki used the World Values Surveys in her analysis, two of the three items she employed in her operationalization of "civic morality" are found in the General Social Survey of 1998. These items measure whether a respondent perceived tax-cheating or providing other forms of false information to government as seriously wrong. Table 6.2 examines the percentage of those who responded that each of these actions was "seriously wrong," the response item reflecting the highest assessment of ethical wrongdoing related to such action, according to the form of religious expression exhibited by the respondent.

Several patterns are evident in the table. First, higher percentages of Americans indicated that it was "seriously wrong" to provide false information to obtain governmental benefits than that it was "seriously wrong" to fail to report all of one's income. Since both actions relate to making

Table 6.2 Civic Morality by Form of Religious Expression
(percent giving highest possible response)

Law-abidingness	Diminished	Privatized	Public	Integrated	*eta*
Taxpayer does not report all income to pay less taxes					
Seriously wrong	24	23	32	39	.15
Provides incorrect information in order to receive government benefits to which one is not entitled					
Seriously wrong	50	44	57	56	.09
Civic Morality Index					
Mean score	6.38	6.28	6.58	6.75	.16

Source: General Social Survey, 1998

[a] Statistically significant at .001 level

false claims, it might seem curious that respondents view the former action as more seriously wrong than the latter. Although further research is required before conclusive claims can be made, one might speculate about two possible reasons why this is the case. On the one hand, the difference could be attributed to respondents believing that they have "earned" their taxed income while being less likely to view government assistance as "earned" or "deserved." On the other hand, everyone is required to submit and pay income tax, but not everyone is eligible for government assistance. As a result, it is likely that more respondents have failed to report all income on their taxes than have provided false information in applications for government assistance. And because it is easier to find blame in someone else than in one's own self, people who have falsified their income may be somewhat less likely to view their actions as "seriously wrong"; thus more respondents may view providing false information to obtain government benefits as seriously wrong than view providing false information to pay less tax as seriously wrong.

Second, it is also clear that one's form of religious expression is related to the likelihood of assessing whether both actions examined in the table are wrong. This conclusion is evident in several ways. Those with public and integrated forms of religious expression are more likely than those with either diminished or privatized forms to view either action as being "seriously wrong." And, those with an integrated form of religious expression are somewhat more likely to view providing false income information on one's taxes as being "seriously wrong" than those with a public form (though no differences are apparent between respondents exhibiting these two forms of religious expression with regard to the false reporting of information related to governmental assistance). For each relationship, the value of *eta* attains statistical significance at the .001 level, indicating that significant differences in the mean scores are evident between and among these different forms of religious expression.

The bottom portion of table 6.2 presents the mean score of an additive index composed of the two variables broken down by form of religious expression. If participation in religious institutions is indeed a seedbed for civic morality, we would expect that respondents in the integrated and public categories would be most likely to score high on the index, reflecting a stronger emphasis on honesty in dealings with government. The mean scores represent the average response on the index for each category of religious expression. The results indicate significant differences in the mean scores, and these differences are also in expected directions—with religionists in the integrated category scoring higher on the index than those with diminished or privatized religious expression.

Of course, it is unclear from the previous analyses whether or not religion has any unique capacity to explain such variation in differences in civic morality. Consequently, a multiple classification analysis was conducted to assess the relative importance of religion in shaping such assessments of wrongdoing after controls have been introduced for various other factors thought to shape responses to this type of question. Letki's analysis revealed that age shaped civic morality, as older people tended to have higher moral standards than young people. Similarly, increased education and family income positively affected one's civic morality, and women were more likely than men to score high on civic morality. In addition to various sociodemographic variables previously employed in such analyses, this MCA also included confidence in public institutions as an independent variable shaping responses to the civic morality index, as "individuals' confidence in key institutional actors has an important effect on their attitudes toward compliance" (Letki 2006, 321).[4] According to Letki's analysis, the more one believes that the legislative body, the civil service, the army, and other institutions related to the state are "trustworthy," the more likely one is "to respect the norms and rules these actors design and implement."

The resulting MCA is shown in table 6.3. Two variables, namely, family income and race, did not attain statistical significance in terms of shaping responses to the civic morality index, while education was only modestly significant at the .05 level. However, the analysis reveals that age and confidence in public institutions are more significantly related to responses on the civic morality index (at a .01 level of statistical significance), while gender and marital status are even more significantly related to civic morality (at a .001 level), as women and those who are married are more likely

Table 6.3 Relative Importance of Religion in Fostering the Virtue of Law-abidingness: A Multiple Classification Analysis

Characteristic	*eta*
Confident in public institutions	.09[b]
Gender	.13[c]
Race	.06
Age	.09[b]
Education	.07[a]
Family income	.04
Marital status	.13[c]
Religious tradition	.15[c]
Form of religious expression	.14[c]
R-square	*.13*

Source: General Social Survey, 1998

[a] Statistically significant at .05 level
[b] Statistically significant at .01 level
[c] Statistically significant at .001 level

to indicate that such behaviors are "seriously wrong" than men and single respondents. However, it is one's religious tradition and one's form of religious expression that exhibit the highest *beta* scores, revealing that, of all the variables included in the analysis, these two religious variables exhibit the strongest relationship to law-abidingness (and each attains statistical significance at the .001 level). Evangelical Protestants exhibit the highest adjusted level of law-abidingness, followed by mainline Protestants, while seculars exhibit the lowest adjusted score on the measure (data not shown). Likewise, those with an integrated mode of religious expression have the highest—and those with a diminished form, the lowest—adjusted score on the index of law-abidingness (data not shown).

External Political Efficacy

While "civic morality," as we have defined it here, measures the trustworthiness of citizens in their interactions with government, a related dimension of law-abidingness is the citizenry's perception of the trustworthiness of governmental institutions. Several decades ago, David Easton (1965) identified the concept of diffuse support, that is, support for the political system itself, which reflects the belief that governmental procedures are fair, trustworthy, and transparent. Such diffuse support is crucially important in a democratic polity, where the overall responsiveness of public institutions is integral to healthy governance.

In the analysis that follows, the concept of external political efficacy is used as an indicator of a citizen's level of diffuse support for the political system (see Iyengar 1980).[5] External efficacy describes a citizen's perception of government's responsiveness, and it is highly correlated with whether citizens perceive their government as corrupt or self-interested. In light of the claims of some scholars that religion acts as a mediating institution between the individual and the state, as well as the research suggesting that a citizen's participation in voluntary associations enhances his or her political efficacy (Joslyn and Cigler 2001), our expectation is that religionists with the most integrated of faith commitments would be most likely to have high levels of external efficacy. The underlying assumption is that support for institutions is transferable; citizens who develop support for one institution (e.g., the church) might possess a disposition to support other institutions as well.

External political efficacy is measured here through an additive index of items related to the responsiveness of government.[6] The relationship between expressions of external political efficacy and one's form of religious expression is examined across time. The results are displayed in table 6.4, and it is the relative standing of each form of religious expression related to such expressions of external efficacy that merits our attention. One pattern among religionists is consistent across surveys: In every survey, regardless of year and survey organization, it was those with an integrated form of religious expression who expressed the highest level of external efficacy, whereas those with a privatized religious expression (National Election Studies) or with a diminished religious expression (General Social Surveys) who expressed the lowest levels of such efficacy.

But does religion have any effect on attitudes of external political efficacy once other factors have been taken into account? To address this question, a MCA of external efficacy for each of the five surveys examined in the previous table was conducted. The results are presented in table 6.5.

Some sociodemographic variables are only marginally related to expressions of external political efficacy. For example, the relative effects of gender failed to attain statistical significance in each of the five surveys examined, while age attained statistical significance in only one of the surveys and marital status in two. On the other hand, education clearly is the variable that affects attitudes of external political efficacy most strongly, as it exhibits the *beta* with the highest magnitude across each of the five surveys

Table 6.4 External Efficacy by Forms of Religious Expression
(percent high efficacy)

Study	Diminished	Privatized	Public	Integrated	*eta*
NES, 1996	23	19	25	26	.08[a]
NES, 2000	25	21	32	29	.10[a]
NES, 2004	34	26	25	35	.05
GSS, 1996	27	30	32	35	.08[a]
GSS, 2004	26	32	33	41	.15[b]

[a] Statistically significant at .05 level
[b] Statistically significant at .001 level

examined. The relative effects of family income were less than that for
education, although the variable attained some level of statistical significance in each survey.

The two religious variables also served to shape expressions of external
efficacy—though in a more modest fashion than education. The magnitude of the *beta* coefficient for religious tradition affiliation attained
statistical significance in two of the five surveys (at the .01 level of significance), with seculars and Jews tending to express the higher levels of
adjusted efficacy and black Protestants tending to express the lowest levels
of such adjusted scores (data not shown). Forms of religious expression
attained statistical significance in four of the five surveys (though it did
so only at the .05 level in two of those cases), with those who exhibit an
integrated form expressing on the whole the highest levels of such adjusted
external efficacy (data not shown). Still the magnitude of the *beta* coefficient for the mode of one's religiosity ranked second in importance in
two of the surveys (National Election Study 2000 and General Social
Survey 2004). Consequently, this analysis suggests (1) that the relationship between religion and attitudes of external political efficacy is not

Table 6.5 Relative Importance of Religion in Fostering External Efficacy:
A Multiple Classification Analysis

Demographic Characteristic	Study				
	GSS 1996	NES 1996	NES 2000	GSS 2004	NES 2004
Gender	.01	.01	.01	.01	.04
Race	.11[b]	.05	.04	.06	.14[c]
Age	.09[b]	.03	.03	.07	.01
Education	.10[b]	.21[c]	.22[c]	.22[c]	.15[c]
Family income	.12[b]	.08[a]	.10[b]	.08[b]	.11[b]
Marital status	.07[a]	.06	.09[a]	.06	.06
Religious tradition	.01	.12[b]	.07	.06	.09[b]
Form of religious expression	.07[a]	.05	.11[b]	.13[c]	.08[a]
R-square	*.05*	*.08*	*.10*	*.12*	*.07*

[a] Statistically significant at .05 level
[b] Statistically significant at .01 level
[c] Statistically significant at .001 level

spurious and (2) that one's form of religious expression is a relatively important contributing factor in shaping attitudes of external political efficacy, though it does not rank as the primary variable.

Interpersonal Trust

Both civic morality and external efficacy focus on dispositions toward public institutions, and we have noted earlier that external political efficacy could actually be viewed as a measure of trust in the working of existing political institutions. Social trust, on the other hand, involves the interpersonal—expectations about the values or behaviors of other persons, specifically whether they are reliable, predictable, competent, or caring.[7]

Interpersonal trust has been of long-standing interest to social scientists, though its definitions and dimensions are matters of dispute (e.g., Levy and Stoker 2000; Jackman and Miller 1998). One area of dispute is the source of interpersonal trust itself. Some scholars have suggested that interpersonal trust is positively related to participation in the voluntary associations of civil society, including religion (Putman 2000), while others have concluded that interpersonal trust results from a citizen's confidence in government, particularly government's stability and power to enforce agreements between citizens (Brehm and Rahn 1997; Levy and Stoker 2000, 493–95).

A related question concerns the scope of interpersonal trust. Consider the interaction of religion and trust. While participation in religious life may generate trust among co-religionists, it does not necessarily mean that such religionists will develop high levels of trust in those outside their own religious group. Or, to state the point in Putnam's terminology, some religious traditions or modes of religious expression may "bond" co-religionists to each other without "bridging" them to outsiders, thereby leaving those co-religionists without a "generalized" social trust. Indeed, some scholars have suggested that the evidence for generalized trust is weak even on those rare occasions in which a citizen belongs to a heterogeneous group, despite that member's exposure to a wide range of people and ideas (Theiss-Morse and Hibbing 2005).

Studies by Veenstra (2002) and Welch et al. (2004) summarize much of the social science literature on the relationship between social trust and religiosity. While different studies point the causality arrow in different directions, Veenstra argues that the relationship between religion and social trust is reciprocal. In his survey of citizens in a Canadian province, Veenstra (2002, 554) finds that "participation in a breadth of secondary associations was significantly related to social and weakly related to political trust." Participation in secondary associations matters, but people "must engage meaningfully in dialogue with others" in order "for lessons regarding trustworthiness to take" (Veenstra 2002, 567). Religious belonging also matters in building social trust, as Veenstra notes that "respondents who claimed no religious affiliation were markedly less trusting than the majority of respondents who claimed affiliation with Protestant or Roman Catholic churches."

Our analysis of interpersonal trust in table 6.6 partially confirms those findings in the case of the American people. The results are based on responses to a question about the trustworthiness of others in each of the surveys listed, with the table presenting the percentages of those respondents in each category who believe that others can generally be trusted. Noteworthy is the fact that respondents in the privatized category are always the least likely to find others trustworthy.

Nevertheless, the relationships between forms of religious expression and expressions of interpersonal trust are relatively weak across the various studies. Moreover, it is unclear whether the variable measuring forms

Table 6.6 Interpersonal Trust by Form of Religious Expression (percent reporting people can be generally trusted)

Study	Diminished	Privatized	Public	Integrated	eta
GSS, 1996	34	34	33	34	.00
NES, 1996	52	44	53	54	.06
GSS, 1998	36	33	38	37	.03
Saguaro, 2000	36	36	36	42	.05[a]
NES, 2000	51	47	50	50	.03
NES, 2004	44	39	49	46	.05
GSS, 2004	38	22	34	36	.08[a]

[a] Statistically significant at .05 level

of religious expression would actually diminish or increase in its relative strength once the effects of other variables are taken into account. Consequently, a MCA was run to control for the effects of other variables, including membership in voluntary associations, as scholars have argued that interpersonal trust is fostered within such associations (e.g., Putnam 1993, 1995a, and 2000).

The analysis is presented in table 6.7. By far the most important variables shaping interpersonal trust are education and race, with age and membership in voluntary associations (and family income to some extent) playing a more secondary role in shaping interpersonal trust. However, the analysis reveals that one's form of religious expression has little, if any, effect on shaping interpersonal social trust.

Just why religion, as measured in terms of forms of religious expression, has little effect in cultivating civic virtue in this particular area of civic life is unclear. Perhaps the relationship between religion and social trust may be more a function of theology than a reflection of one's form of religious

Table 6.7 Relative Importance of Religion in Fostering Social Trust: A Multiple Classification Analysis

Demographic Characteristic	Study		
	NES 1996	NES 2000	NES 2004
Membership in voluntary organization	.11[c]	.09[b]	.10[b]
Gender	.02	.01	.01
Race	.19[c]	.18[c]	.16[c]
Age	.07[b]	.15[c]	.14[c]
Education	.23[c]	.22[c]	.17[c]
Family income	.06	.05	.10[b]
Marital status	.05	.06	.05
Religious tradition	.04	.14[c]	.11[b]
Form of religious expression	.05	.05	.05
R-square	*.17*	*.18*	*.14*

[a] Statistically significant at .05 level
[b] Statistically significant at .01 level
[c] Statistically significant at .001 level

expression. Or perhaps religion is not directly related to expressions of interpersonal trust and is, rather, primarily reflective of one's personal experiences. In any case, interpersonal trust is the only civic virtue examined in which one's form of religious expression did not function as a relatively important explanatory variable.

Political Tolerance

Respect for the rights of others is a complementary virtue to social trust. Such respect is a reciprocal disposition: A respects the rights of B because A expects the same respect from B. Yet the conventional measurement of respect for rights provides little insight into its nature or scope. Surveys periodically ask a battery of questions about respect for the rights of others, but when posed in the abstract, the results tend to be highly skewed in support of respecting such rights. For example, the General Social Survey of 2004 asked respondents to rank on a scale of one to seven whether it is important "that the government respect and protect the rights of minorities." Just as was true with the obedience question discussed earlier in this chapter, over 60 percent of the American people chose the most extreme point that designated "very important."

A potentially more promising approach to assessing respect for the rights of others is to focus on questions that test the limits of a citizen's forbearance of specified groups, that is, their social and political tolerance. Given that tolerance among Americans has been studied by social scientists for more than a half century, a certain conventional wisdom has emerged about the groups most likely or unlikely to exhibit this civic virtue. Probably the one variable most centrally tied to expressions of tolerance is education. For example, Nunn, Crockett, and Williams (1978, 169) state that education is the "single most powerful predictor of tolerance," and Nie, Junn, and Stehlik-Barry (1996, 148–49) conclude that "the more educated [they are], the more likely citizens are to support freedom of expression for many different types of groups under a range of circumstances." Generational differences, as measured in terms of the age of the respondents, is also linked to political tolerance, with younger Americans more likely than older Americans to exhibit attitudes of social and political tolerance (e.g., Glock and Stark 1966).

Conventional scholarly wisdom also holds that religiosity and political tolerance are inversely related—the more religious one is, the less tolerant politically one is likely to be (Woodberry and Smith 1998). A number of studies have linked religion and religious variables to political tolerance (Beatty and Walter 1984; Smidt and Penning 1982; Reimer and Park 2001; Stouffer 1955; Wilcox and Jelen 1990; Woodberry and Smith 1998, 40–42). Generally, social surveys measuring religion in the mass public have used one of three sorting methods in asking questions that make distinctions among religions and between religion and nonreligion: questions about religious belonging (denominational and faith-tradition ties), questions about religious beliefs (positions on theological questions and scriptural authority), and questions about religious behaviors (practices like praying and church attendance that are typically associated with religiosity). The general conclusion of "belonging" studies is that members of churches are less tolerant than nonmembers, and the highest levels of intolerance seem to be found among those who belong to more fundamentalist Protestant churches. Regarding religious behaviors, studies find all pietistic behaviors—high frequencies of praying and Bible reading, and regular church attendance—to be positively associated with intolerance. In regard to religious beliefs, those beliefs most closely linked to American fundamentalism—biblical literalism, a belief in the rapture, a historical Adam and Eve, born-again self-identification, and the need for believers to separate from society—are associated with less support for civil liberties (Green et al. 1994) and greater discriminatory attitudes toward blacks, women, homosexuals, and communists (Kirkpatrick 1993).

Nevertheless, some scholars are beginning to question both the adequacy of the common conceptualization of tolerance and the validity of standard measures of tolerance, thereby bringing into question the conventional wisdom that has emerged based on their use (e.g., Gibson 2006). Many scholars have focused particularly on how one should conceptualize tolerance (e.g., Conyers 2001; Griffiths and Elshtain 2002; Stetson and Conti 2005). To be sure, there are some clear qualities and noncontroversial features of tolerance that most definitions capture. For example, tolerance certainly does not mean that one either stands in agreement or endorses the position(s) held or the action(s) conducted by others. On the contrary, tolerance is "a willingness to permit the expression of ideas or interests one opposes" (Sullivan, Piereson, and Marcus 1982, 2). Neither does tolerance imply indifference to those ideas or interests, since by definition the tolerant person stands in opposition to what he or she tolerates—and often vigorously so. Nor does tolerance necessarily reflect either the lack or presence of prejudice.[8]

Still, when one examines tolerance more fully, the concept becomes murkier. First, there are limits to tolerance; no one tolerates everything under every circumstance. People may support some ideas (agree), oppose other ideas but believe they should be allowed to be expressed (tolerate), and oppose still other ideas or actions while believing that they should not be allowed to be expressed or permitted (do not tolerate). Clearly, not all expressions or actions are to be tolerated or permitted (e.g., murder or rape). Moreover, tolerance may be circumstantial; what ought to be tolerated in one context (e.g., a debate among adults about pornography, complete with illustrations) should not necessarily be tolerated in another context (e.g., a similar debate in an unsupervised middle school classroom).[9]

Kymlicka and Norman (1995, 297) distinguish between virtues that are "civic" and "political," and their distinction bears on the conceptualization of tolerance. The political virtues include the capacity to discern and respect the rights of others in debates about public issues and the willingness to engage in public discourse generally. Certainly these virtues are important within elections and governmental bodies, but for most people they are learned in interactions outside those bodies—in civil society generally, including the individualized spheres of the market and incidental personal interaction. Thus one can make a conceptual distinction between essentially individual actions and attitudes, broader social ones, and those that are specifically political—only the latter category is related to elections, government, and making public policy. In all these actions, tolerance—the willingness to "put up with" an "other" person or group on the same terms one would like oneself to be treated in that sphere—is a virtue.

Gibson (2006) makes a somewhat similar distinction between social tolerance and political tolerance. He contends that questions of prejudice and social distance posed to respondents are more precisely measures of social tolerance, while questions about political activities by groups are measures of political tolerance. He also argues that prejudice against a group (a measure of social intolerance) and intolerance of political activity by members of a particular group are quite independent of each other. Thus, while intuitively it seems logical that there would be a connection between the two, Gibson finds that social intolerance and political intolerance are not necessarily closely connected empirically (Gibson 2006, 25).

Most researchers accept as established fact that increased religiosity leads to increased political intolerance, but the problems in conceptualizing and measuring political tolerance sketched here may affect the standing of conventional wisdom. The General Social Survey (GSS) frequently employs a battery of questions that many have used to assess patterns of political tolerance, and the 2004 GSS employed both its standard measures as well as an alternative battery of questions. Table 6.8 presents data from the 2004 General Social Survey, examining the relationship between forms of religious expression and five categories of people (anti-religionists, communists, homosexuals, militarists, and racists) and whether (1) books they have written promoting their viewpoints should be permitted in public libraries, (2) whether such individuals should be permitted to teach in public schools, and (3) whether they should be allowed to speak in the community. Whereas the former two questions can be viewed to reflect social tolerance, the latter question reflects political tolerance in that it entails constitutionally protected freedom of speech; these items are presented in the top portion of table 6.8. The new GSS battery of three questions related to whether such groups should be granted permission to meet is examined as well, with responses to these questions broken down according to the respondent's form of religious expression, and these questions are presented in the bottom portion of table 6.8.

Several important conclusions can be drawn from the upper portion of table 6.8. First, the extent to which tolerance is willingly granted depends on the type of group under consideration. Racists are the group that, regardless of form of religious expression, consistently obtains the lowest rate of permission to teach, place books in the public library, or speak in public settings. Homosexuals are, relatively speaking, considered to pose far less risk to American society, as their percentages are, in almost every case, the

Table 6.8 Tolerance by Form of Religious Expression
(percent agreeing)

Study	Diminished	Privatized	Public	Integrated	*eta*
Allow to teach					
Anti-religionists	70	66	65	58	.13[a]
Communists	71	76	64	61	.11[a]
Homosexuals	87	85	76	70	.18[a]
Militarists	57	56	56	45	.11[a]
Racists	48	48	48	41	.06
Allow book in library					
Anti-religionists	85	78	68	61	.24[a]
Communists	79	81	70	59	.20[a]
Homosexuals	80	83	76	63	.18[a]
Militarists	77	70	72	58	.19[a]
Racists	74	66	68	55	.17[a]
Allow to speak					
Anti-religionists	86	81	70	69	.19[a]
Communists	76	70	68	64	.12[a]
Homosexuals	91	86	83	74	.19[a]
Militarists	74	70	68	58	.15[a]
Racists	67	67	58	58	.09
Definitely not allow to hold public meeting					
Racists	41	37	40	42	.05
Religious extremists	11	8	5	10	.07
Revolutionaries	48	51	45	53	.05

Source: General Social Survey, 2004

[a] Statistically significant at .001 level

highest found in the table—regardless of one's form of religious expression. The only exception to this pattern is found among those with a diminished form of religiosity, as they are more willing to permit books promoting anti-religionist viewpoints to be placed in the public library than books favorable to homosexuality.

A second important point that can be drawn from table 6.8 is that the nature of the activity, and not just the nature of the group, also affects whether or not an action is likely to be tolerated, a conclusion reached by selecting a specific group (e.g., racists) and the percentages of respondents who believed the group should be allowed to teach, place books in the public library, or be allowed to meet. Regardless of the group examined, the patterns that emerge reveal the greatest tolerance is for permitting groups to speak in public settings (a constitutionally protected freedom) and the least tolerance for allowing members of such groups to teach in public schools.[10]

Third, those who exhibit an integrated form of religious expression consistently are the most hesitant to extend permission to members of groups that they perceive to pose a threat to the health of American public life. In all fifteen comparisons (five groups multiplied by three actions), those with an integrated form of religious expression exhibit the lowest percentage of political tolerance. Conversely, those with a diminished form of religious expression exhibit the highest percentage in twelve of the fifteen comparisons found in the upper portion of table 6.8. In fact, in fourteen of these fifteen comparisons, the differences that emerge are substantial.

Fourth, despite what may appear to be a fairly intolerant stance on the part of those who are more highly religious in terms of their public expression of religious faith (and, more particularly, those with an integrated religiosity), it is interesting to observe that such respondents are not acting solely in terms of self-interest. Note, for example, that those with an integrated religious faith, who despite their greater hesitancy to tolerate particular groups and particular activities, nevertheless are more willing to tolerate those who are labeled anti-religionists than those who are classified as militarists and racists.

Finally, as can be seen from the bottom portion of table 6.8, the format of the survey question has an important effect on whether significant differences emerge among the different forms of religious expression. While statistically significant differences in political tolerance are evident among those with different forms of religious expression in the upper portion of the table (where the survey questions were framed in terms of permitting actions), when one examines the results of the new measure of political tolerance used in the 2004 General Social Surveys (where the survey question asks whether racists, religious extremists, and revolutionaries should be prohibited from holding public meetings), hardly any differences are evident. None of the comparisons exhibit patterns that attain statistical significance, as percentage differences across the various categories of religious expression are quite small.

However, if tolerance is neither indifference nor acceptance, then perhaps tolerance should be examined only among those who stand in opposition to ideas or actions, as tolerance is hardly evident among those who do not oppose such matters in the first place. Consequently, the next analysis is limited to those who clearly stand in opposition to certain kinds of attitudes, behavior, or groups of people. For purposes of this analysis, only those respondents who clearly stated that sexually intimate same-sex relationships are always wrong are examined in table 6.9, focusing on the General Social Surveys of 1987, 1998, and 2004 (these particular surveys contained questions on both the morality of homosexuality and tolerance).

The results are interesting for what they suggest about the current state of political tolerance and what they suggest about the development of tolerance over time. In 1987, for example, there were quite significant differences between integrated religionists and those in the diminished category, especially in terms of social tolerance. There are twenty percentage point differences between the two categories in response to the questions about teaching and books in the library. But note the change over time. By 2004, the differences between the categories had tightened considerably, to the point that the statistical significance of the differences is nonexistent. Note particularly the changes in willingness to grant rights to homosexuals among those who exhibit an integrated form of religious expression. Not only does the percentage of those willing to extend such opportunities to homosexuals increase monotonically over time, but such an increase in willingness to do so outpaces any increases evident within the other forms of religious expression.

The trend undoubtedly relates to increasing societal acceptance of gay and lesbian rights; many religionists are likely part of cross-cutting social networks or have access to information today that they did not possess in the late 1980s, and we know that such cross-cutting networks can have an effect on tolerance (Mutz 2002). But the results also hint that intolerance is not necessarily inherently related to high religious attendance or religious pietism.

Moreover, most examinations of political tolerance are posed in terms of particular groups or actions that are likely to be disliked or disapproved of by respondents who are relatively religious (e.g., anti-religionists and communists). In other words, surveys designed to measure social and political tolerance are themselves often weighted in favor of nonreligious respondents who are not asked to respond to social groups or actions that they are more likely to find objectionable.[11] It is hardly surprising, therefore, that more highly religious people are found to be more intolerant than those who are less religious.

In an effort to provide some relative balance in the objects of political intolerance, we examined those respondents in the General Social Survey of 1998 who held that "people with strong religious beliefs are often intolerant." We then examined the extent to which such respondents held that religious leaders should not be permitted to influence how people vote or what government decisions are made. Certainly, as citizens, religious leaders have the constitutionally protected right to engage in political activities related to freedom of speech (persuasion) and petitioning public officials. Nevertheless, some might argue that opposition to these activities does not constitute political intolerance because it reflects a particular interpretation of the Constitution, the "high wall" of separation between church and state. Of course, that is the point: Political tolerance often raises questions about proper interpretation of the Constitution. And while the question of clergy influencing voting and governmental decisions is somewhat ambiguous in terms of whether the activities performed by religious leaders are committed illegally (e.g., on the pulpit) or legally (off the pulpit), considerable ambiguity exists in the more conventional tolerance measures as well. The items analyzed in table 6.8, for example, do not identify what, specifically, is contained in the hypothetical book to be placed in libraries or what grade levels are to be taught or what speeches are to be permitted.

Consequently, the bottom part of table 6.9 presents the responses to two proposed activities by religious leaders according to the form of religious expression exhibited by the respondents—but only for those respondents who agreed that "people with strong religious beliefs are often intolerant." The results show that the nature of the people considered and the nature of the action proposed clearly shapes respondents' willingness to tolerate

Table 6.9 Political Tolerance by Form of Religious Expression among Those Who Stand in Opposition (percent agreeing)

	Diminished	Privatized	Public	Integrated	eta
Among those who hold that intimate sexual relations between those of the same sex is always wrong					
Allow homosexuals to teach					
GSS, 1987	58	44	47	38	.16[c]
GSS, 1998	61	58	62	56	.06[a]
GSS, 2004	69	79	65	66	.08[b]
Allow books in library					
GSS, 1987	59	48	52	40	.16[c]
GSS, 1998	64	61	56	43	.19[c]
GSS, 2004	59	77	63	55	.12[b]
Allow homosexuals to speak					
GSS, 1987	69	57	61	54	.14[c]
GSS, 1998	75	68	71	64	.10[b]
GSS, 2004	77	79	72	68	.09[b]
Among those who agree that people with strong religious beliefs are often intolerant					
Religious leaders should not influence how people vote					
GSS, 1998	72	78	66	53	.17[c]
Religious leaders should not influence government decisions					
GSS, 1998	73	63	55	45	.23[c]

[a] Statistically significant at .05 level
[b] Statistically significant at .01 level
[c] Statistically significant at .001 level

certain activities. Whereas in the upper portion of table 6.9, those with a diminished or a privatized religious expression tended to be the most tolerant socially and politically, when asked to respond to religious leaders' involvement in politics, those exhibiting these very same religious expressions are the least tolerant politically. Conversely, it is those who exhibit public and integrated forms of religious expression who are now the most tolerant.

Political tolerance is normally a desirable trait. Responsible civic participation requires political tolerance—allowing political participation by groups that one finds personally offensive or from which one is socially distant. But political tolerance has its limits, depending significantly upon the purposes of the groups or individuals acting in the political world, the legitimate interests of the nation to preserve itself, and even one's perspective on democracy itself. How best to operationalize political tolerance in social surveys needs rethinking, as does the conventional wisdom that increased religiosity correlates with decreased political tolerance. While many studies view religiosity as inversely correlated with political tolerance, the data presented above suggest that quite different inferences can be drawn. Future research that is able to transcend the current problem may well reveal, for example, that religious persons are less *socially* tolerant than others (as they may be more likely to view a greater variety of actions as being morally wrong than those who are less religious) but that, when it comes to political discourse and political processes, they may be as *politically* tolerant as their less religious neighbors. It is this ability to make such a distinction—allowing political access to groups that one wants restricted from other social spheres—that constitutes an important civic virtue, not vice.

Work Ethic

The final virtue examined here has economic roots. The idea that life in the marketplace can itself enhance, rather than impede, virtue is a common theme in American intellectual history, as it is often tied to a strong sense of individual freedom. For example, due to the influence of his own "romantic agrarianism" (Schudson 1998, 28), Thomas Jefferson's model of the virtuous republican citizen was the yeoman farmer, whose combination of independence, respect for the land, and duty to community epitomized the best of civic virtue. "Those who labor in the earth," Jefferson effused, "are the chosen people of God, if ever He had a chosen people, whose breasts He has made his substantial deposit for substantial and genuine virtue" (Jefferson 1975, 217). For Jefferson, then, a certain kind of economic activity was responsible for the virtue of the bedrock American citizenry.

Whether or not one agrees with Jefferson, his argument suggests some intriguing possibilities about civic virtue in American public life. In chapter 1 we argued that the state, civil society, and the market have unique characteristics that distinguish each sphere of human activity from the others. We also suggested that each sphere pushes against the boundaries of the others to the point where distinctions among them sometimes blur. Moreover, as Jefferson insisted, it may be that virtues most closely associated with one sphere have reciprocal connections to another.

Consider, for example, the virtue of the work ethic, which is most often associated with economic behavior. As a virtue of liberal democracies, Galston (1991, 45) defines the work ethic as "the sense of obligation to support personal independence through gainful effort with the determination to do one's job thoroughly and well." This definition adds a moral dimension to activity in a market economy. But as Galston suggests, productive work in itself is not a virtuous activity; rather, such work must be accompanied by a twofold disposition: (1) that all physically able people have an obligation to engage in productive labor rather than being intentionally idle and drawing upon state resources to sustain their physical needs and (2) that advancement results through hard work rather than through blind luck.

One might expect that the nature of civil society, and particularly of religion, may well affect a citizen's commitment to the work ethic. Max Weber (1930), for example, argued that the Protestant morality of work was responsible for the development of modern capitalism. While Weber's thesis has been criticized as a historical inaccuracy (e.g., Stark 2005; Delacroix and Nielsen 2001), scholars have nevertheless often linked religion in general with key understandings of work (Chusmir and Koberg 1988). The work ethic, for example, requires a basic belief that one's own behavior has consequences, which religion often teaches. It also assumes a certain measure of confidence in one's own competence, which religion can provide (Verba, Schlozman, and Brady 1995).

Survey results, however, are mixed on the question of religion's role in fostering a work ethic. In various years, the General Social Survey has included a variable that asks respondents to explain how people "get ahead" in the marketplace. They are given three options: hard work, luck, or both hard work and luck in equal measure. We examined responses to the question across four GSS surveys (the years of 1987, 1996, 1998, and 2004) by one's form of religious expression. As shown in table 6.10, most Americans, regardless of their form of religious expression, hold that people get ahead primarily in terms of "hard work." This is true regardless of the year analyzed. But while no significant response differences existed among the different forms of religious expression in 1987, significant differences were evident among the categories in 1996, 1998, and 2004.

By 1998, a respondent's form of religious expression had become significantly related to his or her belief that hard work is the primary means to get ahead economically. It remains unclear, however, whether such a relationship continues to hold when other sociodemographic variables are taken into account. Other factors may well serve to shape such responses. Consequently, a MCA was conducted, with the results presented in table 6.11.

Overall, the data reveal that form of religious expression was either the most important variable or among the most important variables, serving to shape responses that hard work rather than luck or even a combination of luck and work is the means by which one gets ahead economically.

Table 6.10   Work Ethic by Form of Religious Expression, 1987–2004 (percent reporting "get ahead by hard work")

Year	Diminished	Privatized	Public	Integrated	*eta*
GSS, 1987	65	65	60	70	.06
GSS, 1996	67	74	70	72	.06[a]
GSS, 1998	58	68	68	73	.10[b]
GSS, 2004	63	59	69	71	.13[b]

[a] Statistically significant at .01 level
[b] Statistically significant at .001 level

Table 6.11 Relative Importance of Religion in Fostering a Work Ethic: A Multiple Classification Analysis

Demographic Characteristic	Study			
	GSS 1987	GSS 1987	CPS 1990	CPS 1990
Gender	.05	.06	.05	.03
Race	.09[b]	.08	.06	.14[b]
Age	.08[b]	.05	.11[b]	.10
Education	.07[a]	.11[c]	.09[a]	.03
Family income	.08[b]	.05	.07[a]	.09
Marital status	.07[a]	.05	.07[a]	.09
Religious tradition	.07[a]	.06	.07[a]	.12[a]
Form of religious expression	.08[b]	.05	.12[b]	.11[a]
R-square	*.04*	*.03*	*.04*	*.06*

[a] Statistically significant at .05 level
[b] Statistically significant at .01 level
[c] Statistically significant at .001 level

In three of the surveys (1987, 1998, and 2004), the only variable to achieve statistical significance was form of religious expression; the other variables attaining statistical significance did so at a maximum in only two of the four surveys analyzed. Moreover, the *beta* coefficient for the form of religious expression ranked first in magnitude in 1998 and 2004, indicating that it was the most important factor shaping such responses. Thus, of all the variables examined in table 6.11, it would appear that form of religious expression is the one most significantly related to work ethic.

Conclusion

Conceptualizing and measuring civic virtue, and then determining how religion may or may not foster it, is a difficult task. The serious debate about religion in tolerance studies illustrates the point. While religious persons appear to have less social tolerance than nonreligious persons, we have shown that this finding is quite dependent upon how religion and tolerance are being measured. It may be that more careful measures of political tolerance will change conventional wisdom regarding the relationship between religion and this civic virtue. Survey questions can be more thoroughly scrutinized to consider carefully what type of tolerance they are testing, and whether they are testing indifference, prejudice, or some other disposition distinct from tolerance. Asking a wider range of questions about a broader scope of activities seems a better approach to create adequate scales or indexes measuring political tolerance and other tolerances that, although relevant to politics, are clearly distinct.

Findings on social trust, "civic morality," external efficacy, and the work ethic are more straightforward, and the fourfold typology provides additional insight. At the most general level, public and integrated religionists are usually more trusting of both civic/political institutions and others than persons in the diminished or privatized category. Publicly religious people are especially carriers of social trust and are as trusting as (or more trusting) than integrated persons; privately religious people are generally the least trusting category in our fourfold typology. Those in the privatized and diminished categories also exhibit significantly lower confidence and trust in political institutions (measured as external efficacy) than their integrated counterparts. We find similar patterns with respect to efficacy, civic morality, and work ethic.

One cannot conclude from our analysis that civil society, and especially religion as a part of civil society, is entirely responsible for the development of civic virtue. As we suggested, scholars express serious disagreements about the extent of civil society's role in generating efficacy, trust, and tolerance; it is certainly plausible to assume that other factors, including institutional actors such as the state, also play a role as incubators of civic virtue. But the evidence marshaled above makes a strong case that religion—and civil society generally—matters in generating civic virtue, and does so in subtle ways.

Notes

1. Civic virtue is a subset of virtue more generally, which Dagger suggests "refers to the disposition to act in accordance with the standards and expectations that define the role or roles a person performs" (Dagger 1997, 14).

2. Civic virtue is likely to be reciprocally related to the various behaviors we examined in earlier chapters. For example, it is true that civic virtue might serve as a precondition of philanthropic giving, but it may also be true that civic virtue is reinforced, strengthened, or magnified through such giving. The same may be true with regard to group mobilization and the acquisition of civic skills.

3. For a general discussion of these thinkers, see DeLue (2002, chapter 5).

4. Confidence in public institutions was composed of responses given to the following institutions: Congress, the Supreme Court, the executive branch of the federal government, and the military.

5. Scholars conventionally distinguish between internal and external political efficacy. Internal political efficacy taps feelings of personal political effectiveness and competence, whereas external efficacy refers to the belief that political leaders and the structures of government are unresponsive to attempts to shape their endeavors and legislative outcomes. See, for example, Abramson (1983, 141–45).

6. Four items were used to measure external political efficacy in each of the studies analyzed. In the National Election Studies of 1996, 2000, and 2004, they were (a) People like me don't have any say about what the government does, (b) Public officials don't care much what people like me think, (c) How much of the time do you feel that having elections makes the government pay attention to what the people think? and (d) Over the years, how much attention do you feel the government pays to what people think when it decides what to do? In the General Social Surveys, the four items were (a) People like me don't have a say about what the government does, (b) The government doesn't care what people like me think, (c) How likely is it that Congress would give serious attention to your demands? and (d) Most politicians are in politics only for what they can get out of it personally.

7. In fact, while the employed composite measure of external political efficacy is correlated with both measures of social trust and political trust within each of the surveys analyzed in which separate measures of social and political trust are available, in each survey analyzed (the National Election Studies of 1996, 2000, and 2004 and the General Social Survey of 1996), the measure of political trust was more highly correlated with external political efficacy than was the measure of social trust.

8. Prejudice is an adverse opinion held by one person against another person or group of persons who are, or are perceived to be, different in some way. Prejudice is usually irrational, unexamined opposition. Nevertheless, despite prejudicial views that the holders of an "other" view are stupid fools, that one does not want to live next to them, and that one does not want to interact with them,

one may still hold that these "fools" should be allowed to express their opinions in society.

9. Likewise, it might be noted that restricting political expression in the immediate moment, which might seem intolerant, may serve to preserve political tolerance in the longer term. In short, one might prudently choose not to allow groups that would suppress all dissent by the most ruthless methods imaginable if they controlled political power. One might also not tolerate persons who do not allow disagreement about political issues or systems. Intolerance in these instances might advance the more lasting goal of greater tolerance within civic and political institutions.

10. Part of this lack of willingness to provide members of such groups permission to teach is likely tied to the question's failure to identify which educational levels the members would be teaching. It would make a difference if the question were posed in terms of teaching advanced high school or college, or in terms of teaching primary school. Most people view young children as highly vulnerable, and if the respondent answered the question within that framework of reference, the answer would likely be much more restrictive than within the framework of teaching young adults.

11. Perhaps a related but somewhat different example will illustrate these differential assessments. In questions asked periodically about whether one would wish to have people from other social groups living next door as neighbors, respondents who objected to living next door to an African American would likely be viewed as a racist, but no such social stigma would likely be imposed on respondents who answered that they would object to living next door to a religious fundamentalist.

7

❖

Religion, Civic Participation,
and Political Participation

This volume has examined the relationship between religion and civic
responsibility, focusing on religion's role in fostering various behaviors, such as associational involvement, volunteering, and charitable contributions, as well as religion's role in enhancing civic capacities and
cultivating civic virtues. The relationship is complex, but the general patterns found across surveys and over time warrant an empirical conclusion.
Our conclusion is this: Religion, overall, helps to generate and maintain
the behaviors, capacities, and dispositions that we identify as component
parts of civic responsibility. While we acknowledge that religion can foster
conflict and dissension, we nevertheless suggest, on the basis of our findings, that there are good reasons to see the practice of religion largely as a
benefit to democratic citizenship and civic life, regardless of an individual's
specific religious tradition.

Our analysis has been rooted in a distinction between what is political
and what is civic, with our focus more on the latter than the former. Therefore, in the first part of this concluding chapter, we explore the linkages
between the two forms of engagement. Does religion serve to shape civic
participation in ways that are different from religion's effects on political
participation? Or is civic participation the primary means by which religionists are drawn into the political arena? The second part of the chapter provides our concluding reflections on the role of religion in fostering
civic responsibility.

The Changing Nature of American Public Life

We noted in our introduction that social scientists and public intellectuals often equate civic life with political activity. Just as it is important to recognize that participation in religious organizations does not encompass all of religious life, so too it is important to recognize that public life is not limited to political engagement. After all, citizens need not address collective problems through governmental institutions. Consequently, we differentiated between civic and political activity, noting that whereas politics seeks to influence "the selection of governmental personnel and/or the actions they take," civic life reflects "publicly spirited collective action" that is not directly guided "by some desire to shape public policy" (Campbell 2004, 7).

In recent years, there has been a growing discussion among political scientists about the relationship between civic and political life. While some argue that civic engagement is essentially apolitical and distinctive in nature (e.g., Theiss-Morse and Hibbing 2005), others argue that civic engagement and political participation are related, as "a vibrant politics depends on a vibrant civil society" (Macedo et al. 2005, 6–7; see also Zukin et al. 2006). While this debate is ongoing (and often turns on how one understands the term "political"), it appears that social scientists are "increasingly accepting the notion that civic behavior is politically relevant" (Jenkins et al. 2003, 3).[1]

Historically, one important characteristic of American public life has been the relatively high level of civic engagement displayed by the American people. Today there is growing concern over what appears to be an erosion in that engagement. Evidence documenting this decline comes from a number of different vantage points. Perhaps the most prominent and thoroughly documented evidence is the recent decline in most levels of political participation. As noted in the introduction, there has been a substantial decrease in reported political activity over the past several decades,[2] including working for a political party or political candidate and attending political rallies, speeches, or meetings that address public concerns, or working for a political party or election campaign (Putnam 2000, 45). There has also been a slow erosion of voter-turnout rates in American presidential elections, with turnout dropping over the past four decades from approximately 60 percent to 50 percent.

But this decline in public engagement" is not limited to the political sphere; it also appears to have extended to civic life. The records of many long-standing, diverse, voluntary organizations reveal that their levels of membership have declined over the past three decades (Putnam 2000, chapter 3; see also Skocpol 2003). The proportion of the American public who report having served on a committee of a local organization or served as an officer of a club or organization has also declined substantially (Putnam 2000, 45). And Americans appear to be spending less time socializing and visiting with others as well (Putnam 2000, chapter 6).

Though some scholars dispute the contention that America is witnessing an overall decline in civic engagement (e.g., Ladd 1996; Skocpol and Fiorina 1999; Becker and Dhingra 2001),[3] it would seem that Americans are engaging in less face-to-face interaction with others outside their family than they did several decades ago. This decline in social interaction among individuals and within families and voluntary associations raises concerns that America's "social capital" is in decline (Putnam 1995a; Putnam 2000), as any diminution in social ties is likely to lead to a decline in the norms and networks that enable civic engagement. Meanwhile, few if any countervailing data have been generated to demonstrate that political participation has not declined over the past several decades.[4] As a result, "a consistent theme of social and political analysis over the past four decades has been the gradual disengagement of the American citizenry from public life, and especially from traditional political participation" (Zukin et al. 2006, 3).[5]

This decades-long decline in participation in public life, whether civic or political, has prompted considerable discussion about the causes of the decline and its possible remedies. A variety of contributing factors have been identified, both social and political. Some analysts have pointed to increased hours spent watching television and commuting between home and work as a factor depriving individuals of the time they are able to commit to public life (e.g., Putnam 1995b and 2000), others have pointed to the passing of "the long civic generation" (e.g., Goss 1999; Putnam 2000, chapter 14), and still others have suggested that the problem resides more fully in the structures of our political institutions (e.g., Berman 1997; Wuthnow 2003) or the increasing professionalization of leadership in citizens groups (Skocpol 2003).

Another key factor may be related to American individualism, that is, the anti-institutionalism that has always been a part of American public life. As noted earlier, Elshtain (2002, 24) has suggested that religious and political participation are related in that "contemporary distrust of organized politics and organized religion goes hand in hand." Both organized religion and organized politics are public expressions, involving groups of people engaged in a shared enterprise, operating under particular rules, and expressing particular convictions. Accordingly, Elshtain contends, religious believers who devalue religious organizations—especially those who are "spiritual, but not religious"—may also express diminished enthusiasm for organizational endeavors within the civic and political spheres of life.

In the previous chapters, we have shown that privatized religion leads to lower levels of various civic endeavors. What is unclear is whether forms of religious expression significantly shape civic engagement as a whole, or whether they serve to shape only certain specific components of such engagement. Likewise, given the distinction between civic and political participation, it is unclear whether the way in which religion influences civic engagement is similar to the way in which religion may affect political participation.

In the next section we take a more encompassing view of civic participation. The fundamental questions we seek to address are whether the ways in which people are religious are related to the ways in which they engage more broadly in public life, and if so, whether such differences in forms of religious expression are similarly related to civic and political activity.

Civic Participation and Political Participation

To address these questions, we examined those data files that contain variables related to both civic and political participation, along with the requisite questions about the religion of the respondents. In addition, questions related to civic participation had to be asked of respondents generally and not only of those who reported membership in voluntary associations. Toward that end, we utilized three national surveys that contain the required component measures: the National Election Study of 1996, the Saguaro survey of 2000, and the National Election Study of 2004.[6]

Each study contains four questions that assess civic participation and four questions that tap political participation. Fortunately, the four component questions are relatively similar for each composite variable. With regard to civic participation, each of the three studies contains a question tapping whether a respondent was a member of a voluntary association, whether the respondent had volunteered in the past year, and whether the respondent had made a charitable contribution in the past year. The fourth component measure of civic participation is somewhat different across the three studies.[7]

Each study also has four questions that can be used to assess differences in levels of political participation. The items used in the 1996 and 2004 National Election Studies tap the same specific types of political activity,[8] while only some of the items used in the Saguaro 2000 national random survey are similar to the activities found in the National Election Studies.[9]

Relative Frequency

Civic and political participation represent different forms of engagement in public life. Given that voting in the last presidential election is a common measure of political participation, one might anticipate that a significant proportion of the American people would exhibit some level of participation in political life. Participation in major elections generally is viewed as a cultural norm, since most Americans hold that citizens should vote when given the opportunity to cast their ballots on important matters. However, political involvement at the mass level tends to be episodic and geared toward the election cycle, and Americans historically have also exhibited what some have labeled an "anti-politics" bias (Rossiter 1960; Dionne 1991). Consequently one could also reasonably anticipate that relatively few Americans engage in political activity beyond the common act of voting in presidential elections.

While cultural norms related to civic participation are more nebulous, America has been viewed as "a nation of joiners" (Tocqueville 1969; Schlesinger 1944), and much of civic life, in terms of both demands and outcomes, exhibits more immediate and direct effects than does political life. One might therefore anticipate that Americans are more likely to engage in civic than in political activity.

Table 7.1 examines the frequency distribution of related levels of civic and political participation across the three studies in which multiple measures of both variables are available. Since voting in the last presidential election was utilized as component measure of political participation, most respondents reported at least some level of political activity. Nevertheless, both anticipated patterns are evident. First, in all three studies, more Americans reported engaging in some form of civic participation than in some form of political participation. Second, a far higher percentage of Americans reported engaging in three or more acts of civic engagement than in three or more acts of political engagement.

Nature of the Relationship

Civic and political participation are analytically distinct, but one might anticipate that they would be empirically related. What is unclear is the extent to which the two are related, and whether religious factors are similarly related to each type of participation.

Table 7.2 begins to address this issue by examining the relationship between civic and political participation across the three national surveys. As can be seen from the analysis, the two variables are fairly strongly correlated (with correlations falling between .33 and .41). Probably the clearest evidence of a link between the two types of activities emerges among those who did not report any civic participation. In both the 1996 National Election Study and the 2000 Saguaro survey, the vast majority of those who reported no civic activity also reported no political activity. In other words, lack of civic engagement is strongly associated with lack of political engagement. Similarly, the majority of those who exhibit some level of civic engagement also exhibit some level of political participation, and those who

Table 7.1 Distribution of Civic Participation and Political Participation (percent)

Study	Civic participation	Political participation
NES, 1996		
No acts	8	21
One act	15	63
Two acts	33	11
Three or four acts	44	4
Total	101	99
(*n*)	(1521)	(1521)
Saguaro, 2000		
No acts	8	23
One act	17	39
Two acts	24	26
Three or four acts	52	12
Total	101	100
(*n*)	(3003)	(3003)
NES, 2004		
No acts	14	20
One act	28	54
Two acts	26	19
Three or four acts	32	7
Total	100	100
(*n*)	(1066)	(1066)

Component measures of civic participation

NES 1996: (a) membership in some voluntary association, (b) volunteered past year, and (d) worked on a committee to address some community problem

Saguaro: (a) membership in some voluntary association, (b) volunteered within the past year, (c) made a charitable contribution in the past year, and (d) worked on a project related to some community problem

NES 2004: (a) membership in some voluntary association, (b) volunteered within the past year, (c) made a charitable contribution in the past year, and (d) attended a community meeting about some issue

Component measures of political participation

NES 1996: (a) voted in 1996, (b) wore a campaign button or had a yard sign, (c) attended a political meeting of some kind, and (d) contributed to a political candidate or party

Saguaro: (a) voted in 1996, (b) had a yard sign, (c) attended a political rally, and (d) marched in a political demonstration

NES 2004: (a) voted in 2004, (b) wore a campaign button or had a yard sign, (c) worked for a political candidate or party, and (d) contributed money to either a political candidate or party

Table 7.2 Relationship between Civic Participation
and Political Participation (percent)

Index of Political	Index of Civic Participation			
Participation	0	1	2	3+
NES, 1996				
0	62	39	21	10
1	36	55	68	67
2	3	6	9	15
3+	0	0	2	8
Total	101	100	100	100
(*n*)	(117)	(226)	(504)	(666)
			$r = .35^a$	
Saguaro, 2000				
0	61	36	27	11
1	30	45	48	35
2	8	16	20	34
3+	1	3	6	20
Total	100	100	101	100
(*n*)	(213)	(478)	(673)	(1473)
			$r = .41^a$	
NES, 2004				
0	42	27	15	7
1	49	55	56	54
2	8	14	7	14
3+	1	4	7	14
Total	100	100	100	101
(*n*)	(144)	(299)	(276)	(345)
			$r = .33^a$	

[a] Statistically significant at .001 level

tend to be the most engaged civically are also the most likely to be the
most engaged politically.

Nevertheless, while the two kinds of participation are related, they are
also empirically distinct. In fact, some respondents report very high levels
of civic engagement coupled with no political activity, while others report
relatively high levels of political activity coupled with no reported acts of
civic participation, suggesting that some individuals choose to concentrate
their public endeavors primarily within civic life, and others tend to focus
their public endeavors largely within political life.

Modes of Public Involvement

Naturally, individuals participate in public life at varying levels. Recognizing this, several scholars (Zukin et al. 2006) have created a four-fold typology of public engagement based on differences in levels of engagement in civic and political life. In this classification scheme, electoral specialists focus the bulk of their attention on electoral politics, choosing to engage more heavily in electoral than civic endeavors. Civic specialists focus their attention on civic life, engaging more heavily in civic than political activities. Dual activists are those who are highly engaged in both civic and political activities, while the relatively disengaged report little activity in either domain.

For purposes of the analysis presented here, electoral specialists are classified as those who reported at least two or more political acts but less than two civic acts in the past year.[10] The converse is true for civic specialists; they engaged in two or more civic, but fewer than two political, acts. Dual activists are those who reported two or more acts of civic engagement as well as two or more acts of political participation, while the relatively disengaged are those who indicated that they had participated in fewer than two civic as well as fewer than two political activities over the past year.

Table 7.3 examines the distribution of these different forms of engagement in public life across the three surveys. It should be noted that one should not compare the percentage level associated with each pattern over time because the component measures are not identical across the three

Table 7.3 Distribution of the Nature of Engagement in Public Life (percent)

Nature of Engagement in Public Life	NES 1996	Saguaro 2000	NES 2004
Disengaged	22	20	35
Electoral specialist	1	4	6
Civic specialist	64	42	38
Dual activist	14	34	20
Total	101	100	100
(n)	(1513)	(2837)	(1064)

studies. Rather, the data should be examined in terms of general patterns of public engagement and whether these general patterns hold over time.

This classification scheme reveals that most Americans are actively engaged in either some civic or political capacity. Indeed, only about one-fifth to one-third of Americans can be classified as being relatively disengaged. A majority of Americans (though a plurality of Americans in 2004) can be classified as civic specialists, while very few Americans can be classified as electoral specialists.[11] Finally, an important segment, somewhere between one-seventh and one-third of the American people, might be viewed as dual activists—highly involved in both civic and political life.

According to this analysis, Americans are far more likely to focus their efforts on civic than on political life. Most Americans are civic activists, and to the extent that people are engaged politically, they tend to couple their political activism with civic activism, as they are far more likely to indicate that they are dual activists than electoral specialists.

Religion and Public Engagement

To what extent, then, is religion related to differences in public engagement? Are those who exhibit more diminished and privatized forms of religious expression less likely to engage in civic and political life than those who exhibit more public and integrated forms of religious expression? Are those who are relatively religious more likely to specialize in civic than in political life, and do such levels of engagement in civic and political life vary according to their forms of religious expression? These questions are addressed in table 7.4.

Our analysis reveals a relatively strong relationship between one's form of religious expression and the nature of one's engagement in public life. First, those who exhibit a highly privatized form of religious expression were the most likely to be classified as relatively disengaged from both civic and political life. In fact, nearly a majority of the privatized exhibited a pattern of relative disengagement from public life in 2004, despite the fact that there was a significant upturn in voting turnout that year. A majority of privatized religionists were civic specialists in 1996, a plurality were so in 2000, and a little more than one-third were civic activists in 2004.

Table 7.4 Nature of Public Engagement by Form of Religious Expression (percent)

Nature of Public Engagement	Diminished	Privatized	Public	Integrated
National Election Study, 1996				
Disengaged	35	35	14	8
Electoral Specialist	2	1	1	*
Civic Specialist	53	54	75	72
Dual Activist	10	10	10	19
Total	100	100	100	99
			eta = .31[a]	
Saguaro, 2000				
Disengaged	25	36	17	14
Electoral Specialist	4	6	4	3
Civic Specialist	37	40	45	45
Dual Activist	33	19	35	39
Total	99	101	101	101
			eta = .20[a]	
National Election Study, 2004				
Disengaged	43	46	34	26
Electoral Specialist	8	4	6	5
Civic Specialist	32	34	40	44
Dual Activist	17	16	21	24
Total	100	100	101	99
			eta = .18[a]	

* Less than 1 percent

[a] Statistically significant at .001 level

However, those who exhibit high levels of activism in both civic and public life are the least likely to be found within the ranks of those with a privatized religious form of expression. Depending on the survey examined, somewhere between one-tenth and one-fifth of the ranks of the privatized can be classified as dual activists.

Those who exhibit a diminished form of religious expression rival the privatized in their disengagement, but overall a smaller percentage of the relatively disengaged were found among those with a diminished form of religious expression than among those with a privatized form. Of the four forms of religious expression, those with a diminished form were consistently the least likely to be civic specialists.

Those with a public form of religious expression tend to be more engaged in public life than either those with a diminished or a privatized form, but less likely to be engaged than those with an integrated form. Still, those with a public form of religious expression tend to be relatively active. Anywhere from six out of seven (86 percent in 1996) to two out of three (66 percent in 2004) were active in public life in some capacity. The bulk of those who exhibit a public form of religious expression were civic activists, and substantial numbers tended to be dual activists as well.

Those with an integrated form of religious expression are the most likely to participate in public life. As was true among those exhibiting other forms of religious expression, the bulk of integrated religionists were most likely to report that they were civic activists, but of the four categories examined, those with an integrated form of religious expression were the most likely to be dual activists. This pattern holds true across the three surveys examined.

Several important conclusions can be drawn. First, the ways in which people express their religiosity are related to different patterns of civic and political engagement. Those for whom religious faith is highly privatized are the least likely to exhibit any form of activity in public life, whereas those who are inclined to express their religious faith through attendance at public worship services are the most likely to report engagement in both civic and political life.

Therefore, in trying to determine what it may be about religion that serves to shape civic and political engagement, an important starting point is whether religionists participate in public worship activities on a regular basis, because public activity in one sphere is linked to the other. Religious beliefs may also matter, particularly theological concepts that determine the role religion should play in engaging the broader culture. However, such questions are rarely asked in most surveys and consequently are not examined here. In any case, such religious beliefs are more likely to refine than to alter the fundamental relationships revealed here between forms of religiosity and public engagement.

Second, while attendance at religious services is a stronger predictor of civic engagement than is private devotionalism, the prayer variable nevertheless provides important information about the respondent. Devotional life, absent public worship, is associated with withdrawal from public life, whereas frequency of prayer is a *stimulus* for public engagement among those who regularly participate in public worship. Why might that be the case? While some scholars (e.g., Lam 2002) have suggested that devotional activities such as prayer serve to reinforce religious values that promote associational activity, most of the limited research done on the relationship between private prayer and public life has generally pointed to the social-psychological effects of prayer on civic and political engagement.[12] For example, Loveland and his colleagues (2005, 13) conclude that "prayer fosters a cognitive connection to the needs of others," which then "manifests itself in the civic involvement choices of the prayerful." As a result, it is those respondents whose religious life is "integrated" (exhibiting high levels of public worship attendance and high levels of private devotional life) who are the most civically and politically engaged. These results are consistent with the contentions of Wilson and Janoski (1995) that both the depth and type of religiosity are tied, in varying degrees, to civic engagement (as analyzed through volunteer activity in their particular study).

The Unique Contribution of Religion

Once again, the specific role religion plays in public life can be queried. The question here is whether religion continues to be significantly related to civic and political participation once controls have been introduced for others variables. In other words, do respondents' religious affiliations and forms of expression affect the likelihood that they will engage in either civic or political participation beyond what one might expect once factors related to engagement in public life are taken into account?

Table 7.5 addresses this issue, examining civic and political participation separately as dependent variables while assessing the relative strength of the relationship between various independent variables on each form of participation once the effects of the other independent variables have been taken into account. This analysis is once again conducted by means of multiple classification analysis, enabling the use of categorical variables within the context of a multivariate analysis.[13] The relative effects of eight variables on civic and political participation are examined (gender, race, age, education, family income, marital status, religious tradition affiliation,

Table 7.5 Relative Importance of Religion in Fostering Civic and Political Participation: A Multiple Classification Analysis

	NES 1996	Saguaro 2000	NES 2004
Civic Participation			
Gender	.01	.01	.06
Race	.07	.07	.07
Age	.18[c]	.02	.08[a]
Education	.24[c]	.23[c]	.26[c]
Family income	.17[c]	.18[c]	.19[c]
Marital status	.06	.03	.06
Religious tradition	.09	.11[b]	.12[b]
Form of religious expression	.31[c]	.18[c]	.20[c]
R-square	*.31*	*.20*	*.25*
Political Participation			
Gender	.06	.01	.00
Race	.08	.09	.12[c]
Age	.11[b]	.17[c]	.15[c]
Education	.25[c]	.27[v]	.18[c]
Family income	.08	.13[c]	.14[c]
Marital status	.13[c]	.05	.05
Religious tradition	.10[b]	.06	.09[b]
Form of religious expression	.16[c]	.07	.10[b]
R-square	*.17*	*.20*	*.12*

[a] Statistically significant at .05 level
[b] Statistically significant at .01 level
[c] Statistically significant at .001 level

and form of religious expression), as previous research revealed that these variables are related to both civic and political participation (e.g., Conway 1991; Burns, Schlozman, and Verba 2001).

As shown in table 7.5, a number of variables help to explain the likelihood of participation in public life. Most variables that are significantly related to civic participation are also significantly related to political participation. Generally speaking, education, form of religious expression, and family income are the primary variables that shape engagement in public life, as each variable attains statistical significance at the .001 level across all three surveys even when controlling for the effects of all other variables. Form of religious expression exhibits the largest *beta* (.31) in the 1996 National Election Survey but ranks behind education in the magnitude of its *beta* coefficient in the 2000 Saguaro survey and the 2004 National Election Study. In these latter two surveys, form of religious expression and family income exhibit almost identical *beta* coefficients, with each essentially tied as second in relative importance in shaping civic participation.

Of the remaining variables, age and religious tradition rank as modestly important in shaping civic engagement. Each variable attains statistical significance in two of the three surveys, though not consistently at the .001 level of significance. None of the remaining variables—gender, race, and marital status—attain statistical significance in any of the three surveys.

When the focus shifts to political participation, one's form of religious expression continues to remain a relatively significant shaping factor, but its importance does not match that of education, age, or even level of family income. The resultant *beta* coefficients for the level of education variable are statistically significant, and rank highest in relative magnitude, across all three surveys. Age, too, shapes political participation, as in all three surveys it proves to be statistically significant, ranking second in relative importance in two of the three studies. Similarly, family income is statistically significant in two of the three surveys analyzed, ranking third in relative importance in both the 2000 Saguaro and the 2004 NES surveys. While the *beta* coefficient for form of religious expression ranked second in terms of its magnitude in the 1996 National Election Study, its *beta* ranked no higher than fifth in the remaining two studies (though in the 2004 NES its *beta* was still statistically significant). Of the remaining variables, religious tradition affiliation attains statistical significance in two of the three surveys (but only at the .01 level), while marital status and race each attain statistical significance in one of the three surveys.

Overall, therefore, the data presented in table 7.5 demonstrate that the relationship between religion and participation in public life is not spurious, and one's form of religious expression appears to be a stronger factor in shaping civic than in shaping political participation. Even in terms of political participation, though, form of religious expression remains an important explanatory factor, attaining statistical significance in two of the three surveys analyzed.

Because the way in which one expresses one's religiosity is so strongly related to civic participation, and because civic participation is related to political participation, the question arises whether form of religious expression continues to shape political participation after taking into account the effects of civic participation on political participation. As a result, we conducted one final MCA, similar to the one summarized in table 7.5, but with the addition of civic participation as an independent variable shaping political participation. The results of this analysis are presented in table 7.6.

Table 7.6 Relative Importance of Religion in Fostering Political Participation: A Multiple Classification Analysis

	NES 1996	Saguaro 2000	NES 2004
Political participation			
Civic participation	.17[c]	.25[c]	.27[c]
Gender	.06	.01	.02
Race	.06	.06	.10[b]
Age	.09[b]	.17[c]	.13[c]
Education	.20[c]	.21[c]	.12[b]
Family income	.06	.09[b]	.09[b]
Marital status	.13[c]	.05	.04
Religious tradition	.08[a]	.06	.08[a]
Form of religious expression	.12[c]	.02	.07[a]
R-square	*.16*	*.23*	*.17*

[a] Statistically significant at .05 level
[b] Statistically significant at .01 level
[c] Statistically significant at .001 level

Not surprisingly, the variable with the strongest effect on political participation across the three studies is civic participation, with the magnitude of its *beta* coefficient far exceeding all others in every study. However, even with the addition of the civic participation variable, one's form of religious expression continues to be statistically significant, shaping political participation in the 1996 National Election Study and narrowly missing attaining statistical significance at the .001 level in the 2004 National Election Study. Even though form of religious expression is more strongly related to civic participation than to political participation, and even taking into account the effects of civic participation and other independent variables on political participation, the effects of religion on political participation continue to remain fairly substantial (at least in two of the three surveys examined).

Thus, in addition to its effects on membership in voluntary associations, volunteer activity, charitable donations, the formation of civic capacities, and the fostering of civic virtues, religion serves to shape engagement in political life. When measured in terms of form of religious expression, religion has a stronger effect on civic participation than on political participation, but religion's effects on political participation are not negligible.

Religion and Public Life

In the end, the role of religion in democracy remains a controversial and contested matter. Whether on the campaign trail or in the courtroom, whether on television talk shows or in the halls of Congress, religion remains at the center of our debates about the health of the body politic. Some suggest that religious believers pose a danger to public purposes because they seek to impose a single conception of the good on a pluralistic society; others claim that if Americans truly treasure their pluralism religion ought to be a part of public conversation—and that there is ample historical and social scientific evidence that religion can enrich that conversation. The issues that define the debate are profoundly real, and the emotions generated are frequently intense.

Over the past several decades, many Americans have mistakenly come to believe that the *institutional* separation of church and state requires that religion be purely a private and individual matter (Ammerman 2005, 258).[13] The framers of the Constitution feared all forms of concentrated power, and this "impulse to restrain the public presence of religion" is a reflection of legitimate constitutional concerns about the possibility of a state-imposed or de facto form of religious authority. The U.S. Constitution clearly prohibits any state official or agency from compelling or promoting particular religious beliefs or practices. On the other hand, the U.S. Constitution also wisely protects the "free exercise" of any religious impulses within the confines of "acceptable" law and practice. To be sure, the boundary lines for acceptability are difficult to draw (see, e.g., the exchange between Hamilton 2005 and Laycock 2007), but even those commentators who believe the framers bequeathed a "godless" Constitution (Kramnick and Moore 2005) admit the possibility of a "religiously informed politics." Religious groups may enter the public domain, though they should do so with humility, recognizing that "no single group is in charge" and that "no group can accomplish its goals alone" (Ammerman 2005, 259).

The public role of religion, however, is not confined to electoral and interest-group politics or policymaking and implementation. As we have explored in this book, religion generally plays a much deeper role in civic than in political life. Religion serves public, and not just political, purposes in several different ways. First, it contributes to the foundations of democratic society. One might even argue that the absence of religious faith from public life is more dangerous than an excess of religious passion. Religion in America, particularly in its institutional manifestations, is an important "vehicle for the kind of participation essential to the definition of public life" (Cochran 1990, 55). While despotic or totalitarian governments rule by coercion, a free republic is dependent on mass moral restraint. Both liberal and republican strains of democratic thought value internalized order or self-rule over external compulsion. As we found in chapter 6, the combination of public and private religiosity fosters a range of complex dispositions—virtues such as law-abidingness, support for government, tolerance, and a work ethic, among others—that are preconditions of self-rule.

Of course, to exercise self-rule (or self-restraint) often means reining in the pursuit of self-interest. Tocqueville, for example, identified isolated individualism—the single-minded advancement of one's own interests—as a constant threat of democratic egalitarianism. But Tocqueville noted a number of institutions in American life that served to dampen the effects of excessive individualism, that pulled citizens out of their isolated selves and drew them to interact with others, thereby enabling them to see others' interests in light of their own (self-interest "properly understood"). Religious institutions, along with the family, were chief among the institutions of civil society that produced citizens who *chose* to serve the interests of both themselves and others simultaneously, and without the coercive prodding of government.

Contemporary scholars, too, have maintained that neither government coercion nor rational self-interest forms a sufficient basis for social order through self-rule, and some point to religion as a key part of that sufficient basis. For example, sociologist Robert Bellah (1975, ix) has contended that:

> Any coherent and viable society rests on a common set of moral understandings about good and bad, right and wrong, in the realm of individual and social action. It is almost as widely held that these common moral understandings must also rest in turn upon a common set of religious understandings that provide a picture of the universe in terms of which the moral understandings make sense. Such moral and religious understandings produce a basic cultural legitimation for a society which is viewed as at least approximately in accord with them, and a standard of judgment for the criticism of society that is seen as deviating too far from them.

From this perspective, religious life located within civil society both enables and legitimates public moral choices and fosters the basic forms of civility and social restraint that are necessary to collective deliberation in a democracy.

The second way in which religion contributes to public life is through the participatory activities of religion itself. Religion is partly a personal experience that defines an individual's relationship with the sacred; in that sense it is a relatively private matter. But religion is also "public" in myriad ways. Corporate worship is a public occasion, and interaction with other believers occurs in a public space. Participation in these public rituals and spaces shapes the collective experience of a group of believers. Further, relatively well-institutionalized religions provide many opportunities for participation in governance roles, leading worship, education, and personnel committees, or organizing liturgies, celebrations, and institution-sponsored community service or civic projects. Through these public endeavors, members learn to work with others, take responsibility, make collective decisions, compromise and negotiate, express their views, and acknowledge the contrasting views of others. These are elemental civic and political skills in a democracy. In fact, it is reasonable to suggest that churches, which (as noted in chapter 3) are the most prevalent form of voluntary association in the United States, are among the most important sources of those civic skills that help democracy thrive (as established in chapter 5).

The upshot is that religion's private and public aspects serve to "reinforce one another and correct each other's extreme tendencies" (Cochran 1990, 57). The public role that religion plays can be particularly important when the state, the dominant public institution, becomes simply a "large, impersonal, distant provider of goods and services." If public life is to be renewed under such circumstances, and a basis for communal life is to be established, then they will likely be "found outside those great impersonal abstractions of society and state" (Bernstein 1986, 47). Religion provides at least one basis for a renewed public life because it can be a space in which opportunity and responsibility for many kinds of public participation are made available (Cochran 1990, chapter 3). Moreover, religion's influence on volunteering and philanthropic giving, as detailed in chapter 4, illustrates its role in shaping public life.

Unfortunately, the growing privatization of religion and of moral convictions, and their attendant irrelevance to public debate, serves to foster a thin consensus in a complex society in which deeper values and traditions, once part of public debate, are being increasingly pushed into the realm of personal life (Walzer 1994). Religious beliefs have come to be treated largely as personal opinions that should be kept to oneself, matters that are inappropriate in public deliberation (Carter 1993; Casanova 1994). The assumption is that public order is best maintained in civil society by encouraging people not to speak explicitly about beliefs that require religious commitment perhaps not shared by others (Audi 1997). Yet by denying the appropriateness of expressing one's basic convictions, this privatization of religious and moral convictions serves, in turn, to reduce the "motivation for banding together, for organizing around deeply held values, and attempting to bring these commitments to bear on public issues" (Wuthnow 1999b, 22).

Finally, religion contributes to public life in a third way by providing another voice (or voices) in our pluralistic culture. Many religious traditions call adherents to engage in "prophetic politics"—to speak out against evil in all its forms, including its political forms, and to live out models of social life that better reflect sacred purposes (e.g., the Christian notion of "the kingdom of God"). In its public role, religion may serve as one of the voices to which political power should be responsive in the formulation of public policy. A democratic polity cannot restrict and, in fact, should welcome moral insights into issues involving important ethical questions. Such moral perspectives act as counterweights to crudely pragmatic and amoral thinking. By reminding the state of its ethical obligations, religion can pay an important public role in democratic life.

Religion can also help protect democratic society from movement toward greater statism and potential totalitarianism. Democratic governments are based on the principle of limited government, and religion serves as a major bulwark against the authority of a state attempting to exceed its rightful boundaries. Totalitarian states generally attack institutional or corporate religious expression rather than individual religious belief because religious institutions express and "promulgate belief in a transcendent reality by which the state can be called to judgment," and in so doing, "such institutions threaten the totalitarian proposition that everything is to be within the state, nothing is to be outside the state" (Neuhaus 1984, 82). By seeking to reduce religion simply to privatized conscience, the totalitarian state attempts to restrict the public square to only two actors—the state and the individual. In this circumstance, "religion as a mediating structure—a community that generates and transmits moral values—is no longer available" (Neuhaus 1984, 82).

From the beginning of American history, the practices of religion and democracy have been intertwined in an uneasy yet mutually beneficial alliance. The promise of the institutional disestablishment of religion was twofold: On the one hand, it ensured that democracy could flourish without the dominance of a single religious power; on the other hand, it made possible that religion *in general* could flourish by forbidding the state to support any specific religion. Still, disestablishment did not separate religion from politics, nor could it. All public policies embody particular normative goals and values; in this sense, all governments and policies "legislate morality." Whether or not they are derived from a particular religious faith, one's values affect the way one views the purposes of government, the policy goals it should pursue, and the kinds of procedures to be employed. It is therefore inevitable that religious values, like all other values, help to shape political life.

Nor does disestablishment require the separation of religion from civic life more generally. Indeed, the analyses in this volume have revealed different ways in which religion shapes our public responsibilities well beyond our politics, as well as beyond our specific religious traditions. While we do not claim that our discussion is definitive—much more can and will be said about the relationship between religious and public life—we hope that our efforts here will stimulate further inquiry into the public role of religion in the United States and beyond.

Notes

1. Putnam examined twelve different acts of political and community participation for the years 1973–74 and 1993–94, and over the course of this twenty-year period, he found a drop of 25 percent in those who reported participating in at least one of these twelve activities (Putnam 2000, 45).

2. Turnout in presidential elections declined by nearly a quarter between 1960 (62.8 percent) and 1996 (48.9 percent), with turnout in off-year and local elections declining by approximately the same proportion (Putnam 2000, 32). Turnout in the 2000 presidential election was roughly similar to that of the 1996 election. Of course, the exception to this general pattern was the upswing in voter turnout in the 2004 presidential election, when the turnout rate was once again at the 60 percent mark. But see MacDonald and Popkin 2001.

3. Again, perhaps the strongest piece of counterevidence is the strong upturn in voter turnout in the 2004 presidential election.

4. One other counterargument to the thesis of decline is the argument that what has changed is not so much the total level of activity as the mix of particular activities in which they are publicly engaged. Engagement in public life may have not so much declined as "spread to a wider variety of channels," with the mix of public activities in which citizens are participating different today than in the past (Zukin et al. 2006, 3) and with the totality of such engagement having become more civic and less political.

5. The General Social Survey of 2004 contains questions tapping civic and political participation. However, one major component measure of civic participation, namely, membership within voluntary associations, was asked of one-half of the respondents, and the other civic participation questions were asked of the other half of the respondents. As a result, we were unable to create a measure of civic participation that is roughly equivalent to the measures of civic engagement utilized in the three studies employed for this analysis.

6. The nature of these specific questions can be found at the bottom of table 7.1.

7. While the focus of the specific activity remained the same, the NES 1996 and 2004 surveys differed in how they posed the question tapping the activities.

8. These differences in the nature of political activities examined can be found at the bottom of table 7.1.

9. The procedure employed in classifying respondents into the various categories of public engagement follows that employed by Zukin and his colleagues (2006). While the component measures employed are for the most part similar, they are not identical. Moreover, while the analysis here employs four component variables for both civic and political participation, the Zukin measure of political engagement employed five.

10. Because Zukin and his colleagues include a fifth component measure for political engagement, it was potentially easier for respondents to report a minimum of two political activities. As a result, their findings report a higher level of electoral specialists than the findings reported here (Zukin et al. 2006, 64).

11. For example, Harris (1999, 82) has argued that prayer may "empower individuals with a sense of competence and resilience, inspiring them to believe in their own ability, with the assistance of an acknowledged sacred force, to influence or affect governmental affairs, thus—in some instances—to act politically." Likewise Poloma and Gallup (1991, 178) have contended that prayer heightens an "awareness that lessens the separation between the private religious side and the public political side of life."

12. For more information on multiple classification analysis, see the discussion related to table 3.7 in chapter 3.

13. Of course, what constitutes acceptable restrictions by law is open to some difference of opinion. Usually these restrictions occur when there are "compelling state interests" related to practices or behavior. The state, for example, may have a compelling state interest to protect the health and life of innocent children from parents who abuse them. It would be reasonable for the state to prohibit any use of child sacrifice within one's religious practice. Other forms of restrictions may be far more controversial and "unacceptable." For example, restricting the freedom of churches to disqualify job candidates based on the applicant's religious characteristics would be far less likely to be an "acceptable" law and practice.

Appendix A: Description of Surveys Employed

American National Election Study (NES)

The American National Election Study is a national random survey conducted by the Institute for Social Research at the University of Michigan with funding from the National Science Foundation. The NES has been fielded biennially since 1948. Every year, the survey includes a range of questions about Americans' political activities and attitudes, with special attention to voting behavior and partisanship.

Arts and Religion Survey, 1999 (A and R)

The Arts and Religion Survey was conducted in 1999 with support from the Pew Charitable Trusts. Administered by the Gallup Organization, the national representative survey (n = 1,530 American adults) gathered extensive data about respondents' views on the relationship between religion and creative arts. Wuthnow (2003) discusses key findings.

Citizen Participation Study, 1990 (CPS)

The American Citizen Participation Study was a national survey conducted in 1990 (n = 2,517 American adults) and funded by the National Science Foundation and several private foundations. Designed to gather information about both political and nonpolitical civic participation in the United States, the survey asked a range of questions about respondents' conventional political behavior (e.g., voting, monetary contributions, campaign volunteering) and participation in voluntary associations. The ACPS also asked a battery of demographic questions, including questions on church activity and religious affiliation. Verba, Schlozman, and Brady (1995) discuss many of ACPS's key findings about the development of civic skills.

Civic Involvement Survey, 1997 (CIS)

The Civic Involvement Survey was conducted in 1997 with support from the Lilly Endowment and Pew Charitable Trusts. Administered by the Gallup organization, the national representative survey (*n* = 1,528 American adults) gathered extensive data about patterns of civic involvement in the United States. The survey also included questions about respondents' religious beliefs and practices. Wuthnow (1998a) discusses key findings.

General Social Survey (GSS)

The General Social Survey is a national random survey conducted by the National Opinion Research Center (NORC) at the University of Chicago with funding from the National Science Foundation. The GSS was first conducted in 1972; since 1994, the NORC has administered the survey biennially. A set of core questions, which are asked in every survey, allows researchers to assess trends in key social indicators over time, including respondents' demographic characteristics and attitudes about institutions and culture. The core questions usually include measures of religious affiliation, belief, and behavior (most notably religious attendance). Every year, the GSS also includes unique modules that focus on particular social phenomena or attitudes.

Giving and Volunteering, 1996 (GVS)

The Giving and Volunteering Survey was conducted biennially from 1990 to 2001 for Independent Sector, a coalition of charitable and other nonprofit organizations. The survey seeks to gather comprehensive information about the giving practices of the American people, including financial contributions to charities and volunteering habits (and the interrelations between the two). In 1996, the Gallup Organization administered the survey to a representative sample of 2,719 American adults.

God and Society in North America, 1996 (G and S)

The God and Society in North America Survey was a cross-national survey of religion and civic/political engagement in the United States and Canada. The Angus Reid Group administered the survey by telephone to a representative sample of 3,000 Canadian and 3,023 American adults. The Pew Charitable Trusts funded the survey.

International Social Survey Program: Religion II, 1998

The International Social Survey Program is on ongoing program of cross-national collaboration that develops topical modules as supplements to regular national surveys. In 1998, the module addressed religion. The number of respondents surveyed varied by country.

Religion and Politics Survey, 2000

The Religion and Politics survey was conducted by Princeton University's Survey Research Center in 2000 with support from the Pew Charitable Trusts. The survey gathered information on religious and political views of a random national sample of 5,603 American adults. The survey was part of a larger project assessing the role of mainline Protestantism in public life. Wuthnow and Evans (2002) discuss some of the key findings.

Religion and Public Life, 2001

The Religion and Public Life Survey was conducted for the Pew Center for People and the Press in 2001. The survey (n = 2,041) focused specifically on the general public's attitudes toward faith-based social service organizations. The Pew Center discussed the key findings in a survey report (Pew Center 2001).

Saguaro Social Capital Benchmark Survey, 2000

The Saguaro Social Capital Benchmark Survey was conducted in 2000 for the Civic Engagement in America Project at Harvard's John F. Kennedy School of Government with major support from the Ford Foundation. The random national survey included 3,003 respondents and focused on the nature and scope of "social capital" in the United States. The role of religion in generating social capital was a key dimension of the survey, which included extensive measurements of religious belief and participation. As a benchmark, the survey is intended as a basis for future comparative analysis about social capital.

Appendix B: Variation in Questions and Question Wording on Membership in Voluntary Associations

	GSS 1987	Verba 1990	G&S 1996	NES 1996	Wuth 1997	Sag 2000	GSS 2004
Fraternal groups	X	X		X	X		X
Civic				X			
Civic or service clubs	X	X			X		X
Social service			X				
Service/charitable groups				X			
Charity or social welfare						X	
Service or fraternal						X	
Veterans' groups	X	X	X	X	X	X	X
Political clubs or organizations	X		X		X	X	X
Political issue organizations				X	X		
Liberal/conservative				X			
Party/candidate				X			
Environmental clubs or organizations			X		X		
Neighborhood associations		X	X			X	
Community				X			

(*continued*)

	GSS 1987	Verba 1990	G&S 1996	NES 1996	Wuth 1997	Sag 2000	GSS 2004
Sports groups or clubs	X				X	X	X
Recreational			X				
Hobby or sports		X		X			
Hobby or garden clubs	X				X	X	X
Youth groups	X	X	X		X	X	X
Children				X			
Senior citizens		X	X			X	
Elderly				X			
Ethnic, racial, or national	X	X			X	X	X
Ethnic				X			
School service groups	X				X		X
School groups such as PTA						X	
School fraternities or sororities	X				X		X
Health, fitness clubs					X		
Health-related			X				
Health services organizations		X					
Self-help						X	
Literary, art, or music		X		X	X	X	
Literary, art, discussion, or study	X						X
Discussion or study					X		
Education, arts, music, or cultural		X	X				
Educational, tutoring, or literacy					X		
Education				X			
Culture				X			
Farm organizations	X				X		X
Professional or academic	X	X			X		X

	GSS 1987	Verba 1990	G&S 1996	NES 1996	Wuth 1997	Sag 2000	GSS 2004
Professional or business			X				
Professional, trade, farm, or business						X	
Business				X			
Church		X		X	X		
Religious or church-related			X				
Church-affiliated groups	X				X		X
Organization affiliated with religion						X	
Other religious				X			
Consumer groups/ buying clubs					X		
Therapeutic or counseling groups			X		X		
Self-help				X			
Women's rights		X	X	X			
Other	X	X		X	X	X	X
Labor unions	X	X	X	X	X	X	X

Appendix C: Question Wording Related to Volunteering by Survey

Survey on Giving and Volunteering Survey, 1996

Q5: Listed on this card are examples of the many different areas in which people do volunteer activity. By volunteer activity I mean not just belonging to a service organization, but actually working in some way to help others for no monetary pay. In which, if any, of the areas listed on this card have you done some volunteer work in the past twelve months:

a. Health organizations
b. Education
c. Religious organizations
d. Human services
e. Environment
f. Public/society benefit
g. Recreation—adults
h. Arts, culture, & humanities
i. Work-related organizations
j. Political organizations/campaigns
k. Youth development
l. Private & community foundations
m. International/foreign
n. Informal—alone
o. Other

God and Society in North America, 1996

Asked only of those respondents who reported that they were a member of or affiliated with the group noted: Do you do any voluntary work of any kind for this group?

a. Professional or job-related groups
b. Social service groups for the elderly, poor, or disabled
c. Religious or church-related groups
d. Environmental groups
e. Youth work (scouts, guides, youth clubs)
f. Community-based or neighborhood associations
g. Health-related groups
h. Recreational groups
i. Senior citizen groups
j. Veterans' groups
k. Women's groups
l. Political groups
m. A small group that meets regularly and provides support or caring for those who participate in it
n. Education, arts, music, or cultural organizations

National Election Study, 1996

V961257: What about you, were you able to devote any time to volunteer work in the last 12 months?

Civic Involvement Survey, 1997

During the past year, have you spent any time volunteering for any of the following:

a. A neighborhood or homeowners' association
b. Distributing food to the needy
c. A shelter for abused women or children
d. A neighborhood crime watch program
e. AIDS-related activity
f. Environmental projects
g. Building houses for the poor
h. A community development corporation
i. A violence prevention effort
j. A political campaign
k. Activities related to schools
l. Community organizing
m. Youth activities
n. Arts or cultural activities
o. Church-related activities
p. Informal volunteering

General Social Survey, 1998

VOLWKPOL: Have you done any voluntary activity in the past 12 months in any of the following areas? Political activities.

VOLWKCHR: Have you done any voluntary activity in the past 12 months in any of the following areas? Charitable activities.

VOLWKREL: Have you done any voluntary activity in the past 12 months in any of the following areas? Religious and church-related activities.

VOLWKOTH: Have you done any voluntary activity in the past 12 months in any of the following areas? Any other kind of voluntary activities.

Arts and Religion Survey, 1999

Q106: Approximately how many hours do you spend volunteering each week?

Q174: Do you, yourself, happen to be involved in any charity or social service activities, such as helping the poor, the sick, or the elderly?

Saguaro Benchmark Survey, 2000

Q58: How many times in the past twelve months have you volunteered?

Q59: I'm going to list some of the types of organizations where people do volunteer work. Just tell me whether you have done any volunteer work for each in the past twelve months:

a. for your place of worship
b. for health care or fighting particular diseases
c. for school or youth programs
d. for any organization to help the poor or elderly
e. for any arts of cultural organizations
f. for any civic group

Religion and Politics Survey, 2000

Q22: During the past twelve months, have you done volunteer work at a church or other place of worship?

Q23: During the past twelve months, have you done volunteer work for an organization other than a church or place of worship?

Religion and Public Life Survey, 2001

Q5: In the past year have you volunteered your time to any political organizations or candidates?

Q9: In the past year have you volunteered your time to any child or youth development programs, such as day care centers, schools, tutoring, scouts, or little league?

Q11: In the past year have you volunteered your time to any arts or cultural organization?

Q13: In the past year have you volunteered your time to any neighborhood, civic, or community group such as a block association or a neighborhood watch?

Q15: In the past year have you volunteered your time to any organization to help the poor, sick, elderly, or homeless?

General Social Survey, 2002

VOLCHRTY: During the past 12 months, how often have you done each of the following things: Done volunteer work for a charity?

National Election Studies, 2004

V045171: In the last 12 months, were you able to devote any time to volunteering?

General Social Survey, 2004

VOLCHRTY: During the past 12 months, how often have you done each of the following things: Done volunteer work for a charity?

Appendix D: Question Wording Related to Charitable Giving by Survey

Survey on Giving and Volunteering Survey, 1996

Q25a: For each of the areas in which you contributed money, which categories on this card best describe how much you and members of your family gave (in 1995)?

God and Society in North America, 1996

On this year's tax return, will you make a claim for charitable donations which you made?

National Election Study, 1996

V961264: How about you, were you able to contribute any money to church or charity in the last 12 months?

General Social Survey, 1998

GIVECONG: During the last year, approximately how much money did you and the other family members in your household contribute to each of the following: To your local congregation?

GIVEREL: During the last year, approximately how much money did you and the other family members in your household contribute to each of the following: To other religious organizations, programs, or causes?

GIVEOTH: During the last year, approximately how much money did you and the other family members in your household contribute to each of the following: To nonreligious charities, organizations, or causes?

Arts and Religion Survey, 1999

During the last year, approximately how much money did you and the other family members in your household contribute to each of the following:

a. Your local congregation
b. Other religious organizations, programs, or causes
c. Arts or cultural organizations
d. Other nonreligious charities, organizations, or causes

Saguaro Social Capital Benchmark Survey, 2000

Q37: During the past 12 months, approximately how much money did you and the other family members in your household contribute to:

a. All religious causes, including your local religious congregation
b. All nonreligious charities, organizations, or causes

General Social Survey, 2002

GIVCHRTY: During the past 12 months, how often have you done each of the following things: Given money to a charity?

National Election Studies, 2004

V045172: In the last 12 months, have you made any contribution of money to church?

General Social Survey, 2004

GIVCHRTY: During the past 12 months, how often have you done each of the following things: Given money to a charity?

References

Abramson, Paul. 1983. *Political Attitudes in America: Formation and Change*. San Francisco: W. H. Freeman and Company.

Ackerman, Bruce. 1980. *Social Justice in the Liberal State*. New Haven, CT: Yale University Press.

Ackerman, Bruce A., and James S. Fishkin. 2004. *Deliberation Day*. New Haven, CT: Yale University Press.

Ahlstrom, Sidney. 1960. "Theology and the Present-Day Revival." *Annals of the American Academy of Political and Social Science* 332 (November): 20–36.

———. 1963. "Thomas Hooker: Puritanism and Democratic Citizenship." *Church History* 32 (4): 415–31.

Allport, Gordon, and J. M. Ross. 1967. "Personal Religious Orientation and Prejudice." *Journal of Personality and Social Psychology* 5:432–43.

Almond, Gabriel, and Sidney Verba. 1963. *The Civic Culture: Political Attitudes and Democracy in Five Nations*. Princeton, NJ: Princeton University Press.

Ammerman, Nancy. 1997. "Organized Religion in a Voluntaristic Society." *Sociology of Religion* 58 (3): 203–15.

———. 2005. *Pillars of Faith: American Congregations and Their Partners*. Berkeley, CA: University of California Press.

Anders, Sarah F. 1955. "Religious Behavior of Church Families." *Journal of Marriage and Family Living* 17:54–57.

Andolina, Molly W., Krista Jenkins, Cliff Zukin, and Scott Keeter. 2003. "Habits from the Home, Lessons from School: Influences on Youth Civic Engagement." *PS: Political Science and Politics* 36 (2): 275–80.

Astin, Alexander W. 2000. "The Civic Challenge of Educating the Underprepared Student." In *Civic Responsibility and Higher Education*, ed. Thomas Ehrlich, 124–46. Phoenix, AZ: Oryx Press.

Audi, Robert. 1997. "Liberal Democracy and the Place of Religion in Politics." In *Religion in the Public Square*, eds. Robert Audi and Nicholas Wolterstorff, 1–66. Lanham, MD: Rowman & Littlefield.

———. 2000. *Religious Commitment and Secular Reason*. New York: Cambridge University Press.

Auslander, Gail, and Howard Litwin. 1988. "Sociability and Patterns of Participation: Implications for Social Service Policy." *Journal of Voluntary Action Research* 17:25–37.

Barber, Benjamin. 1984. *Strong Democracy: Participatory Politics for a New Age*. Berkeley, CA: University of California Press.

———. 1998. *A Place for Us: How to Make Society Civil and Democracy Strong*. New York: Hill and Wang.

Beatty, Kathleen, and Oliver Walter. 1984. "Religious Preference and Practice: Reevaluating Their Impact on Political Tolerance." *Public Opinion Quarterly* 48 (Spring): 318–29.

Becker, Penny Edgell, and Pawan Dhingra. 2001. "Religious Involvement and Volunteering: Implications for Civil Society." *Sociology of Religion* 62 (3): 315–35.

Beiner, Ronald, ed. 1995. *Theorizing Citizenship*. Albany: SUNY Press.

Bekkers, Rene, and T. N. M. Schuyt. 2007. "And Who Is Your Neighbor?: Explaining the Effect of Religion on Charitable Giving and Volunteering." Working paper, Department of Philanthropic Studies, Vrije Universiteit Amsterdam.

Bellah, Robert. 1975. *The Broken Covenant: American Civil Religion in Time of Trial*. New York: Seabury Press.

Bellah, Robert, Richard Madsen, William Sullivan, Ann Swidler, and Steve Tipton. 1985. *Habits of the Heart: Individualism and Commitment in American Life*. Berkeley, CA: University of California Press.

Berger, Peter, and Richard John Neuhaus. 1977. *To Empower People: The Role of Mediating Structures in Public Policy*. Washington, DC: AEI Press.

Berkowitz, Peter. 1999. *Virtue and the Making of Modern Liberalism*. Princeton, NJ: Princeton University Press.

Berman, Sheri. 1997. "Civil Society and Political Institutionalization." *American Behavioral Scientist* 40 (5): 562–74.

Bernstein, R. 1986. "The Meaning of Public Life." In *Religion and American Public Life: Interpretations and Explorations*, ed. Robin Lovin, 29–52. Mahwah, NJ: Paulist Press.

Berry, Jeffrey. 1999. *The New Liberalism: The Rising Power of Citizen's Groups*. Washington, DC: Brookings Institute Press.

Berry, Jeffrey, and Clyde Wilcox. 2007. *The Interest Group Society*, 4th edition. New York: Longman.

Bibby, Reginald, and Merlin Brinkerhoof. 1974. "Sources of Religious Involvement: Issues for Future Empirical Investigation." *Review of Religious Research* 15:71–79.

Boyte, Harry, and Nancy Kari. 2000. "Renewing the Democratic Spirit in American Colleges and Universities: Higher Education as Public Work." In *Civic Responsibility and Higher Education*, ed. Thomas Ehrlich, 27–59. Phoenix, AZ: Oryx Press.

Braiker, Brian. 2007. "God's Numbers." *Newsweek*, March 30, 2007, www.msnbc.msn.com/id/17879137/site/newsweek (accessed October 1, 2007).

Brehm, John, and Wendy Rahn. 1997. "Individual-level Evidence for the Causes and Consequences of Social Capital." *American Journal of Political Science* 41:999–1023.

Brooks, Arthur C. 2003. "Religious Faith and Charitable Giving." *Policy Review* 121 (October–November): 39–50.

———. 2006. *Who Really Cares: The Surprising Truth about Compassionate Conservatism*. New York: Basic Books.

Bruce, Steve. 2002. *God Is Dead: Secularization in the West*. Oxford: Blackwell.

Bryce, James. 1910. *The American Commonwealth*, Vol. 2, 4th edition. New York: Macmillan Publishing Company.

Burns, Nancy, Kay Schlozman, and Sidney Verba. 2001. *The Private Roots of Public Action: Gender, Equality, and Political Participation*. Cambridge, MA: Harvard University Press.

Campbell, David. 2004. "Community Heterogeneity and Participation." Paper presented at the annual meeting of the American Political Science Association, Sept. 2–5.

———. 2006. *Why We Vote: How Schools and Communities Shape our Civic Life*. Princeton, NJ: Princeton University Press.

Campbell, David, and Steven Yonish. 2003. "Religion and Volunteering in America." In *Religion as Social Capital: Producing the Common Good*, ed. Corwin E. Smidt, 82–106. Waco, TX: Baylor University Press.

Carter, Stephen L. 1993. *The Culture of Disbelief: How American Law and Politics Trivialize Religious Devotion*. New York: Basic Books.

Casanova, Jose. 1994. *Public Religions in the Modern World*. Chicago: University of Chicago Press.

Cassel, Carol, and Celia Lo. 1997. "Theories of Political Literacy." *Political Behavior* 19 (4): 317–35.

Chaves, Mark. 1994. "Secularization as Declining Religious Authority." *Social Forces* 71:749–74.

Chopyak, Jill. 2001. "Citizen Participation and Democracy." *National Civic Review* 90 (Winter): 375–83.

Chusmir, Leonard H., and Christine S. Koberg. 1988. "Religion and Attitudes Toward Work: A New Look at an Old Question." *Journal of Organizational Behavior* 9 (3): 251–62.

Cimino, Richard, and Don Lattin. 1998. *Shopping for Faith: American Religion in the New Millennium*. San Francisco: Jossey-Bass.

"The Civic Mission of Schools." 2003. A Report of the Carnegie Corporation of New York and CIRCLE: The Center for Information and Research on Civic Learning and Engagement. www.civicmissionofschools.org/campaign/documents/CivicMissionofSchools.pdf (accessed May 18, 2007).

Cnaan, Ram, Stephanie Boddie, Charlene McGrew, and Jennifer Kang. 2006. *The Other Philadelphia Story: How Local Congregations Support Quality of Life in Urban America*. Philadelphia, PA: University of Pennsylvania Press.

Cochran, Clarke. 1990. *Religion in Public and Private Life*. New York: Routledge.

Cohen, Jean. 1999. "Does Voluntary Association Make Democracy Work?" In *Diversity and Its Discontents: Cultural Conflict and Common Ground in Contemporary American Society*, eds. Neil Smelser and Jeffery Alexander, 263–91. Princeton, NJ: Princeton University Press.

Cohen, Jean, and Andrew Arato. 1992. *Civil Society and Political Theory*. Cambridge, MA: MIT Press.

Colby, Anne, and Thomas Ehrlich, with Elizabeth Beaumont, Jennifer Rosner, and Jason Stephens. 2000. "Introduction: Higher Education and the Development of Civic Responsibility." In *Civic Responsibility and Higher Education*, ed. Thomas Ehrlich, xxi–xliii. Phoenix, AZ: Oryx Press.

Conway, M. Margaret. 1991. *Political Participation in the United States*, 2nd edition. Washington, D.C.: Congressional Quarterly Press.

Conyers, A. J. 2001. "Rescuing Tolerance." *First Things* August/September: 43–46.

Crawford, Sue E. S., and Laura R. Olson, eds. 2001. *Christian Clergy in American Politics*. Baltimore: Johns Hopkins University Press.

Curtis, James. 1971. "Voluntary Association Joining: A Cross-National Comparative Note." *American Sociological Review* 36:872–80.

Dagger, Richard. 1997. *Civic Virtues: Rights, Citizenship, and Republican Liberalism*. New York: Oxford University Press.

Davie, Grace. 1994. *Religion in Britain since 1945: Believing without Belonging*. Oxford: Blackwell.

Dekker, Gerard. 1993. "Is Religious Change a Form of Secularization? The Case of the Reformed Churches in the Netherlands." Paper presented at the 22nd International Conference for the Sociology of Religion, Budapest, Hungary, July 1993.

Delacroix, Jacques, and Francois Nielsen. 2001. "The Beloved Myth: Protestantism and the Rise of Industrial Capitalism in Nineteenth-Century Europe." *Social Forces* 80:509.

Delli Carpini, Michael X., and Scott Keeter. 1996. *What Americans Know about Politics and Why It Matters*. New Haven, CT: Yale University Press.

DeLue, Stephen M. 2002. *Political Thinking, Political Theory, and Civil Society*, 2nd edition. New York: Longman.

Dionne, E. J., Jr. 1991. *Why Americans Hate Politics*. New York: Simon & Schuster.

———. 2001. "Religion's Third Renegotiation with the Public Square." In *Religion and the Public Square in the 21st Century*, ed. Ryan Streeter, 23–30. Indianapolis, IN: Hudson Institute, Inc.

Djupe, Paul, and J. Tobin Grant. 2001. "Religious Institutions and Political Participation in America." *Journal for the Scientific Study of Religion* 40 (2):303–14.

Dworkin, Ronald. 1985. *A Matter of Principle*. Cambridge, MA: Harvard University Press.

Easton, David. 1965. *A Systems Analysis of Political Life*. New York: John Wiley.

Eberly, Don. E. 1994. *Restoring the Good Society: A New Vision for Politics and Culture*. Grand Rapids, MI: Baker Books.

———. E. 1998. *America's Promise: Civil Society and the Renewal of American Culture*. Lanham, MD: Rowman & Littlefield.

Ecklund, Elaine. 2005. "Models of Civic Responsibility: Korean Americans in Congregations with Different Ethnic Composition." *Journal for the Scientific Study of Religion* 44 (March): 15–28.

Edgell, Penny. 2006. *Religion and Family in a Changing Society*. Princeton, NJ: Princeton University Press.

Edwards, Michael. 2004. *Civil Society*. Malden, MA: Polity Press.

Ehrenberg, John. 1999. *Civil Society: The Critical History of an Idea*. New York: New York University Press.

Elshtain, Jean Bethke. 1995. *Democracy on Trial*. New York: Basic Books.

———. 2002. "Religion and American Democracy." In *Religion, Politics, and the American Experience: Reflections on Religion and American Public Life*, ed. Edith Blumhofer, 16–26. Tuscaloosa: University of Alabama Press.

Fowler, Robert Booth. 1989. *Unconventional Partners: Religion and Liberal Culture in the United States*. Grand Rapids, MI: Eerdmans.

———. 1999. *Enduring Liberalism: American Political Thought since the 1960s*. Lawrence, KS: University Press of Kansas.

Fowler, Robert Booth, Allen D. Hertzke, Laura R. Olson, and Kevin R. denDulk. 2004. *Religion and Politics in America*, 3rd edition. Boulder, CO: Westview Press.

Fung, Archon. 2003. "Associations and Democracy: Between Theories, Hopes, and Realities." *Annual Review of Sociology* 29:515–39.

Gallup, George, Jr., and Jim Castelli. 1989. *The People's Religion: American Faith in the 90's*. New York: Macmillan Publishing Company.

Gallup, George, Jr., and D. Michael Lindsay. 1999. *Surveying the Religious Landscape: Trends in U.S. Beliefs*. Harrisburg, PA: Morehouse Publishing.

Galston, William A. 1991. *Liberal Purposes: Goods, Virtues, and Diversity in the Liberal State*. New York: Cambridge University Press.

———. 1992. "Introduction." In *Virtue: Nomos XXXIV*, eds. William A. Galston and John W. Chapman. New York: New York University Press.

———. 1995. "Liberal Virtues and the Formation of Civic Character." In *Seedbeds of Virtue: Sources of Competence, Character, and Citizenship in American Society*, eds. Mary Ann Glendon and David Blankenhorn, 35–60. Lanham, MD: Madison Books.

———. 2000. "Civil Society and the 'Art of Association.'" *Journal of Democracy* 11:64–70.

———. 2001. "Political Knowledge, Political Engagement, and Civic Education." *Annual Review of Political Science* 4:217–34.

Gautier, Mary L. 1998. "Church Elites and Restoration of Civil Society in the Communist Societies of Central Europe." *Journal of Church and State* 40:289–318.

Gibson, James. 2006. "Enigmas of Intolerance: Fifty Years after Stouffer's *Communism, Conformity, and Civil Liberties*." *Perspectives on Politics* 4:1 (March): 21–34.

Glendon, Mary Ann. 1991. *Rights Talk*. New York: Free Press.

Glendon, Mary Ann, and David Blankenhorn, eds. 2005. *Seedbeds of Virtue: Sources of Competence, Character, and Citizenship in American Society*. Lanham, MD: Madison Books.

Glock, Charles, and Rodney Stark. 1966. *Christian Beliefs and Anti-Semitism*. New York: Harper & Row.

Goss, Kristin. 1999. "Volunteering and the Long Civic Generation." *Nonprofit and Voluntary Sector Quarterly* 28 (December): 378–415.

Greeley, Andrew. 1997. "The Other Civic America: Religion and Social Capital." *The American Prospect* 32:68–74.

Green, John C. 2007. *The Faith Factor: How Religion Influences American Elections*. Westport, CT: Praeger.

Green, John C., James L. Guth, Lyman A. Kellstedt, and Corwin E. Smidt. 1994. "Uncivil Challenges? Support for Civil Liberties among Religious Activists." *The Journal of Political Science* 22:25–49.

Green, John C., Lyman A. Kellstedt, Corwin E. Smidt, and James L. Guth. 2007. "How the Faithful Voted: Religious Communities and the Presidential Vote." In *A Matter of Faith: Religion in the 2004 Presidential Election*, ed. David Campbell, 15–36. Washington, DC: Brookings Institution Press.

Greenawalt, Kent. 1988. *Religious Conviction and Political Choice*. New York: Oxford University Press.

Grenville, Andrew. 2000. "'For By Him All Things were Created . . . Visible and Invisible': Sketching the Contours of Public and Private Religion in North America." In *Rethinking Church, State, and Modernity: Canada between Europe and America*, eds. David Lyon and Marguerite Van Die, 211–27. Toronto: University of Toronto Press.

Griffiths, Paul J., and Jean Bethke Elshtain. 2002. "Proselytizing for Tolerance: Parts I and II." *First Things* November: 30–36.

Guth, James L., John C. Green, Lyman A. Kellstedt, and Corwin E. Smidt. 2006. "Faith and Public Policy: A View from the Pews." *The Review of Faith & International Affairs* 3 (Fall): 3–10.

Guth, James L., John C. Green, Corwin E. Smidt, Lyman A. Kellstedt, and Margaret M. Poloma. 1997. *The Bully Pulpit: The Politics of Protestant Clergy*. Lawrence: University of Kansas Press, 1997.

Guth, James L., Lyman A. Kellstedt, Corwin E. Smidt, and John C. Green. 2006. "Religious Influences in the 2004 Presidential Election." *Presidential Studies Quarterly* 36 (June): 223–42.

Hadden, Jeffrey. 1989. "Desacralizing Secularization Theory." In *Secularization and Fundamentalism Reconsidered: Religion and the Political Order*, Vol. 3, eds. Jeffry Hadden and Anson Shupe, 3–26. New York: Paragon House.

Hamilton, Marci. 2005. *God vs. the Gavel: Religion and the Rule of Law*. New York: Cambridge University press.

Harris, Fred. 1999. *Something Within: Religion in African-American Political Activism*. New York: Oxford University Press.

Hausknecht, Murray. 1962. *The Joiners: A Sociological Description of Voluntary Association Membership in the United States*. New York: Bedminister Press.

Himmelfarb, Gertrude. 1999. *One Nation: Two Cultures*. New York: Alfred A. Knopf.

Hodgkinson, Virginia A., Murray S. Weitzman, Eric A. Crutchfield, Aaron J. Heffron, and Arthur D. Kirsch. 1996. *Giving and Volunteering in the United States*. Washington, DC: Independent Sector.

Hodgkinson, Virginia A., Murray S. Weitzman, and Arthur D. Kirsch. 1990. "From Commitment to Action: How Religious Involvement Affects Giving and Volunteering." In *Faith and Philanthropy in America: Explor-*

ing the Role of Religion in America's Voluntary Sector, eds. Robert Wuthnow and Virginia A. Hodgkinson, 93–114. San Francisco, CA: Jossey-Bass.

Hoge, Dean R., Benton Johnson, and Donald A. Luidens. 1994. *Vanishing Boundaries: The Religion of Mainline Protestant Baby Boomers*. Louisville, KY: Westminster/John Knox Press.

Hoge, Dean R., and David A. Roozen, eds. 1979a. *Understanding Church Growth and Decline*. New York: Pilgrim Press.

———. 1979b. "Research on Factors Influencing Church Commitment." In *Understanding Church Growth and Decline, 1950–1978*, eds. Dean R. Hoge and David A. Roozen, 42–68. New York: Pilgrim Press.

Hollenbach, David. 2003. *The Global Face of Public Faith: Politics, Human Rights, and Christian Ethics*. Washington, D.C.: Georgetown University Press.

Hyman, Herbert, and Charles Wright. 1971. "Trends in Voluntary Association Membership of American Adults." *American Sociological Review* 36 (April): 191–206.

Independent Sector. 1999. *Giving and Volunteering in the United States: Executive Summary*. www.indepedentsector.org/GranV/default.htm (accessed May 15, 2007).

———. 2001. *Giving and Volunteering in the United States: Executive Summary*. www.independentsector.org/programs/research/GV01main.htlm (accessed May 15, 2007).

Iyengar, Shanto. 1980. "Subjective Political Efficacy as a Measure of Diffuse Support." *Public Opinion Quarterly* 44 (2): 249–56.

Jackman, Robert, and Ross A. Miller. 1998. "Social Capital and Politics." *Annual Review of Political Science* 1:47–73.

Jackson, Elton, Mark Bachmeier, James Wood, and Elizabeth Craft. 1995. "Volunteering and Charitable Giving: Do Religious and Associational Ties Promote Helping Behavior?" *Nonprofit and Voluntary Sector Quarterly* 24 (Spring): 59–78.

Jefferson, Thomas. 1975. "Notes on the State of Virginia." In *The Portable Jefferson*, ed. M. D. Peterson. New York: Penguin.

Jenkins, Krista, Molly Andolina, Scott Keeter, and Cliff Zukin. 2003. "Is Civic Behavior Political? Exploring the Multidimensional Nature of Political Participation." Paper given at the annual meeting of the Midwest Political Science Association, April 3–6, Chicago.

Jones, Keely. 2006. "Giving and Volunteering as Distinct Forms of Civic Engagement: The Role of Community Integration and Personal Resources in Formal Helping." *Nonprofit and Voluntary Sector Quarterly* 35 (June): 249–66.

Joslyn, Mark, and Allan Cigler. 2001. "Group Involvement and Democratic Orientations: Social Capital in the Postelection Context." *Social Science Quarterly* 82 (June): 357–68.

Keck, Margaret, and Kathryn Sikkink. 1998. *Activists beyond Borders*. Ithaca, NY: Cornell University Press.

Kellstedt, Lyman A., and John C. Green. 1993. "Knowing God's Many People: Denominational Preference and Political Behavior." In *Rediscovering the Religious Factor in American Politics*, eds. David C. Leege and Lyman A. Kellstedt, 53–71. Armonk, NY: M. E. Sharpe.

Kellstedt, Lyman, John Green, James Guth, and Corwin Smidt. 1996. "Grasping the Essentials: The Social Embodiment of Religion and Political Behavior." In *Religion and the Culture Wars: Dispatches from the Front*, eds. John Green, James Guth, Corwin Smidt, and Lyman Kellstedt, 174–92. Lanham, MD: Rowman & Littlefield.

———. 1997. "Is There a Culture War? Religion and the 1996 Election." Paper presented at the annual meeting of the American Political Science Association. Washington, D.C., September.

Kirkpatrick, Lee A. 1993. "Fundamentalism, Christian Orthodoxy, and Intrinsic Religious Orientation as Predictors of Discriminatory Attitudes." *Journal for the Scientific Study of Religion* 32(3): 256–68.

Knoke, David. 1986. "Associations and Interest Groups." *Annual Review of Sociology* 12:1–21.

Kramnick, Isaac, and R. Laurence Moore. 2005. *The Godless Constitution: A Moral Defense of the Secular State*. New York: Norton.

Kwak, Nojin, Dhavan Shah, and R. Lance Holbert. 2004. "Connecting, Trusting, and Participating: The Direct and Interactive Effects of Social Associations." *Political Research Quarterly* 57 (December): 643–52.

Kymlicka, Will, and Wayne Norman. 1995. "Return of the Citizen: A Survey of Recent Work on Citizenship Theory." In *Theorizing Citizenship*, ed. Ronald Beiner, 283–322. Albany, NY: State University of New York Press.

———. 2000. *Citizenship in Diverse Societies*. New York: Oxford University Press.

Ladd, Everett C. 1996. "The Data Just Don't Show Erosion of America's Social Capital." *The Public Perspective* 7 (4): 7–16.

Lam, Pui-Yan. 2002. "As the Flocks Gather: How Religion Affects Voluntary Association Participation." *Journal for the Scientific Study of Religion* 41 (September): 405–22.

Lambert, Ronald, James Curtis, Barry Kay, and Steven Brown. 1988. "The Social Sources of Political Knowledge." *Canadian Journal of Political Science* 21 (June): 359–74.

Laycock, Douglas. 2007. "A Syllabus of Errors." *Michigan Law Review* 105:1169.

Layman, Geoffrey. 2001. *The Great Divide: Religious and Cultural Conflict in American Party Politics*. New York, NY: Columbia University Press.

Layman, Geoffrey, and John C. Green. 2005. "Wars and Rumors of Wars: The Contexts of Cultural Conflict in American Political Behavior." *British Journal of Political Science* 36 (1): 61–89.

Lazerwitz, Bernard. 1961. "Some Factors Associated with Variations in Church Attendance." *Social Forces* 39:301–309.

———. 1962. "Membership in Voluntary Associations and Frequency of Church Attendance." *Journal for the Scientific Study of Religion* 2 (October): 74–84.

Lemon, M., B. Palisi, and P. Jacobson. 1972. "Dominant Statuses and Involvement in Formal Voluntary Associations." *Journal of Voluntary Action Research* 1(2): 30–42.

Letki, Natalia. 2006. "Investigating the Roots of Civic Morality: Trust, Social Capital, and Institutional Performance." *Political Behavior* 28 (Dec.): 305–25.

Levy, Margaret, and Laura Stoker. 2000. "Political Trust and Trustworthiness." *Annual Review of Political Science* 3:475–507.

Lichterman, Paul, and C. Brady Potts. 2005. "The Civic Life of American Religion: An Introductory Statement." Paper read at the Civic Life of American Religion: Citizens and Believers in a Diverse Society, May 1, University of Southern California.

Loveland, Matthew, David Sikkink, Daniel Myers, and Benjamin Radcliff. 2005. "Private Prayer and Civic Involvement." *Journal for the Scientific Study of Religion* 44 (March): 1–14.

Luskin, Robert. 1987. "Measuring Political Sophistication." *American Journal of Political Science* 31 (4): 856–99.

MacDonald, Michael, and Samuel Popkin. 2001 "The Myth of the Vanishing Voter." *American Political Science Review* 95 (Dec.): 963–74.

Macedo, Stephen. 1990. "Liberal Civic Education and Religious Fundamentalism: The Case of God v. John Rawls?" *Ethics* 105:468–96.

———. 1995. *Liberal Virtues: Citizenship, Virtue, and Community in Liberal Constitutionalism.* New York: Oxford University Press.

———. 2000. *Diversity and Distrust: Civic Education in a Multicultural Democracy.* Cambridge, MA: Harvard University Press.

Macedo, Stephen, Yvette Alex-Assensoh, Jeffrey M. Berry, Michael Brintnall, David E. Campbell, Luis Ricardo Fraga, Archon Fung et al. 2005. *Democracy at Risk: How Political Choices Undermine Citizen Participation, and What We Can Do about It.* Washington, DC: Brookings Institution Press.

Macintyre, Alasdair C. 1984. *After Virtue: A Study in Moral Theory.* Notre Dame, IN: University of Notre Dame Press.

Madison, James. 1987/1788. "Federalist 55: The Total Number of the House of Representatives." In *The Federalist Papers: James Madison, Alexander Hamilton, and John Jay*, ed. Isaac Kramnick. New York: Penguin Putnam.

Mathews, David. 2000. "How Concepts of Politics Control Concepts of Civic Responsibility." In *Civic Responsibility and Higher Education*, ed. Thomas Ehrlich, 149–63. Phoenix, AZ: Oryx Press.

Milbrath, Lester. 1965. *Political Participation: How and Why Do People Get Involved in Politics?* Chicago: Rand McNally.

Miller, Melissa K. 2003. *The Joiners: Voluntary Organizations and Political Participation in the United States.* Doctoral dissertation, Northwestern University.

Minkoff, Debra. 1997. "Producing Social Capital: National Social Movements and Civil Society." *American Behavioral Scientist* 40 (March/April): 606–19.

Moberg, David. 1962. *The Church as a Social Institution: The Sociology of American Religion.* Englewood Cliffs, NJ: Prentice-Hall.

Mooney, Christopher E. 2001. *The Public Clash of Private Values: The Politics of Morality Policy.* Chatham, NJ: Chatham House.

Mutz, Diana. 2002. "Cross-Cutting Social Networks: Testing Democratic Theory in Practice." *American Political Science Review* 96 (March): 111–26.

Nagel, Thomas. 1991. *Equality and Partiality.* Oxford, UK: Oxford University Press.

National Commission on Civic Renewal. 1998. "A Nation of Spectators: How Civic Disengagement Weakens America." College Park, MD: University of Maryland.

Nemeth, Roger, and Donald Luidens. 2003. "The Religious Basis of Charitable Giving in the United States." In *Religion as Social Capital: Producing the Common Good*, ed. Corwin E. Smidt, 107–20. Waco, TX: Baylor University Press.

Neuhaus, Richard. 1984. *The Naked Public Square: Religion and Democracy in America*, 2nd edition. Grand Rapids, MI: Eerdmans.

Neuman, W. Russell. 1986. *The Paradox of Mass Politics*. Cambridge, MA: Harvard University Press.

Nie, Norman, Jane Junn, and Kenneth Stehlik-Barry. 1996. *Education and Democratic Citizenship in America*. Chicago: University of Chicago Press.

Nozick, Robert. 1974. *Anarchy, State, and Utopia*. New York: Basic Books.

Nunn, Clyde, Henry Crockett, and J. Allen Williams. 1978. *Tolerance for Conformity: A National Survey of Americans' Changing Commitment to Civil Liberties*. San Francisco, CA: Jossey-Bass.

Olsen, Marvin E. 1970. "Social and Political Participation of Blacks." *American Sociological Review* 35:682–96.

Ostrom, Eleanor. 1997. "Task Force to Set Agenda for Civic Education Program." *PS: Political Science and Politics* 30 (4): 744.

Park, Jerry Z., and Christian Smith. 2000. "To Whom Much Has Been Given . . . : Religious Capital and Community Voluntarism among Churchgoing Protestants." *Journal for the Scientific Study of Religion* 39(3): 272–86.

Pascal, Blaise. 2004. *Pensees*. Trans. W. F. Trotter. Whitefish, MT: Kessinger Press.

Peterson, Steven. 1992. "Church Participation and Political Participation: The Spillover Effect." *American Politics Quarterly* 20 (1): 123–39.

Pew Center for People and the Press. 2001. "Faith-Based Funding Backed, But Church-State Doubts Abound." Report. April 10, 2001. Washington, DC: Pew Center for People and the Press.

Poloma, Margaret, and George C. Gallup. 1991. *Varieties of Prayer*. Philadelphia: Trinity International Press.

Popenoe, David. 1995. "The Roots of Declining Social Virtue." In *Seedbeds of Virtue: Sources of Competence, Character, and Citizenship in American Society*, eds. Mary Ann Glendon and David Blankenhorn, 71–104. Lanham, MD: Madison Books.

Post, Robert C., and Nancy L. Rosenblum. 2002. "Introduction." In *Civil Society and Government*, eds. Nancy L. Rosenblum and Robert C. Post, 1–25. Princeton, NJ: Princeton University Press.

Presser, Stanley, and Mark Chaves. 2007. "Is Religious Service Attendance Declining?" *Journal for the Scientific Study of Religion* 46 (3): 417–23.

Putnam, Robert. 1993. *Making Democracy Work: Civic Traditions in Modern Italy*. Princeton, NJ: Princeton University Press.

———. 1995a. "Bowling Alone: America's Declining Social Capital." *Journal of Democracy* 6 (January): 65–79.

———. 1995b. "Tuning In, Tuning Out: The Strange Disappearance of Social Capital in America." *PS: Political Science and Politics* 28 (December): 631–43.

———. 2000. *Bowling Alone: The Collapse and Revival of American Community*. New York: Simon & Schuster.

———. 2003. *Better Together: Restoring the American Community*. New York: Simon and Schuster.

Quinley, Harold E. 1974. *The Prophetic Clergy: Social Activism among Protestant Ministers*. New York: Wiley.

Rawls, John. 1971. *A Theory of Justice*. Cambridge, MA: Harvard University Press.

———. 1993. *Political Liberalism*. New York: Columbia University Press.

———. 1999. *The Law of Peoples*. Cambridge, MA: Harvard University Press.

Regnerus, Mark, Christian Smith, and David Sikkink. 1998. "Who Gives to the Poor? The Influence of Religious Tradition and Political Location on the Personal Generosity of Americans toward the Poor." *Journal for the Scientific Study of Religion* 37(3):481–93.

Reimer, Sam, and Jerry Z. Park. 2001. "Tolerant (In)civility? A Longitudinal Analysis of White Conservative Protestants' Willingness to Grant Civil Liberties." *Journal for the Scientific Study of Religion* 40 (December): 735–45.

Roof, Wade Clark. 1999. *Spiritual Marketplace: Baby Boomers and the Remaking of American Religion*. Princeton, NJ: Princeton University Press.

Roof, Wade Clark, and William McKinney. 1987. *American Mainline Religion: Its Changing Shape and Future*. New Brunswick, NJ: Rutgers University Press.

Rose, Arnold. 1954. *Theory and Method in the Social Science*. Minneapolis, MN: University of Minnesota Press.

Rossiter, Clinton. 1960. *Parties and Politics in America*. Ithaca, NY: Cornell University Press.

Rotolo, Thomas. 2000. "A Time to Join, A Time to Quit: The Influence of Life Cycle Transitions on Voluntary Association Membership." *Social Forces* 78 (March): 1133–61.

Sandel, Michael. 1982. *Liberalism and the Limits of Justice*. New York: Cambridge University Press.

———. 1996. *Democracy's Discontents: America in Search of a Public Philosophy*. Cambridge, MA: Harvard University Press.

Sanders, Thomas, with Robert Putnam. 2006. "Social Capital and Civic Engagement of Individuals over Age Fifty in the United States." In *Civic Engagement and the Baby Boomer Generation: Research, Policy, and Practice Perspectives*, eds. Laura Wilson and Sharon Simson, 21–39. New York: Hayworth Press.

Schlesinger, Arthur. 1944. "Biography of a Nation of Joiners." *The American Historical Review* 50 (1): 1–25.

Schlozman, Kay, Sidney Verba, and Henry Brady. 1999. "Civic Participation and the Equality Problem." In *Civic Engagement in American Democracy*, eds. Theda Skocpol and Morris Fiorina, 427–60. Washington, D.C.: Brookings Institution Press.

Schudson, Michael. 1998. *The Good Citizen: A History of American Civic Life*. New York: Martin Kessler Books.

Scott, John, Jr. 1957. "Membership and Participation in Voluntary Associations." *American Sociological Review* 22 (June): 315–25.

Singer, Jefferson, Laura King, Melanie Green, and Sarah Barr. 2002. "Personal Identity and Civic Responsibility: 'Rising to the Occasion' Narratives and Generativity in Community Action Student Interns." *Journal of Social Issues* 58 (3): 535–57.

Skocpol, Theda. 1999. "How Americans Became Civic." In *Civic Engagement in American Democracy*, eds. Theda Skocpol and Morris Fiorina, 27–80. Washington, DC: Brookings Institution Press.

———. 2003. *Diminished Democracy: From Membership to Management in American Civic Life*. Norman, OK: University of Oklahoma Press.

Skocpol, Theda, and Morris Fiorina. 1999. *Civic Engagement in American Democracy*. Washington, DC: Brookings Institution Press.

Smidt, Corwin E. 1999. "Religion and Civic Engagement: A Comparative Analysis." *The Annals of the American Academy of Political and Social Science* 565 (September): 176–92.

———. 2001. "Religion and American Public Opinion." In *In God We Trust? Religion and American Political Life*, ed. Corwin E. Smidt, 96–117. Grand Rapids, MI: Baker Academic.

———. 2003. *Religion as Social Capital: Producing the Common Good*. Waco, TX: Baylor University Press.

———, ed. 2004. *Pulpit and Politics*. Waco, TX: Baylor University Press.

———. 2007. "Evangelical and Mainline Protestants at the Turn of the Millennium: Taking Stock and Looking Forward." In *From Pews to Polling Places in the American Religious Mosaic*, ed. Matthew Wilson, 29–51. Washington, D.C.: Georgetown University Press.

Smidt, Corwin E., John Green, James Guth, and Lyman Kellstedt. 2003. "Religious Involvement, Social Capital, and Political Engagement: A Comparison of the United States and Canada." In *Religion as Social Capital: Producing the Common Good*, ed. Corwin E. Smidt, 153–69. Waco, TX: Baylor University Press.

Smidt, Corwin, and James Penning. 1982. "Religious Commitment, Political Conservatism, and Political and Social Tolerance in the United States: A Longitudinal Analysis." *Sociological Analysis* 43:231–46.

Smith, Christian, and Melissa Lunquist Denton. 2005. *Soul Searching: The Religious and Spiritual Lives of American Teenagers*. New York: Oxford University Press.

Smith, David Horton. 1975. "Voluntary Action and Voluntary Groups." *Annual Review of Sociology* 1:247–70.

———. 1994. "Determinants of Voluntary Association Participation and Volunteering: A Literature Review." *Nonprofit and Voluntary Sector Quarterly* 23 (September): 243–63.

Smith, Paul H., ed. 2000. *Letters of Delegates to Congress, 1774–1789*. Vol. 4. Washington, DC: Library of Congress.

Smith, Tom W. 1990. "Trends in Voluntary Group Membership." *American Journal of Political Science* 34 (August): 646–61.

Stark, Rodney. 2005. *Victory of Reason: How Christianity Led to Freedom, Capitalism, and Western Success*. New York: Random House.

Stark, Rodney, and Charles Glock. 1968. *American Piety: The Nature of Religious Commitment*. Los Angeles: University of California Press.

Steele, David. 1994. "At the Front Lines of the Revolution: East Germany's Churches Give Sanctuary and Succor to the Purveyors of Change." In *Religion, The Missing Dimension of Statecraft*, eds. Douglas Johnson and Cynthia Sampson, 119–52. Oxford: Oxford University Press.

Stetson, Brad, and Joseph G. Conti. 2005. *The Truth about Tolerance: Pluralism, Diversity, and the Culture Wars*. Downers Grove, IL: InterVarsity Press.

Stolle, Dietland, and Marc Hooghe. 2004. "Inaccurate, Exceptional, One-Sided or Irrelevant?: The Debate about the Alleged Decline of Social Capital and Civic Engagement in Western Societies." *British Journal of Political Science* 35:149–67.

Stolle, Dietland, and Thomas Rochon. 1998. "Are All Associations Alike?: Member Diversity, Associational Type, and the Creation of Social Capital." *American Behavioral Scientist* 42 (September): 47–65.

Stoltzenberg, Ross M., Mary Blair-Loy, and Linda J. Waite. 1995. "Religious Participation in Early Adulthood: Age and Family-Life Cycle Effects on Church Membership." *American Sociological Review* 60:84–103.

Stouffer, Samuel. 1955. *Communism, Conformity, and Civil Liberties: A Cross-Section of the Nation Speaks Its Mind*. New York: Doubleday.

Streeter, Ryan. 2002. "Introduction: Voluntary Associations and the Primacy of Moral Habits." In *The Soul of Civil Society: Voluntary Associations and the Public Value of Moral Habits*, eds. Don Eberly and Ryan Streeter, vii–xiii. Lanham, MD: Lexington Books.

Sullivan, John L., James Pierson, and George E. Marcus. 1982. *Political Tolerance and American Democracy*. Chicago: University of Chicago Press.

Theiss-Morse, Elizabeth, and John R. Hibbing. 2005. "Citizenship and Civic Engagement." *Annual Review of Political Science* 8:227–49.

Thumma, Scott, Dave Travis, and Warren Bird. 2007. "Megachurches Today 2005: Summary of Research Findings." Hartford Institute for Religion Research. http://hirr.hartsem.edu/megachurch/megastoday2005_summaryreport.html (accessed Feb. 1, 2007).

Tocqueville, Alexis de. 1969. *Democracy in America*. Garden City, NY: Doubleday and Company.

Ulzurrun, Laura Morales Dies de. 2002. "Associational Membership and Social Capital in Comparative Perspective: A Note on the Problems of Measurement." *Politics & Society* 30 (September): 497–523.

Veenstra, Gerry. 2002. "Explicating Social Capital: Trust and Participation in the Civil Space." *Canadian Journal of Sociology* 27(4): 547–72.

Verba, Sidney. 1965. "Organizational Membership and Democratic Consensus." *Journal of Politics* 27 (August): 467–97.

Verba, Sidney, and Norman Nie. 1972. *Participation in America: Political Democracy and Social Inequality*. New York: Harper & Row.

Verba, Sidney, Kay Schlozman, and Henry Brady. 1995. *Voice and Equality: Civic Voluntarism in American Politics*. Cambridge, MA: Harvard University Press.

Wald, Kenneth, Lyman Kellstedt, and David Leege. 1993. "Church Involvement and Political Behavior." In *Rediscovering the Religious Factor in American Politics*, eds. David Leege and Lyman Kellstedt, 121–38. Armonk, NY: M. E. Sharpe.

Wald, Kenneth, Adam Silverman, and Kevin Fridy. 2005. "Making Sense of Religion in Political Life." *Annual Review of Political Science* 8:121–43.

Walzer, Michael. 1983. *Spheres of Justice: A Defense of Pluralism*. New York: Basic Books.

———. 1994. *Thick and Thin: Moral Argument at Home and Abroad*. Notre Dame, IN: University of Notre Dame Press.

———. 1995. "The Concept of Civil Society." In *Toward a Global Civil Society*, ed. Michael Walzer, 7–67. Providence, RI: Berghahn.

———. 2004. *Political and Passion: Toward a More Egalitarian Liberalism*. New Haven, CT: Yale University Press.

Warren, Mark A. 2003. "Faith and Leadership in the Inner City: How Social Capital Contributes to Democratic Renewal." In *Religion as Social Capital: Producing the Common Good*, ed. Corwin E. Smidt, 49–68. Waco, TX: Baylor University Press.

Warren, Mark E. 2001. *Democracy and Association*. Princeton, NJ: Princeton University Press.

Weber, Max. 1930. *The Protestant Ethic and the Spirit of Capitalism*. Trans. Talcott Parsons. Crows Nest, NSW, Australia: Allen and Unwin.

Weigel, George. 1992. *The Final Revolution: The Resistance Church and the Collapse of Communism*. Oxford: Oxford University Press.

Welch, Michael R., David Sikkink, Eric Sartain, and Carolyn Bond. 2004. "Trust in God and Trust in May: The Ambivalent Role of Religion in Shaping Dimensions of Social Trust." *Journal for the Scientific Study of Religion* 43(3): 317–43.

White, R. H. 1969. "Toward a Theory of Religious Influence." *Pacific Sociological Review* 2 (1): 23–28.

Wilcox, Clyde, and Ted Jelen. 1990. "Evangelicals and Political Tolerance." *American Politics Quarterly* 18 (January): 25–46.

Wilson, James Q. 1995. "Liberalism, Modernism, and the Good Life." In *Seedbeds of Virtue: Sources of Competence, Character, and Citizenship in American Society*, eds. Mary Ann Glendon and David Blankenhorn, 17–34. Lanham, MD: Madison Books.

Wilson, John. 2000. "Volunteering." *Annual Review of Sociology* 26:215–40.

Wilson, John, and Thomas Janoski. 1995. "The Contribution of Religion to Volunteer Work." *Sociology of Religion* 56 (2): 137–52.

Wilson, John, and Marc Musick. 1997. "Who Cares?: Toward an Integrated Theory of Volunteer Work." *American Sociological Review* 62 (October): 694–713.

———. 1998. "The Contribution of Social Resources to Volunteering." *Social Science Quarterly* 79 (December): 799–814.

Wolfe, Alan. 1989. *Whose Keeper?: Social Science and Moral Obligation*. Berkeley, CA: University of California Press.

———. 1998. *One Nation, After All*. New York: Viking.

Woodberry, Robert D., and Christian S. Smith. 1998. "Fundamentalism et al: Conservative Protestants in America." *Annual Review of Sociology* 24:25–56.

Wright, Charles, and Herbert Hyman. 1958. "Voluntary Association Memberships." *American Sociological Review* 23 (June): 284–94.

Wuthnow, Robert. 1990. "Religion and the Voluntary Spirit in the United States: Mapping the Terrain." In *Faith and Philanthropy in America: Exploring the Role of Religion in America's Voluntary Sector*, eds. Robert Wuthnow, Virginia Hodgkinson et al., 3–21. San Francisco, CA: Jossey-Bass.

———. 1991. *Acts of Compassion: Caring for Others and Helping Ourselves.* Princeton, NJ: Princeton University Press.

———. 1996. *Christianity and Civil Society: The Contemporary Debate.* Valley Forge, PA: Trinity Press International.

———. 1998a. *After Heaven: Spirituality in America since the 1950s.* Berkeley, CA: University of California Press.

———. 1998b. *Loose Connections: Joining Together in America's Fragmented Communities.* Cambridge, MA: Harvard University Press.

———. 1999a. "Mobilizing Civic Engagement: The Changing Impact of Religious Involvement." In *Civic Engagement in American Democracy,* eds. Theda Skocpol and Morris Fiorina, 331–63. Washington, D.C.: Brookings Institution Press.

———. 1999b. "Democratic Liberalism and the Challenge of Diversity in Late-Twentieth-Century America." In *Diversity and Its Discontents: Cultural Conflict and Common Ground in Contemporary American Society,* eds. Neil Smelser and Jeffery Alexander, 19–35. Princeton, NJ: Princeton University Press.

———. 2002. "Reassembling the Civic Church: The Changing Role of Congregations in American Civil Society." In *Meaning and Modernity: Religion, Polity, and Self,* eds. Richard Madsen, William Sullivan, Ann Swidler, and Steven Tipton, 163–80. Berkeley, CA: University of California Press.

———. 2003. "Can Religion Revitalize Civil Society? An Institutional Perspective." In *Religion as Social Capital: Producing the Common Good,* ed. Corwin E. Smidt, 191–209. Waco, TX: Baylor University Press.

———. 2004. *Saving America?: Faith Based Services and the Future of Civil Society.* Princeton, NJ: Princeton University Press.

———. 2005. *America and the Challenges of Religious Diversity.* Princeton, NJ: Princeton University Press.

Wuthnow, Robert, and John H. Evans. 2002. *The Quit Hand of God: Faith-Based Activism and the Public Role of Mainline Protestantism.* Berkeley: University of California Press.

Yamane, David. 1997. "Secularization on Trial: In Defense of a Neosecularization Paradigm." *Journal for the Scientific Study of Religion* 36:109–22.

Zaller, John. 1992. *The Nature and Origins of Mass Opinion*. New York: Cambridge University Press.

Zukin, Cliff, Scott Keeter, Molly Anderson, Krista Jenkins, and Michael Delli Carpini. 2006. *A New Engagement? Political Participation, Civic Life, and the Changing American Citizen*. New York: Oxford University Press.

Index

The letter *t* following a page number denotes a table.

Name Index